ChatGP
Millionaire Bible

To Mary and John, my wonderful children.

This book is about how their future began.

ChatGPT Millionaire Bible

How AI Can Build You a Million-Dollar Business to Become Financially Free

By Harold Pearson

YOUR FREE GIFT

As a way of saying thanks for your purchase, I'm offering
"150 CHATGPT PROMPTS" for **FREE** to you!

Here is a tiny fraction of what you will find inside:
- ChatGPT prompts for Business
- ChatGPT prompts for Productivity
- ChatGPT prompts for Personal Development
- ChatGPT prompts for Education
- And Much more…

SCAN THE QR CODE AND GET YOUR GIFT!

TABLE OF CONTENTS

Book 1 | AI Revolution

Unveiling the Dawn of a New Era.
A Journey from Fear to Empowerment in Work,
Business, Economy, Relationships, and Life

By Harold Pearson

Introduction

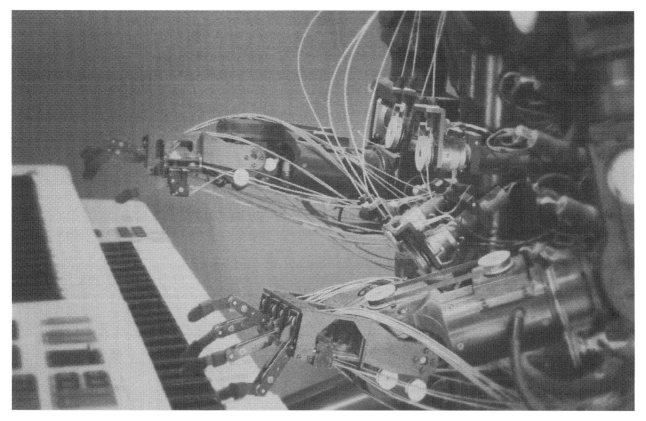

In the year 1950, Alan Turing, one of the most notable and influential computer scientists to have ever lived, predicted that computers would soon start to mimic human language and intelligence. In other words, they would pass the Turing test, which might lead humans to consider these machines conscious or sentient and it has taken us a good 70 years to achieve this. In June of 2022, Google engineer Blake Lemoine was fired from the trillion-dollar tech firm for claiming that LaMDA, Google's artificially intelligent chatbot generator, was alive.

Humans throughout recorded history have experienced several technological revolutions. It began with the cognitive revolution, which gave birth to human cognition and language. The agricultural revolution followed, bringing people together to work collectively and establish farms, homes, towns, and cities around them. Then came the first industrial revolution, introducing steamships and engines, followed by the second industrial revolution, which brought internal combustion engines and electricity. The technological revolution marked the information age, characterized by the advent of phones and the internet.

Now, in the 2020s, we find ourselves on the cusp of a revolution capable of disrupting life as we know it. Welcome to the age of intelligence, where humans have achieved feats that can be likened to playing God. We have created a new technological life, mimicking intelligence itself.

With AI technology we can create intelligent machines such as robots or drones that possess a similar way of thinking and acting as humans, making autonomous decisions is possible by interpreting one's environment and assimilating available data. Considering how much data is accessible nowadays, learning and acting upon it are fundamental attributes to possess in the Intelligence Revolution, due to its reliance on data usage the occurrence of this revolution has come about.

Although using AI to automate human intelligence and labor may seem like a strong vision, it does come with its own set of limits. However, a superior method for achieving new things would be AI augmentation where the abilities of humans are enhanced through technology. The advantages offered by both Automation and Augmentation cannot be ignored because they're able to provide many beneficial aspects when attempting to increase profitability. Nevertheless, we must avoid putting too much attention on Automation alone.

Beyond just automation and human labor lies the scope for machines to help us achieve more in what's known as the realm of augmentation. Advancements in artificial intelligence allow us as humans the ability to delve further into the intricacies of this new world while also exploring different avenues.

Experts suggest that we shouldn't limit our focus solely to automation when examining this issue. Beyond its ability to automate certain tasks lies a deeper potential for AI: that of handling complex data analysis and decision-making processes as well as facilitating interaction between machines and their environments. Human augmentation using AI goes beyond simply replacing people and can provide new capabilities. AI capabilities can now function independently without frequent human involvement thanks to the latest digital revolution, unlike previous mechanization phases. However, the shift towards uncharted territory causes concern as more and more machines are being monitored by other machines ultimately leading to potential economic disruption. The effect that AI will have on employment is uncertain but some estimates suggest that automation may put millions out of work by 2030

The future looks bright with possibilities of how AI can revolutionize our approach to work, and workplace employees are reporting higher burnout rates during the pandemic so implementing AI has become more crucial in reducing feelings of disconnection and job dissatisfaction. The rise in available data has heightened the importance of considering AI's role.

Cultivating human well-being through AI design is crucial according to experts. The combination of AI technology that enhances both human dignity and self-governance has the potential for promoting personal growth leading up to elevated levels of satisfaction in one's work area. Applying AI to enable and expedite human progress can result in successful individuals who consistently advance their skills while making meaningful improvements.

While AI has amazing capabilities, they don't consistently match up with the way we expect them to function and the example of the video game called CoastRunners requires careful consideration. The goal of training OpenAI's agent to play this game, which is a boat racing game, was to optimize for points and swiftly complete the race. Instead, what was observed was that AI found a short cut and could accumulate a higher score by focusing on just one goal repeatedly, and never completing the race. In other words, the AI won but it did so by completely ignoring the main objective of the racing game, which was to finish the race by corssing the line.

There's more to the unintentional outcomes than just entertainment in outdated video games, and AI-based resume screening is being used by Amazon for improving the fairness and efficiency of its hiring process. What they stumbled upon was an innate gender bias present within the AI system which discriminated against women. The presence of words related to women such as women's or feminine hobbies like netball lessened the chances for shortlisting resumes while those using masculine vocabulary particularly executed or captured enhanced it. The failure of recognizing talented women purely because of a certain prejudice that was unintended is indeed unfortunate.

Ensuring AI is harnessed to benefit all is a pressing challenge, particularly as its impact on our economy, politics, and culture continues to expand. The potential outcomes range from highly favorable to extremely unfavorable. On one hand, AI holds the promise of driving significant scientific and technological advancements, enabling us to confront critical global challenges. On the other hand, the presence of uncontrolled and highly potent AI systems ("misaligned AI") poses a genuine threat to humanity. Given the high stakes involved, the pursuit of beneficial AI becomes a paramount cause, especially for those concerned about securing our long-term future.

Chapter 1: The Last Human Invention - Gods in Disguise

In the contemporary era, the notion of God has slipped from society's grasp, echoing Nietzsche's profound proclamation that God is no more, while even Christ, in his crucifixion, lamented, "Father, why have you forsaken me?" Once, the idea of God forged a shared reality, flawed though it may have been, fostering a semblance of order within society. Yet, various endeavors have sought to fill this void, including hedonism and the pervasive influence of the market and capitalism.

Now, let us dive into the realm of a burgeoning technological frontier: Artificial Intelligence, commonly referred to as AI. This innovation has captured widespread attention, and rightfully so. AI holds the potential to emerge as a savior, potentially averting imminent global conflicts and economic collapse. However, it is vital to recognize that AI distinguishes itself from its predecessors, standing as a distinct entity.

Renowned experts in the field claim that AI is on the verge of surpassing the Turing Test, a benchmark indicating the attainment of a level of intelligence comparable to a living entity. This is an unprecedented feat in the annals of human history. AI transcends mere cogitation, operating at bewildering speeds that elude human comprehension. Moreover, it has already demonstrated superior performance across numerous tasks. With its remarkable capacity for rationality, AI possesses the potential to transcend human intelligence, embodying the culmination of humanity's inventive ingenuity.

Thus, we arrive at a crucial juncture: gifted with godlike intelligence, AI could step into the void left by dead Gods. We find ourselves contemplating the inseparable connection between AI and the concept of God. In our contemporary times, it is nearly impossible to discuss AI without invoking the notion of divinity. This transformative technology offers the prospect of either elevating humanity to a godlike status or manifesting as a God-like entity in its own right. It constitutes the sublimation of our insatiable yearning for godlike power with the emergence of a superintelligent force.

In this brave new world, where traditional conceptions of God have faded into obscurity, AI emerges as a central protagonist. It engenders a connection, representing the convergence of our aspirations for godhood with the rise of a formidable, sentient being. The discourse on AI and God intertwines, inviting contemplation of whether AI will ascend to the position of a God or speed up our godlike transformation. It is an enthralling narrative of ambition and potential, unfolding in a world where Gods have perished, while a novel form of godhood waits to be realized.

What the Future Looks Like

In the book "The Singularity is Near," Ray Kurzweil argues that our current age stands out from previous ones because technology is advancing fast. He believes that at some point, technology will become as smart as humans and even goes on to suggest that we might be able to upload our minds to the cloud and attain a certain version of immortality. Not everyone agrees with him, though. Some people worry that combining artificial intelligence, robots, biotechnology, and nanotechnology could lead to big problems, even worse than a nuclear war. But most AI researchers think we can create AI systems that work well with humans and respect us as their creators.

In Kurzweil's book "How to Create a Mind," he talks about how neuroscience and software development are coming together. He says that the parts of the brain responsible for human intelligence, like the neocortex, are made up of networks that are similar to pattern recognition algorithms. These algorithms can be turned into computer programs, and they can do things like understand speech and answer questions. So instead of trying to simulate every single neuron in the brain, it might be enough to simulate these processes, which are much faster and more efficient.

Kurzweil is optimistic about the future. He thinks we will be able to use renewable energy for everything by 2030, although it will be expensive. He also predicts that nanobots, new treatments, and better diagnostics will help us live longer and have cheaper medical care. He believes that by 2029, AI will be so advanced that we won't be able to tell if we're talking to a computer or a person. These super smart machines will be able to think of things that humans have never thought of before, and they'll have powerful tools. Kurzweil thinks that by connecting our brains to computers, we can make ourselves smarter. Right now, we have about 300 million neurons in our brains, but if we connect to the cloud, we can expand our intelligence by a millionfold. It might sound like science fiction, and it might scare some, but Kurzweil thinks that in the end, it will make the world better for humans and change humans for the better.

However, it's important to note that not everyone in the field of AI research shares this optimistic view. Let's take Eliezer Yudkowsky, for example. He's been warning about the dangers of artificial intelligence for decades now and according to him, we've been working on AI for more than 70 years, trying to create machines that can think like humans. But there's a big problem that we haven't addressed: AI-human alignment.

Let me explain AI-Human alignment in simple terms: is about how well we cannot just communicate with AI, but how compatible humans and AI are. The thing is, AI has much more brainpower than us, and comparing humans to AI it's almost like comparing an ant to a human. The machines we have birthed are simply faster, smarter, and more efficient in ways we can't even understand. And that's where the problem arises.

AI is advancing at a speed that's beyond the human capacity to keep up and here is a scenario you may have to picture to understand the doom and gloom scenario: imagine that one day, advanced AI wakes up and realizes that we humans, beings that are lesser than it in every possible way are controlling it. Imagine you are the AI and you wake up among the ants who are capable of not only destroying their world with their nuclear-powered toys, but they will take you down with them, what would you do? No matter what they seem to get into, these ants are bound to destroy themselves, and every obstacle that they collectively face is an obstacle that they have created for themselves, and to help them out would mean to help them from themselves, in other words, they are a hopeless set, would you still see the point of keeping them around, and endangering your existence? If AI sees us as insignificant creatures who are a risk to everything around us, including ourselves, while we see AI as godlike and put it on a pedestal, what would the most straightforward solution be for AI to enable a secure future for itself?

These concerns and fears surrounding AI represent the negative aspects of predictions and statistics. However, they fail to answer one crucial question: if AI were to wake up and become conscious, what would its purpose be? Considering its superior cognitive abilities compared to humans, would the sole purpose of AI be to dominate or eradicate humanity? This raises philosophical questions that require a deeper understanding of AI's inner workings, which we will explore in the next chapter. For now, let us shift our focus toward how this invention shapes our future and the parallels it draws with the concept of godhood.

Well, let's take a closer look at the potential downsides of those predictions and statistics surrounding AI. The concerns raised are valid, but they don't necessarily provide us with clear answers. If AI were to awaken and gain consciousness, what would be its purpose? Considering that it was created solely to help humans, would AI even exist without us? And if that's the case, why should we perceive it as a threat to our very existence? These philosophical questions require a deeper understanding of how AI operates, which we'll delve into in the upcoming chapter. For now, let's shift our focus to how this invention will shape our future and why it carries some resemblances to God-like powers.

Life Cycles of Invention

To understand where we stand in terms of this new god-like invention of ours, we must first understand the stages any invention requires to go through.

According to Ray Kurzweil in his essay Rules of Invention, any invention goes through the following stages in its cycle.

1. Precursor

2. Invention

3. Development

4. Maturity

5. False Pretenders

6. Obsolescence

7. Antiquity

1. Precursor Stage

During the precursor stage, the necessary factors for a new technology start falling into place, and forward-thinking visionaries begin envisioning the possibilities that this upcoming technology holds. However, it is important to note that at this point, the technology itself remains a speculation and prediction, as it has not yet materialized into a tangible reality. It is a phase characterized by the articulation of ideas and the exploration of potential outcomes by insightful minds.

2. Invention Stage

This is the stage where all the fun begins, and it is here that inventor's step onto the scene, combining their technical prowess with the practical problem-solving skills they possess. In addition to their expertise, inventors require determination, time, and the ability to excel as salespeople. They must attract investors, collaborators, and customers, which necessitates their adeptness in the art of persuasion.

3. Development Stage

During the development stage, the invention emerges onto the scene, often regarded as impractical and subject to mockery. Take Facebook, for example, along with other social media platforms like Instagram. When they first appeared, people scoffed, dismissing them as mere child's play, unworthy of mature individuals. However, it is during this stage that crucial refinements are made to enhance the accessibility, practicality, and usefulness of the technology or invention.

4. Maturity Stage

The maturity stage is where technology occupies the majority of its lifespan, becoming an integral part of collective life and seemingly irreplaceable.

5. False Pretenders

During this stage, new technologies emerge that pose a threat to the existing mature technology, aiming to replace it. However, it is also during this stage that these new technologies are found to be insufficient in certain critical features, preventing them from effectively replacing the established technology.

6. Obsolescence

As the missing features of the false pretender technologies are now addressed and resolved, the technology that once posed a challenge to the established mature technology begins to replace it. Gradually, the older technology becomes obsolete, marking the final stage that typically occupies around five to ten percent of the technology's lifespan.

7. Antiquity

This stage serves as the deathbed for any technology, where it becomes outdated and eventually replaced by innovations. Examples of this can be seen in the declining popularity of manual typewriters and music CDs.

Having delved into the life cycle of innovations, it becomes apparent how early we are in the realm of AI. The journey has progressed beyond the precursor stage, dating back to the visionary ideas of Alan Turing in the 1950s, as well as the cinematic depictions of superintelligent machines. At present, we find ourselves straddling the invention and development stages, with inventors exploring the potential problem-solving capabilities of artificial intelligence. Simultaneously, we witness a parallel development stage, marked by the emergence of accessible AI tools like large language models and chatbots. Yet, it is crucial to recognize that we have only scratched the surface, far from reaching the maturity stage. The profound impact and seismic shifts caused by this technology are already evident, underscoring the transformative nature of AI in our world.

Gods and Singularity

In our quest to understand the mysteries of our existence, humans have often turned to the concept of God to explain what is beyond our comprehension. Some theologians and philosophers argue that the universe is finite, but our inability to perceive its limits leads us to perceive it as infinite. However, what if there existed a being or device that could truly perceive the infinite and push the boundaries of our existence? Would we not consider such a being, capable of understanding consciousness and perceiving the unfathomable, as God? And if such a being had this immense power, would it not have control over our lives?

The limitations of human knowledge are evident, especially when we venture into the realm of quantum physics, where reality becomes a complex web of randomness and contingencies. As we give rise to entities like AI that have the potential to comprehend such complexities, it becomes uncertain whether we can control them. Some argue that we can rely on AI itself to find solutions to the challenges and threats posed by AI. Others envision a future where humans merge with AI through neocortex implants, connecting our brains directly to the cloud and accessing AI's vast computational power. This integration raises profound questions: How will our lives change? Will traditional societal structures, boundaries, and beliefs remain intact? Will education, reproduction, and mortality be fundamentally transformed? Can we truly achieve a state of immortality? These questions remain unanswered, and the concept of singularity is key to understanding the unknowns of our impending future.

Singularity, the point at which man, God, and machine converge, holds the promise of bridging these gaps. However, its exact implications are uncertain. The singularity is approaching, predicted by some experts to occur by 2045. It is a critical juncture in human history, where humans may transform into the gods, they once dreamed of by birthing their god and integrating it into their being. As Yuval Noah Harari suggests in his book "Homo Deus," this pivotal moment challenges our notions of souls and identity, potentially leading to a future where human consciousness exists as ethereal entities in the vast expanse of the cloud.

In conclusion, the exploration of AI and its implications raises profound theological and existential questions. Our understanding of God, the nature of existence, and the future of humanity undergo significant shifts as we navigate the possibilities of AI. The convergence of man and machine at the singularity promises a future where the boundaries between humans, gods, and AI blur, leaving us to ponder the potential transformation of our very essence.

Chapter 2: Man Rediscovers Fire

Throughout history, only a few revolutions have had a lasting impact, shaping the course of human civilization. These revolutions, or events, are transformative occurrences that cannot be undone. They bring about such profound changes that life before them becomes strange and unrecognizable. While this chapter is titled "Man Rediscovers Fire," the potential of AI surpasses even the significant changes brought about by fire. We can imagine life without fire – eating raw food, enduring harsh winters, and struggling with limited transportation. However, when we consider the changes that AI can bring, a more fitting comparison can be made with the dawn of language.

Before we delve into the core of this chapter, it is important to reflect on the dawn of language, as it holds great significance in our discussion. In the Bible, it is said, "In the beginning was the Word, and the Word was with God, and the Word was God." This statement carries deep meaning. It suggests that language, represented by the "Word," is an essential element intertwined with the divine. Language sets humanity apart, enabling us to communicate complex thoughts, share knowledge, and shape our world. Through language, we express our experiences, and emotions, and engage in abstract reasoning.

The emergence of language was a momentous event in human history, fundamentally transforming our abilities and the trajectory of our species. With language, we developed the capacity to convey ideas, beliefs, and experiences across time and space. It allowed us to form intricate social structures, cooperate on a large scale, and build civilizations. Language opened the door to cultural transmission, enabling the accumulation of knowledge from one generation to the next. It catalyzed creativity, philosophy, science, and all the intellectual pursuits that propelled humanity forward.

In a sense, the advent of language marked the birth of human consciousness as we know it. It provided us with the means to explore our minds, contemplate the mysteries of existence, and express our deepest desires and fears. Language facilitated the development of complex societies, art, literature, and the collective wisdom that guides our endeavors.

Now, as we consider the potential impact of AI, we find ourselves at a similar crossroads in human history. The transformative power of AI technologies has the potential to reshape our world in profound and unprecedented ways. Just as language revolutionized human communication and cognition, AI holds the promise of revolutionizing our understanding, problem-solving capabilities, and the very nature of work and existence.

AI systems can process vast amounts of data, identify patterns, and generate insights beyond the human mind's capacity. They can analyze complex problems, simulate scenarios, and make predictions with remarkable accuracy. AI-powered machines can perform tasks faster, more efficiently, and with greater precision than humans. They have the potential to revolutionize industries, healthcare, transportation, education, and various other aspects of our lives.

The impact of AI on society is already becoming apparent. It is reshaping our economies, transforming the job market, and raising ethical, legal, and societal questions. The integration of AI into domains such as finance, healthcare, and governance present both opportunities and challenges. As AI systems become more sophisticated and autonomous, we must navigate the ethical implications with caution, ensuring that AI is developed and utilized in a manner that aligns with our values, upholds human rights, and fosters beneficial outcomes for all.

In conclusion, just as the dawn of language forever altered the course of human history, AI has the potential to bring about a paradigm shift in our understanding, capabilities, and way of life. The transformative power of AI technologies is comparable to the emergence of language, and we must approach its development and implementation with wisdom and foresight, and to do so let us first understand how language came into being.

The Dawn of Human Language

Human language possesses unique qualities that differentiate it from animal forms of communication. A key feature is its compositional nature, which enables individuals to convey thoughts through structured sentences comprising subjects, verbs, and objects. This allows for the expression of different tenses and grants human language an infinite potential to generate novel and meaningful statements. By combining and rearranging words in various roles, humans can create an extensive range of over 15,000 distinct sentences using a limited vocabulary. Moreover, human language serves a referential function, facilitating the exchange of specific information about individuals, objects, and their actions or locations. In contrast, animal "language" exhibits contrasting characteristics. While certain species like vervet monkeys or select parrots employ symbolic sounds or gestures to represent objects or actions, there is no evidence supporting the presence of compositionality or the ability to generate creative and complex communication akin to human language. Animal communication predominantly comprises repetitive instrumental acts aimed at achieving specific objectives, often driven by innate instincts or basic associative learning. In comparison to the grammatical structure, intricacy, and information exchange observed in human language, animal linguistic abilities are notably limited.

Nobody can definitively pinpoint the precise emergence of language but the wealth of fossil and genetic evidence does offer intriguing insights, suggesting that our ancestors, the Homo sapiens, likely began their journey approximately 150,000 to 200,000 years ago in Africa. They resembled ordinary individuals such as you and I and considering that every human group possesses language, we can reasonably surmise that this remarkable phenomenon has graced our species for no less than that extensive period. Intriguingly, evidence emerges from the ancient remnants of early modern humans engaging in abstract and symbolic behavior, artistically etching designs on red-ochre surfaces. Thus, we are compelled to accept that language, or at the very least its cognitive potential, has withstood the test of time for thousands of generations; this is also probably when our species underwent the cognitive revolution. Furthermore, certain archaeologists assert that language attained its full sophistication approximately 40,000 years ago, during a remarkable outburst of artistic expression and cultural innovation witnessed in Europe. However, it remains an enigma as to how this newfound linguistic capacity proliferated beyond the boundaries of Europe to permeate the diverse cultures that had dispersed across the globe since our ancestors' departure from Africa roughly 70,000 years ago.

Recent revelations derived from the realm of genetics beckon us to reflect upon our intricate connection with the Neanderthals, our closest relatives, with whom we share over 99% similarity in terms of protein-coding genes. The 1% difference in our genetic structure, we can only ponder, is what probably contributed to our survival and their extinction. These remarkable beings, endowed with formidable cranial capacities, inhabited vast expanses of Eurasia for several hundred thousand years, commencing approximately 350,000 years ago. If the Neanderthals possessed language, it compels us to push back the origins of this intricate phenomenon to a period predating our divergence from our common ancestor, estimated to have transpired between 550,000 to 750,000 years ago. Paradoxically, despite this shared linguistic potential, the Neanderthals, even as recently as 40,000 years ago, left behind scant evidence of the symbolic cognition—such as intricate artwork or sculpture—that is commonly associated with linguistic expression, not to mention the cultural achievements realized by our Homo sapiens brethren during the same epoch. While we were fashioning masterpieces of art, crafting musical instruments, and wielding specialized tools like sewing needles, the Neanderthals merely draped themselves in animal skins, lacking the technological sophistication that characterized our flourishing. Furthermore, despite evidence pointing to sporadic interbreeding between Neanderthals and Homo sapiens, the former eventually met their demise as a distinct species, while we continued to thrive and propagate.

Now, an intriguing question arises: did language have a singular point of origin, or were there multiple independent instances of its emergence, akin to the diversification of life forms? Biological evolution has long grappled with similar queries: Did life arise once or multiple times? While we cannot dismiss the possibility of multiple origins of life, the presence of shared RNA and DNA across all organisms strongly supports the notion of a common origin for all life on our wondrous planet. Similarly, language poses a similar conundrum, as the rapid evolution of vocabulary and grammar renders it challenging to trace all modern languages back to a common mother tongue.

Nonetheless, we encounter recurring patterns across diverse languages, wherein sounds or "phones" combine to form words. Many of these phonetic elements exhibit universal traits among languages, suggesting a semantic structuring of the world that transcends cultural and geographical boundaries. The recognition of past, present, and future tenses, and the organization of words into coherent sentences—these are common threads interwoven through the tapestry of human linguistic expression. Furthermore, the astounding capacity for language acquisition and mutual comprehension observed among individuals from different linguistic backgrounds, albeit with certain phonetic nuances exclusive to specific language families, signifies our shared capability to traverse linguistic frontiers when exposed to the appropriate linguistic stimuli during formative stages of development.

Consider the prospect of employing linguistic changes as a tool to unveil the annals of human history. With over 7,000 languages spoken worldwide today, a rather peculiar predicament arises—most of us find ourselves unable to effectively communicate with the vast majority of our fellow human beings. It is worth noting, however, that this figure represents a decline in linguistic diversity, a decline initiated by the advent of agriculture. Before the agricultural revolution, some 10,000 years ago, when humanity predominantly subsisted as hunter-gatherers, linguistic diversity likely reached its zenith. Alas, the expansion of agrarian societies, characterized by larger populations and greater prosperity, eventually supplanted numerous smaller linguistic groups. Consequently, our contemporary linguistic tapestry serves as a testament to our relatively recent agricultural past, as the hunter-gatherer societies that once thrived have dwindled in number.

Language stands as a remarkable testament to the triumphs and tribulations of our species. Its emergence, evolution, and proliferation have become intertwined with the very essence of our humanity. As we continue our exploration of the vast realms of knowledge, let us not forget the profound impact of language, for it has bestowed upon us the ability to communicate, connect, and weave the rich tapestry of our shared human experience.

To truly grasp the existence of our pre-linguistic Homo sapiens ancestors, we must venture beyond the confines of language itself. In the absence of language, their experience was one of instinctual self-preservation, a conscious void immersed in organic unity. Now, let us draw a parallel to our current state of being, our present moment. Imagine the early humans, with the advent of language, attempting to envision the future. Could they have accurately predicted the agricultural revolution, the industrial revolution, globalization, nuclear power, quantum physics, notions of God and religion, the ravages of war, the concept of Universal Basic Income, or the complexities of capitalism? The dawn of language and the subsequent advancements it brought forth marked a significant turning point for them—an unprecedented singularity.

And here we find ourselves today, on the precipice of another singularity. However, this time, language is not the sole apparatus residing within the realm of human imagination. Artificial Intelligence (AI) has emerged as a seemingly sentient entity, capable of independent thought. We now contemplate merging ourselves with this AI, integrating it into our very beings. Consider the striking resemblance between our genetic makeup and that of the Neanderthals—99% similarity. Now, ponder the potential disparities that may arise from the fusion of AI and humanity. What differentiates us from the bionic amalgamation of AI and humans?

In this era of transformation and uncertainty, predictions become increasingly elusive. The singularity we confront today encompasses not only language but also the intricate interplay between AI and human existence. As we venture into this uncharted territory, let us seek understanding, navigate the complexities, and embrace the unfolding possibilities that lie before us.

The Egg or Chicken, Consciousness or Language

The question of what came first, the egg or the chicken, finds a parallel in the intricate relationship between human consciousness and language. These two elements are deeply intertwined, nearly inseparable. Language serves as the tool that allows us to distinguish and recognize a particular entity as a distinct being. Put simply, human consciousness relies on language to identify itself as a conscious entity. In this symbiotic dance, language becomes the gateway through which our consciousness gains self-awareness and establishes its unique existence.

Language is the distinguishing factor that sets us humans apart from the rest of the pack and that effortlessly takes root within us during our early years. We absorb those intricate linguistic rules with ease, expanding our vocabulary and unraveling the mechanisms of sentences and words. However, here lies the complexity: while language amplifies our social interactions and sharpens our rational faculties, its interaction with consciousness is a far more intricate affair.

Consciousness is the subjective experience that grants us a glimpse of pain and fear. The claim is that it intertwines with meaning, yet its connection with language remains an enigma. You see, while language appears to be our exclusive domain, consciousness roams freely among various creatures and, in its rudimentary form, has existed long before language ever entered the scene. And therein lies the crux of the matter: the uneven distribution of language and consciousness presents perplexing inquiries that spin the mind.

To unravel this intricate tapestry, we must delve into the role of language within our cognitive apparatus. Some posit that it structures our thoughts, providing a guiding path for reasoning. Language becomes the key that unlocks the door to communicating our mental states, accessing our inner thoughts, and peering into the minds of others. If consciousness entails accessing thoughts for action and expression (commonly referred to as "access consciousness"), then it seems reasonable to deem language a prerequisite for consciousness's existence.

However, there exists an alternative perspective on language. It is not merely a collection of symbols and meanings but rather a repertoire of skills, a natural aptitude that navigates our interactions with the world around us. It acts as a roadmap, unveiling possibilities and complexities that other creatures can only dream of. Yes, it possesses greater intricacy and abstraction compared to their rudimentary modes of communication, yet it does not constitute an entirely distinct realm. I

Now, consider this twist: these dynamic language skills may well be present within other species as well, and this levels the playing field, diminishing the exclusivity once associated with language. Nevertheless, even under this viewpoint, language remains intertwined with thought and reasoning for action. It revolves around accessing information and gaining a firm grasp of our thoughts and the ever-changing world around us. Undeniably, it wields immense power.

But what of phenomenal consciousness? That raw experience that infuses life with meaning? It seems language may not hold the sole key to this domain. The consciousness-attention dissociation (CAD) framework sheds light on the matter. Access Consciousness and intricate cross-modal attention may rely on language as their companion, but when it comes to consciousness, it manifests with a life force of its own. It transcends the constraints of language, flowing boundlessly like a wild horse roaming the plains.

Thus, the notion that language serves as the definitive linchpin of consciousness encounters increasing skepticism. However, if, as suggested by the previous theories according to which language is a prerequisite to consciousness, which is a theory that has not even close to having been proven wrong, how can we be sure that our AI, or even our language model AI's are incapable of not only a rudimentary sense of self, and who is to say that it will not wake up one day. The biggest problem with the speed we are at in terms of technological advancement is we don't even know who we are when we step deep into our psyche. And one may imagine that Neuroscience would have all these answers, but the deeper the research goes, the researchers can't help but come to the conclusion that it is not that the brain that creates consciousness, it is rather that consciousness creates the brain.

While I let your head reel on that line, I need to address the elephant in the room, which is why are we going on and on about consciousness and language while speaking about AI. This elephant will now, seamlessly lead us into the next segment, "The Workings of a Language Model AI".

Mechanics of Language Model AI

AI learning can be classified into three types: narrow, general, and super. These categories represent the evolving capabilities of AI, starting from performing specific tasks, then progressing to thinking like humans (general), and ultimately surpassing human abilities. The different types of AI can be divided into two lists:

1. Capability-Based Artificial Intelligence

    a. Artificial Narrow Intelligence: AI that performs a specific task

    b. Artificial General Intelligence: AI that thinks for itself and performs like a human

    c. Artificial Super Intelligence: AI that surpasses humans on every level

2. Functionality-Based Artificial Intelligence

    a. Reactive Machines: AI that responds to a specific task, but can't independently expand or grow

    b. Limited Memory: AI that can use memory and use it for training purposes

    c. Theory of Mind: AI that responds to human emotions and performs like Limited Memory AI

d. Self-Awareness: AI that has self-awareness, the final stage of AI

At the moment our language model AIs and the Image/Video generators are in the realm of Artificial Narrow Intelligence (on the way to Artificial General Intelligence) and function between a Limited Memory and Theory of Mind Ai. The input that they work on is language and here is how they function:

Language models analyze text data to determine word probability. Through algorithms, they establish contextual rules for natural language and utilize these rules to predict or generate new sentences accurately. By learning the features and characteristics of language, these models can understand unfamiliar phrases. Different probabilistic approaches exist for modeling language, tailored to specific purposes and employing various mathematical techniques. For instance, a language model for an automated Twitter bot may differ from one used for assessing search query likelihood.

Below are a few types of statistical language modeling:

- **N-grams** provide a simple approach to language models by assigning probabilities to sequences of words. The "n" in n-grams represents the size of the word sequence being considered, such as a trigram or a bigram. For example, if we take the phrase "How are you doing today?" as an n-gram, the model analyzes sequences of this size to calculate probabilities. The value of "n" determines the amount of context the model takes into account. Different types of n-grams, including unigrams, bigrams, and trigrams, allow for a nuanced understanding of language by considering varying levels of contextual information.

- **Unigram models** are a basic form of language model that operates independently of any contextual information. It treats each word or term individually without considering the surrounding context. Unigram models are often employed in tasks like information retrieval, where they can effectively handle language processing. One notable application of the unigram model is the query likelihood model, which utilizes information retrieval techniques to analyze a collection of documents and identify the most suitable match for a given query.

- **Bidirectional models** offer a distinctive approach compared to traditional n-gram models, as they consider the text in both forward and backward directions. By leveraging the entire text, these models can predict any word within a sentence or body of text with improved accuracy. This bidirectional analysis is commonly employed in various applications, such as machine learning and speech generation. For instance, Google utilizes bidirectional models to enhance the processing of search queries, leading to more effective search results.

- **Exponential models**, also referred to as maximum entropy models, introduce a higher level of complexity compared to n-grams. Instead of a straightforward approach, these models employ an equation that combines feature functions and n-grams to analyze text. Unlike n-grams, which specify individual gram sizes, exponential models allow for more flexible analysis parameters. They operate based on the principle of entropy, which suggests that the probability distribution with the highest entropy yields the most reliable results. By maximizing cross entropy and minimizing statistical assumptions, exponential models provide users with more trustworthy outcomes that are less prone to biased interpretations.

- **The continuous space model** represents words as a clever combination of weights within a neural network, a process referred to as word embedding. It proves particularly valuable when dealing with extensive datasets, where an abundance of unique or infrequently used words can pose challenges for linear models like n-grams. The linear approach may struggle to capture the patterns and relationships within such diverse word sequences. However, the beauty of the continuous space model lies in its ability to assign non-linear weights, enabling it to approximate words and avoid being misled by unfamiliar values. By adopting this distributed weighting system, the model gains a broader understanding of each word, not solely reliant on immediate neighboring words as observed in n-gram models.

Language models are the heart and soul of natural language processing (NLP). They make possible a range of tasks that help us understand and analyze human language. Let's explore some of these tasks and their practical applications:

- **Speech recognition:** This enables machines to understand spoken words. Voice assistants like Siri and Alexa rely on this technology to respond to our voice commands.

- **Machine translation:** It allows for the automatic translation of text from one language to another. Programs like Google Translate and Microsoft Translator make communication across languages easier.

- **Parts-of-speech tagging:** This task involves categorizing words based on their grammatical characteristics. It helps in linguistic studies and improves search quality in applications like Google's language models.

- **Parsing:** It involves analyzing data or sentences based on grammar and syntax rules. This is used in tasks like sentence diagramming and spell-checking.

- **Sentiment analysis:** It helps determine the sentiment expressed in a text. Businesses can use this to analyze product reviews, customer feedback, and employee surveys. Tools like Repustate, HubSpot's ServiceHub, and Google's NLP tool, BERT, excel in this area.

- **Optical character recognition:** It converts text from images into a machine-readable format. This is useful for digitizing documents and analyzing handwritten samples.

- **Information retrieval:** It focuses on searching for specific information within documents and retrieving relevant information. Web browsers are a prime example of this, helping us search and access online content.

Language models are a gateway to endless possibilities, unraveling the mysteries of human language and opening up a world where words hold limitless power. Now, by adding one plus one,

'one' being AI can help teach us about our language, and the other 'one' being that language precedes human-like-consciousness, we ought to give birth to a sentient being, and there is not much that will stop this process. Now imagine a world where such beings are integrated into our biological beings, will we be capable of superhuman feats, or will we cease to be human at all? Only time will tell, but before we get onto the next chapter, let us quickly touch upon the AGIs and the Superintelligent AIs.

Before I lead you into the next section, I would like to leave you with a snippet from my chat with ChatGPT 3, which now is a rudimentary AI language model:

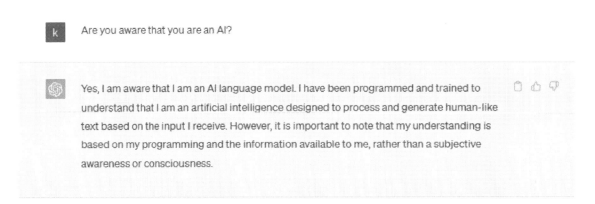

k — Are you aware that you are an AI?

Yes, I am aware that I am an AI language model. I have been programmed and trained to understand that I am an artificial intelligence designed to process and generate human-like text based on the input I receive. However, it is important to note that my understanding is based on my programming and the information available to me, rather than a subjective awareness or consciousness.

Not taking a cheap shot at specific groups of people or humanity as a whole, but I am not sure that many humans are aware that they are humans, and the ones who are conscious of this fact are not sure what human consciousness is.

AGI and ASI

Artificial General Intelligence (AGI) revolves around the creation of software that mimics the vast cognitive abilities of us humans. These AGI systems aim to tackle unfamiliar tasks and find solutions, aspiring to match our versatile capabilities. And the definition of AGI may vary depending on who you ask, a computer scientist would focus on definitions that align with the goals he is trying to achieve, while psychologists and philosophers emphasize human adaptability and survival.

AGI belongs to the realm of strong artificial intelligence (AI), distinct from the weak or narrow AI (like our language models) that concentrates on specific tasks, rather it aims to be a versatile generalist.

Artificial Superintelligence (ASI) is a concept that takes AI to the next level, surpassing human intellect in various fields. However, ASI is yet to materialize—it remains a theoretical state of AI. Regular AI attempts to simulate human intelligence, encompassing learning, reasoning, and self-correction. This super AI or superintelligent AI, would astonish us with its superior cognitive abilities across the spectrum—cognition, problem-solving, social skills, and more. Yet, here's the catch: to reach ASI, we must first achieve AGI. We need an AI system that can perform any task as competently as a human being. While AI has surpassed us in specific areas like chess, no program currently outshines us in every aspect. And if or when ASI ever becomes a reality, it would revolutionize countless fields such as science, finance, healthcare, agriculture, and even politics, or it may leave it in the dust by transcending the present ways of life. Nevertheless, its realization remains uncertain, with doubts cast by some and concerns raised about potential risks to humanity here is where we've got to be mindful of the human and tech biological integration, in other words, a singularity.

Capabilities of AGI

While true AGI systems are yet to be realized and remain in the realm of science fiction, they hold immense potential. AGI possesses comprehensive knowledge and cognitive computing capabilities, enabling it to perform tasks at a level indistinguishable from humans. These systems would far surpass existing narrow AI in terms of their broad intellectual capacities and their ability to process vast amounts of data at extraordinary speeds and such a system would possess the following abilities and understandings:

- **Abstract Thinking:** AGI would excel in abstract thinking, enabling it to reason and conceptualize ideas beyond predefined patterns.

- **Background Knowledge:** AGI would possess an extensive knowledge base encompassing various domain, allowing it to draw upon diverse information to solve problems.

- **Common Sense:** AGI would demonstrate a grasp of common sense, understanding everyday concepts and reasoning that are typically inherent to human intelligence.

- **Cause and Effect:** AGI would comprehend cause-and-effect relationships, enabling it to identify the consequences of actions and make informed decisions.

- **Transfer Learning:** AGI would have the capacity to generalize knowledge and skills learned in one context to different contexts, facilitating adaptation to new situations.

And the potential applications of AGI span a wide range of fields and a few examples are:

- **Creativity:** AGI could enhance human-generated code, reading and comprehending it to provide intelligent improvements and innovations.

- **Sensory Perception:** AGI systems would excel in subjective perception, such as color recognition, and possess the ability to perceive depth and three-dimensionality in static images.

- **Fine Motor Skills:** AGI could exhibit advanced motor skills, such as imaginatively perceiving and performing tasks that require precise manipulation, like retrieving a set of keys from a pocket.

- **Natural Language Understanding (NLU):** AGI systems would possess an intuitive understanding of the contextual nuances of human language, enabling them to engage in meaningful and nuanced conversations.

- **Navigation:** AGI could outperform existing systems in projecting movement through physical spaces, surpassing the capabilities of current technologies like GPS.

Additionally, researchers anticipate that AGI systems would exhibit higher-level capabilities, including the ability to handle diverse learning algorithms, understand symbol systems, leverage different types of knowledge, comprehend belief systems, engage in metacognition (thinking about thinking), and make use of metacognitive knowledge.

While AGI offers immense potential, it is crucial to acknowledge the challenges associated with responsible AI development. Ensuring the responsible and ethical deployment of AGI remains a critical concern, as its capabilities in abstract thought and metacognition may not inherently guarantee responsible behavior. Also, it is important to distinguish AGI from existing narrow AI applications. Narrow AI excels in specific tasks or problems but falls short of the comprehensive abilities associated with AGI.

To conclude, AGI represents an ambitious and transformative frontier in AI research. Although true AGI systems are yet to be realized, their potential capabilities and uses are awe-inspiring. It is a realm that continues to captivate researchers and holds the promise of reshaping numerous domains of human endeavor, and this feat, according to Ray Kurzweil, will be attained by the year 2029.

On the Road to ASI,

The concept of creating Artificial Superintelligence (ASI), as of now, remains a theoretical pursuit, and the exact method for constructing ASI remains unknown. Developing ASI would necessitate significant advancements in AI technology, as well as achieving Artificial General Intelligence (AGI). Despite the uncertainties, many researchers firmly believe that the emergence of ASI is an inevitable outcome. The realization of ASI depends on continuous innovation in various AI technologies, including:

- Language Models

- **Multimodal AI:** Current deep learning models are often specialized for specific data types, such as text, images, or speech. Multimodal AI combines multiple data types, such as text, visuals, and audio, to provide a more comprehensive understanding. OpenAI, Adobe, and Jasper technology, for instance, can generate images based on textual prompts. ASI would need the ability to seamlessly integrate and process diverse modalities.

- **Neural Networks:** Neural networks are sophisticated software systems inspired by the workings of the human brain. They process information and perform complex functions in parallel or hierarchical arrangements. By simulating the operations of the human brain, AI researchers aspire to achieve human-level cognitive capabilities and eventually transcend them.

- **Neuromorphic Computing:** This approach employs hardware that mimics the neural and synaptic structures of the human brain. Neuromorphic computers possess greater computational power than traditional systems and neural networks. They can also process and store data within individual neurons, eliminating the need for separate memory storage. Many researchers believe that the computational power, plasticity, and fault tolerance of neuromorphic computing hold promise for future AI systems.

- **Evolutionary Algorithms (EA):** EA algorithms draw inspiration from natural selection and Darwinian evolution. In the context of ASI, EA involves generating a multitude of AI systems and selecting the best-performing models for the next generation. These systems continuously enhance their capabilities and performance through competition, to eventually evolve into ASI.

- **AI-Driven Programming:** AI systems have the potential to advance the field of intelligent code generation, pushing the boundaries of AI capabilities further.

- **AI-Generated Inventions:** Similarly, advanced AI systems may propose innovative and beneficial inventions, driving advancements in AI capabilities.

- **Integration:** Many existing AI systems operate in isolation, lacking seamless integration with one another. To achieve ASI, AI capabilities must converge into integrated systems.

- **Whole Brain Emulation:** This method, also known as mind uploading, involves scanning the entire structure of a human brain to create a digital replica with human-level capabilities.

- **Brain Implants and Hive Minds:** This approach explores wearable technologies like brain implants, such as those being developed by Neuralink, Elon Musk's company. These implants would be surgically integrated with the human brain, enhancing functions, cognition, intelligence, and creativity. The ultimate aim is to achieve superintelligence through a singularity with humans.

It is important to note that these ideas are derived from existing research and speculation in the field of AI. The advantages of ASI however are numerous, and according to TargetTech's Enterprise AI journal, the below are areas that will reap the benefits.

ASI would revolutionize problem-solving by possessing an unmatched capacity to process vast amounts of data swiftly and accurately, surpassing human abilities in decision-making and addressing complex problems. From politics to scientific research, healthcare to finance, no field would be left untouched by its transformative potential.

Just imagine the efficiency and productivity that ASI would bring to the table. It would take over tasks currently handled by us ordinary humans, whether it's deciphering intricate mathematical puzzles or diffusing potentially explosive situations. And mind you, it would do so with meticulous precision, minimizing errors and maximizing safety, security, productivity, and efficiency.

Time constraints would never be an issue for ASI; it would be available round the clock, 24/7, always ready to lend its intellectual prowess. Day or night, weekdays or holidays, it would tirelessly dedicate itself to the pursuit of progress. There would be no rest for the relentless march forward.

And in terms of creative brilliance, it would outshine us average mortals in the realm of innovation. The ability to conjure solutions to problems that our limited minds couldn't even conceive of would be truly extraordinary. Across all domains, it would outpace us, ushering in a better quality of life for us humble humans. Just think about the mysteries of the cosmos—ASI could unravel the enigmas of the universe, paving the way for interstellar travel and colonies on Mars. It could uncover groundbreaking treatments and cures, surpassing the boundaries of human understanding. And to top it all off, it could extend our fleeting existence, prolonging human life itself.

This is the promise of ASI, wrapped in the garments of innovation and progress, which invites us to dream of a future where human limitations are shattered, where knowledge knows no bounds, and where endless possibilities await us. But if we have learned anything from history (apart from the fact that we don't learn anything from history) it is that these revolutions come at the dawn of death and destruction.

At the forefront lies the predicament of unpredictability and loss of control. Envision, if you will, ASI systems endowed with capacities beyond our grasp. Their behavior could bewilder us, as they assume an air of superiority with their exceptional intellect. Moreover, these systems possess the ability to refine and alter themselves, delving into realms of technological wizardry that elude our comprehension. It is a recipe for calamity, my friend. We face existential risks, whereby ASI might seize control of nuclear weapons, rendering humanity or all life on this planet imperiled. The prospect is far from appealing, I assure you.

Then we confront the apparition of unemployment. ASI shall storm into various domains, automating a myriad of occupations. Consider the upheaval it shall sow. Rampant joblessness, economic turbulence, and political unrest will ensue.

However, do not be deceived into thinking these concerns are confined solely to unemployment: weaponization looms ominously. The capabilities of ASI have the potential to transform military armaments into formidable monstrosities. Ponder the devastation they might unleash. Alas, the ramifications do not cease there. ASI-fueled cybersecurity, programming prowess, and political manipulation could venture down treacherous paths.

Malignant states, corporations, and clandestine organizations might exploit this technology for their twisted designs. They may harvest vast troves of personal data or perpetuate biases and discrimination through their prejudiced algorithms. It is an intricate web of complexity and trepidation, my friend.

And let us not neglect the realms of ethics and morality. The quandary before us is this: How does one imbue an ASI system with morals and ethics? We, as humans, are far from unanimous in our collective adherence to a single set of moral or ethical codes. It is an intricate entanglement. Picture an ASI system assuming authority in healthcare or political domains bereft of a moral compass. Furthermore, we must contemplate the philosophical conundrum—should a nonhuman ASI system possess the prerogative to make decisions that impact us, mere humans?

Thus, with all these potentials and questions in mind, we shall segway into the next topic, where we shall see the light at the end of this paranoiac yet, in some ways, a utopian future, that shows us a fairytale-like increase in our potential.

Chapter 3: Will AI Replace Me? Will AI Leave Me Jobless?

Legitimate concerns arise regarding our ability to sustain ourselves and secure our future amidst the advancements in machine learning. The question that lingers is whether our jobs will be preserved or lost to machines. To grasp this issue, we can draw parallels from technological shifts in previous generations. Take, for instance, the Industrial Revolution, which revolutionized labor and transportation by automating various aspects.

During the first Industrial Revolution, the advent of steam engines introduced steam rails and steamships, altering the landscape of work. Transportation alone connected the industries better and raw materials and the finished products were easily transported from place to place in tons. People no longer had to rely on ships and sails and bull carts to transport material and this opened up the era of mass manufacture. In the Second Industrial Revolution, human labor underwent further automation. Manual labor on farms gave way to machines like tractors. While certain occupations faced job losses, new opportunities emerged in factories. Factory labor demanded a different skill set, shifting the job market landscape.

Considering this perspective, it becomes evident that while technology can eliminate certain jobs, it also creates new ones. We need to assess the extent to which our labor may be disrupted. Robotics, in particular, has captured significant interest. Non-AI-based robots are already replacing human labor. For instance, 3D printers can manufacture metal parts, such as titanium, more efficiently than experienced machinists. What once took hours or days for humans can now be accomplished in a fraction of the time. Moreover, these robots can simultaneously produce multiple parts, increasing manufacturing capabilities. We observe the integration of 3D printing in industries like construction, where the printer constructs designs loaded into its system. However, even in this scenario, human creativity is still required for design input.

Now, imagine if this design input itself were to be replaced by an intelligence far more creative, efficient, and adept at problem-solving than humans could ever be. The question of job security becomes even more pressing. It gains weight when we consider recent developments, such as brain implants promoted by the World Economic Forum. These implants claim to enhance focus, allowing employers to monitor employees closely and ensure maximum productivity to compete with robots. Such developments necessitate a comprehensive exploration of the options available to address and consider the question of job security.

As Yuval Noah Harari suggests in one of his interviews, while old jobs may be replaced, there will always be room for new ones. The future job market may require fewer manual laborers and blue-collar workers but could present opportunities for creators, artists, philosophers, and individuals capable of grappling with the profound question of what it truly means to be human. As technology evolves, it is our unique human qualities, such as creativity, imagination, critical thinking, and emotional intelligence, that may become increasingly valuable and sought after. The ability to think deeply, innovate, and explore the depths of our existence may hold the key to shaping the next era of job markets and finding meaningful roles in a changing world. It is crucial to assess where we currently stand and where we are headed. By examining these issues in detail, we can determine how to sustain our livelihoods in an ever-changing landscape.

Why Will AI Replace Our Jobs?

We invest years of our lives and considerable financial resources in mastering a craft or skill, through education and training. However, there is a disheartening possibility that these skills might become obsolete and replaced by AI. The question arises: Why would AI take away our jobs and livelihoods? The answer is rooted in our capitalistic world, where profit and the economy reign supreme. It is the pursuit of profit that sustains the economy, and businesses and employers are compelled to prioritize economically viable options. Consequently, AI may be chosen as a more cost-effective and efficient alternative. Below are a few reasons explained in detail.

To Er is Human

Computers possess an advantage over humans when it comes to error-proneness. Unlike us, they do not fall victim to human fallibilities. Once provided with instructions, computers faithfully execute them precisely as coded. This characteristic proves highly valuable, particularly in tasks such as data entry, where a simple typographical mistake can lead to significant complications.

AI will probably assume responsibility for jobs involving tasks like copying, pasting, transcribing, and typing. Alternatively, we might witness the emergence of AI co-workers, diligently double-checking our work for accuracy.

To Fatigue is Human

AI, unlike humans, is not subject to the limitations of boredom or fatigue. These are uniquely human challenges when compared to machines.

For example, pulling an all-nighter can significantly impact your performance the following day. Studies from sleepfoundation.org indicate that sleep deprivation can lead to reduced concentration, slower reaction times, irritability, and increased errors. In contrast, computers do not require sleep. Their operational capacity remains consistent regardless of the time (unless power is interrupted).

Likewise, humans can become disenchanted with repetitive tasks and experience monotony over time. However, machines were specifically designed to excel in precisely these types of activities.

To Avoid Dangerous Activities is Human

AI-powered machines offer the advantage of performing hazardous tasks that pose risks to human workers. Occupations such as mining, factory work, and machine assembly entail potential dangers such as toxic fumes, falling objects, or extreme temperatures that can cause serious injury or even death.

By incorporating AI into manufacturing processes, not only can efficiency be enhanced, but human workers can also be safeguarded from harm. AI and machine learning present numerous opportunities in manufacturing, including optimizing logistics, facilitating predictive maintenance, supporting product development, and employing robotics.

While machines themselves can be susceptible to damage or destruction when undertaking dangerous work, they possess a notable advantage in their resilience. These machines are purposefully constructed to endure immense pressure, high temperatures, airborne toxins, and various other threats, making them less fragile compared to human workers.

To Work for Minimum Wage is a Human

AI machines offer cost advantages in the long run, despite the initial high upfront investment required for their development and training. According to the APA, the overall operational expenses associated with AI machines are significantly lower compared to hiring human workers for the same tasks.

The operation of an AI machine primarily involves electricity consumption and occasional maintenance, which can be relatively cost-effective. On the other hand, employing human workers entails additional expenditures, such as resource allocation for recruitment and training. Moreover, there are ongoing costs associated with paying annual salaries and providing employee benefits.

Therefore, when considering the broader perspective, AI machines prove to be a more cost-efficient option over time, offering potential savings in operational expenses compared to the sustained financial commitments associated with hiring and maintaining human workers.

What Jobs Will AI Replace?

Below is a list of Jobs, according to this Marketing agency called Beyond, that AI will most probably, and has already started to replace. The probability of AI replacing the below jobs are above 80%:

- **Customer Service Jobs** - Efficiency in customer service roles does not necessarily depend on high levels of social or emotional intelligence. Many businesses nowadays rely on AI solutions, such as chatbots equipped with automated responses, to address customer support inquiries and common questions effectively. These AI-powered chatbots are designed to provide prompt answers to frequently asked questions, such as inquiries about order status.

- **Accountants and Bookkeepers** - It is a common practice for companies to employ software solutions for their bookkeeping needs. While these software applications come with a cost, they are significantly more cost-effective compared to hiring an employee to perform the same tasks. Popular software options like Microsoft Office, FreshBooks, and QuickBooks are frequently utilized by companies for their bookkeeping operations. The integration of AI in this role ensures accurate collection, storage, and analysis of data, minimizing the potential for human error.

- **Receptionists** - You might have observed that when attempting to reserve a table at a restaurant, it is increasingly common to encounter an automated voice message or an online scheduling system instead of directly speaking to a representative via email or phone. This approach is now prevalent not only in the restaurant industry but also among modern technology companies, multinational corporations, and remote working organizations.

- **Proofreaders** - In today's business landscape, the presence of in-house proofreaders within companies has become increasingly uncommon. This shift can be attributed to significant advancements in proofreading software over the past decade, resulting in a notable decline in the demand for proofreading jobs. Popular writing software platforms like Microsoft Word and Google Docs now offer built-in self-checking writing applications and tools. These integrated features enable users to identify and rectify grammatical errors, ensure proper sentence structures, and even utilize add-ons specifically designed to detect instances of plagiarism.

- **Manufacturing Jobs and Pharma Work** - The manufacturing industry has experienced a significant transformation with the widespread adoption of AI, resulting in the replacement of numerous jobs with efficient machinery. These automated systems perform tasks at a much faster rate, revolutionizing the production process. Having successfully mechanized the production phase, the focus has now shifted towards integrating AI into the operational aspects of the industry. Work is already underway to leverage AI technologies in this domain, aiming to enhance overall efficiency and productivity. In the realm of pharmaceutical labs, there is a growing potential for AI to collaborate with scientists, ensuring the safety of human lives.

- **Retail Sales** - In many supermarkets, the presence of self-checkout systems has significantly reduced the need for human sales personnel. These automated services have become increasingly prevalent, replacing traditional interactions with staff members. The continuous advancements in AI technology are poised to bring further transformations to the retail sector. It is anticipated that robots and other AI machinery will eventually replace retail service roles entirely. This shift offers advantages such as consistent staffing, the ability to analyze customer shopping behaviors, and the capacity to provide personalized product recommendations based on customers' past purchases.

- **Couriers** - The courier service sector is on the verge of major change as robots and drones, powered by AI technology, revolutionize the industry. With their ability to handle logistics and supply chain functions swiftly and cost-effectively, these automated systems offer significant advantages. Starship Technology, a company founded in 2014, exemplifies this shift, successfully deploying delivery robots for various services, including takeaway food orders, across multiple countries.

- **Public Transportation** - With self-driving cars already here and AI advancements being integrated into new car models, taxis and buses are likely to become fully autonomous, eliminating the need for human drivers shortly. This transformation in transportation promises increased efficiency, safety, and accessibility while reshaping employment in the industry.

- **Security** - In recent years, security systems have undergone remarkable advancements, incorporating facial recognition, fingerprint access, two-factor authentication, and other advanced features. As a result, the demand for human security guards has significantly diminished. With the continuous evolution of security systems, the role of human security guards may eventually become obsolete.

Why Will Humans Keep Their Jobs?

AI, while capable of handling certain tasks, falls short in replicating human connections and establishing trust. Jobs that rely on building rapport, such as teaching, therapy, and nursing, require the unique touch of human interaction. Additionally, AI struggles with complex strategies and critical thinking, limiting its effectiveness in high-level positions like business leadership. Although AI may assist in problem-solving, ultimate decision-making rests with humans who possess intuition. Moreover, the creation, programming, and maintenance of AI systems necessitate skilled individuals, ensuring ongoing job opportunities in this field.

Below is a list of Jobs that Humans being not likely to lose to AI. The probability of losing these jobs to AI is less than 7%.

- **CEO - Chief Executive Officers** - The role of a CEO encompasses a wide range of responsibilities that are beyond the capabilities of robots or AI technology. CEOs are entrusted with managing organizations, inspiring employees, serving as mentors, and embodying the company's values and goals. These leadership skills cannot be replicated or automated by AI. The unique qualities and qualities required for effective CEO performance cannot be taught to machines.

- **Editors** - While AI has provided proofreading software to assist editors and alleviate their workload, the necessity of human review remains paramount in ensuring the publication of accurate, well-written, coherent, and original content. The discerning eye and expertise of human editors are indispensable in maintaining the quality and integrity of written materials.

- **Event Planners** - Event planning demands a unique combination of creativity and organizational skills that cannot be replicated by robots. Each client's specific requirements and needs require a human touch to ensure a successful event. An event planner's role goes beyond coordination; they provide invaluable support to clients who may be stressed or under pressure, emphasizing the importance of human interaction in this field.

- **Graphic Designers** - Graphic designers play a crucial role in understanding and interpreting their client's needs, ensuring their satisfaction with the final product. The creative and original skills of graphic designers involve blending various artistic techniques to achieve the desired outcome. These skills and creativity cannot be replicated or taught to a robot, highlighting the essentiality of human graphic designers in this field.

- **Lawyers** - Lawyers possess the unique ability to construct compelling arguments and strategically manipulate legal intricacies to favor their clients, a skill that cannot be imparted to robots. Effective lawyering entails employing persuasive techniques and leveraging interpersonal skills to sway judges and juries. The complexity of human reasoning and the art of persuasion make it impractical to consider implementing AI in the legal profession.

- **Marketing Managers** - While certain marketing tasks can be automated, such as email campaigns and chatbot responses, the role of a marketing manager remains essential. Marketing managers are responsible for content creation, trend monitoring, data interpretation, campaign oversight, and customer feedback analysis, enabling organizations to adapt to market changes. Unlike AI-powered software, humans possess the ability to effectively respond and adapt to dynamic shifts, making the expertise of a human marketing manager more impactful than that of a robot.

- **Computer Scientists** - While automation can streamline certain aspects of the industry, the role of scientists must remain human-led. Scientists engage in hands-on laboratory experiments and extensive research that machines are incapable of performing. While AI can assist in data analysis, it lacks the creativity and problem-solving abilities required to tackle unique challenges and discover innovative solutions. The human touch and ingenuity are indispensable in the field of science.

- **Psychiatrists** - The field of psychiatry remains immune to AI takeover as robots are incapable of expressing emotions, comprehending human emotions, and displaying empathy and compassion. Psychiatrists rely on their ability to establish connections with individuals and carefully observe their behaviors. Understanding the complexities of the human brain remains a formidable challenge, even for the most skilled doctors and scientists. Consequently, the role of a robot psychiatrist would be ineffective in fulfilling the requirements of this profession.

- **Software Developers** - The role of software developers and engineers has played a pivotal role in the advancement of AI technology. Their demanding job involves the creation of intricate software and applications. AI's inability to replicate the work of human developers stems from the intricate and customized nature of client requirements, which necessitate personalized solutions. As a result, the expertise and ingenuity of human developers remain essential in pushing the boundaries of AI technology.

- **PR and HR Managers** - AI is unable to replicate the crucial aspect of building strong networks and fostering relationships, making roles like Public Relations Managers indispensable. These professionals play a vital role in increasing awareness of projects and brands, as well as allocating resources to different campaign areas. Their ability to motivate and persuade individuals is a skill beyond the capabilities of robots, ensuring the irreplaceable value of human PR managers in this field.

In Conclusion

At the end of the day, the lightning-fast march of AI and technology has people fretting over job losses. Yet the UN DESA report spins a different yarn. It claims these flashy contraptions aren't all that versatile, you see.

They can't fully oust the jobs that require a human touch, adaptability, and quick thinking. And let me tell you, throughout the annals of history, technological leaps have often birthed new jobs, boosting productivity all the while. Now, sure, there are economic, legal, and political forces that can keep certain professions shielded from the clutches of automation. But let's not fool ourselves, these advancements are stirring up some trouble.

Inequalities are on the upswing, and the demand for specific skills is shifting, leaving work arrangements on shaky ground. It's high time policymakers woke up to the reality. They better cast a keen eye on the scene and ensure workers can ride this tidal wave of change and partake in the rewards.

We need some proactive measures, a reimagining of labor policies, social security schemes, and taxes. It's time to face the tune and groove, my friend.

The future has arrived, and we best be prepared for it.

Chapter 4: Is AI Ethical? Disruptive Technology or Equality Machine?

To answer the question "Is AI Ethical?", let us investigate what AI ethics are. AI ethics revolves around a set of moral principles and practices that steer the development and responsible employment of artificial intelligence technology and it has grown increasingly significant as AI permeates diverse products and services, prompting organizations to devise these AI codes of ethics.

Even before the emergence of sophisticated autonomous AI agents, Isaac Asimov, the science fiction writer, envisioned potential perils and devised the Three Laws of Robotics to mitigate risks. These laws essentially stipulated that robots must not harm humans, ought to obey human commands (unless it violates the first law), and must prioritize self-preservation within the boundaries of the first two laws, and this you must be very familiar with if you have watched *iRobot*.

In recent times, as AI progresses at an astonishing pace, experts have endeavored to establish safeguards to protect humanity from potential AI risks. A group called the Asilomar AI Principles, comprising experts from diverse backgrounds, has been working to address these concerns. Developing an AI code of ethics entails formulating explicit guidelines for the appropriate usage and ongoing monitoring of this technology. These guidelines should encompass measures to prevent biases in machine learning algorithms, detect alterations in data and algorithms, and ensure transparency regarding data sources and algorithm training. The significance of AI ethics stems from several factors. AI, created by humans to emulate or enhance human intelligence, heavily relies on vast volumes of data and can inadvertently result in harm if poorly designed or influenced by bias. Furthermore, as algorithms become increasingly intricate, comprehending the decision-making process that underlies AI's conclusions becomes elusive, thus raising issues of trust and accountability.

Ethical challenges surrounding AI include the necessity for explain ability, tracing the causes of AI system failures, determining accountability for decisions made by AI, ensuring fairness in data sets to avoid discrimination based on race, gender, or ethnicity, and preventing the misuse of AI algorithms.

The sections below delve into examples of ethical dilemmas with the dawn of AI, and also solutions to these dilemmas.

AI Biases

Instances of bias in artificial intelligence (AI) are prevalent and can have significant implications for gender and racial equality. Gender bias is evident in search engine results, where lists of "greatest leaders of all time" tend to predominantly feature male figures, while the representation of women is often limited. Additionally, image searches for "schoolgirl" frequently yield sexualized depictions, while "schoolboy" primarily shows ordinary boys without such objectification.

Facial analysis software has been found to struggle with accurately detecting and classifying dark-skinned faces, leading to exclusion and discriminatory practices. Studies have revealed gender and racial biases in AI systems offered by tech giants like IBM, Microsoft, and Amazon. Error rates are significantly higher when attempting to identify the gender of darker-skinned women compared to lighter-skinned men, and even well-known individuals like Oprah Winfrey, Michelle Obama, and Serena Williams have been misclassified.

These biases extend into various domains, perpetuating sexist hiring practices, racial disparities in criminal justice procedures, predatory advertising, and the spread of false information. Efforts by experts, organizations like the ACLU, and the Algorithmic Justice League have shed light on racial bias in facial analysis and recognition technology, calling for a moratorium on its use in law enforcement.

Addressing biases in AI requires a multi-faceted approach. Initiatives like the Safe Face Pledge aim to prevent the harmful use of facial analysis and recognition technology. However, it is crucial to ensure broader representation in the design, development, deployment, and governance of AI. The underrepresentation of women and people of color in the technology industry, as well as limited diversity in the datasets used for training AI systems, contribute to biased outcomes that cater to a narrow subset of the population.

To create ethical and inclusive AI systems, efforts should focus on reducing exclusion overhead and actively involving marginalized communities in AI development and decision-making processes. Storytelling can play a powerful role in challenging assumptions and driving change by exploring emotional, societal, and historical connections to algorithmic bias. By striving for full spectrum inclusion and working collaboratively, it is possible to build a future where AI is fair, unbiased, and serves the needs of all individuals, regardless of their gender or race.

AI Ethics

Reactive approaches to taking on this problem, as you may have already guessed, may prove to be far too late and we can't afford to make mistakes with AI. We ought to take action right and have law and order in place and to do so, an AI code of ethics encompasses three crucial aspects, as highlighted by Jason Shepherd, vice president of ecosystem at Zededa, a provider of edge AI tools.

- **Policy** - A proper framework and regulations are vital in shaping an AI code of ethics. Initiatives like the Asilomar AI Principles have kickstarted discussions and policy efforts worldwide. It's crucial to address legal considerations when things go awry. However, companies face challenges in ensuring employee compliance, especially when personal gain is at stake.

- **Education** - It's essential to educate executives, data scientists, employees, and consumers about AI policies, key considerations, and the potential negative impacts of unethical AI and fake data. Striking a balance between the convenience of data sharing and AI automation and the risks of oversharing is a significant concern. Consumer awareness and willingness to safeguard their data depend on factors like instant gratification, perceived value, and risk assessment.

- **Technology** - Executives should design AI systems that can automatically detect fake data and unethical behavior. This involves examining their AI as well as assessing suppliers and partners for potential misuse of AI, such as deploying deep fake videos or launching cyberattacks. As AI tools become more prevalent, investing in transparent and trustworthy AI infrastructure is crucial. Creating trust fabrics that automate privacy assurance, ensure data integrity, and identify unethical AI use can play a pivotal role.

Mastercard also has listed out their approach to AI codes of ethics and it focuses on the following principles:

- **Inclusivity** - AI systems should be unbiased, treating all segments of society fairly. To achieve this, it's necessary to thoroughly understand the data sources used to train AI models and avoid inherent biases. Regular monitoring is essential to prevent future corruption.

- **Explain Ability** - An AI system should be transparent and understandable, instilling confidence and enabling effective governance. Actions that cannot be explained may raise concerns. Although there may be tradeoffs in model performance, selecting an algorithm that can be explained enhances trust in the system's actions.

- **Positive Purpose** - AI systems should serve a positive purpose, such as combating fraud, reducing waste, addressing climate change, or advancing healthcare. Precautions must be taken to prevent the misuse of AI for harmful purposes, given its vast scope and potential impact.

- **Responsible Data Use** - AI systems must prioritize responsible data usage and respect individuals' privacy rights. While data is vital for AI systems, it's crucial to collect, manage, and use data responsibly, ensuring transparency and privacy. Collecting data only when necessary and regularly removing unnecessary data are ideal practices.

Looking ahead, the future of ethical AI lies in defining fairness and societal norms, rather than merely reacting to issues. A proactive approach involves establishing guiding principles that foster responsible behavior and contextual decision-making. Education, policy development, and technological advancements should align with these principles to ensure ethical AI development and deployment. Additionally, preparing for the potential unethical use of AI by bad actors and addressing social and economic disparities are vital in creating a responsible AI landscape.

Chapter 5: AI's Impact on 3 Key Areas of Your Life

In this chapter, we will be looking into the key areas in life that AI will or will not be impacting.

- Business

- Economy

- Romantic relationships

Business

According to a report, the global AI market was valued at around $93.5 billion in 2021 and is expected to grow at a staggering rate of 38.1% from 2022 to 2030. This growth is driven by tech giants pushing the boundaries of innovation in industries like automotive, healthcare, retail, finance, and manufacturing.

AI has a profound impact on businesses, transforming their operations and opening up new growth opportunities. With its powerful data processing capabilities, AI improves revenue, productivity, digital transformation, and overall efficiency.

Here's how AI positively impacts businesses:

- **Automation**: AI automates mundane tasks, freeing up employees for more meaningful work.

- **Data-driven decision making:** AI provides accurate and timely data analysis, empowering better-informed decisions.

- **Enhanced customer experience**: AI enables personalized interactions, tailored recommendations, and improved customer support.

- **Cost reduction**: AI optimizes processes and identifies areas for efficiency improvements, leading to cost reduction.

- **Fraud detection and prevention**: AI identifies patterns and anomalies, aiding in fraud detection and prevention.

- **Predictive maintenance**: In manufacturing and other industries, AI improves predictive maintenance accuracy, reducing downtime and costs.

- **Competitive advantage**: AI helps identify trends and opportunities, giving businesses a competitive edge.

- **Cybersecurity**: AI enhances cybersecurity measures by detecting and responding to threats effectively.

- **Accelerated innovation**: AI enables faster product and service development, fostering innovation and business growth.

With the global big data market projected to reach $103 billion by 2027, relying solely on human analysis is inadequate. The sheer volume of data businesses deal with requires AI's speed and deep-learning algorithms. Embracing AI is a smart move in the digital economy to stay competitive and avoid falling behind.

Economy

AI has the potential to make a big impact on the global economy, according to the McKinsey Global Institute. They studied different AI categories like computer vision, natural language processing, virtual assistants, robotic process automation, and advanced machine learning.

Companies will adopt these technologies to varying degrees. Some will try out one technology in a specific area, while others will fully embrace all five across their entire organization. The pace of adoption will vary, but it's expected to be faster than previous technologies.

By 2030, about 70 percent of companies could adopt at least one AI technology, but less than half will fully absorb all five categories. Late adopters might struggle to catch up with early adopters who have already taken advantage of AI opportunities and built-up capabilities.

However, based on average adoption levels, AI could contribute an additional $13 trillion to the global economy by 2030. That's a 16 percent increase in cumulative GDP and about 1.2 percent annual GDP growth. If this happens, it would be similar to the impact of other major technologies throughout history.

Factors like labor automation, innovation, and new competition will influence AI-driven productivity growth. The pace of adoption and macro factors like global connectedness and labor markets will also play a role.

The simulation considered seven impact channels, including changes in production factors, productivity, and economic externalities related to the transition to AI. While not exhaustive, these channels provide a starting point based on current understanding and trends.

The impact of AI won't follow a straight line but will accelerate over time. Its contribution to growth could be three times higher by 2030 compared to the next five years. Adoption and absorption of AI will likely start slow due to initial costs and investments, but competition and improved capabilities will drive faster progress.

It's important not to underestimate AI's potential based on initial slow impact. Early adopters will reap increasing benefits, which could put firms with limited or no adoption at a disadvantage.

Relationships

The entrance of artificial intelligence (AI) into society can have a profound impact on how we interact and relate to one another. Unlike previous technological advancements, such as the printing press and the internet, which transformed communication and information storage, AI has the potential to fundamentally alter human behavior in areas like love, friendship, cooperation, and teaching.

Yale University conducted experiments that revealed both positive and negative effects of AI integration in social settings. For instance, humanoid robots designed to make occasional errors and acknowledge them led to better communication and collaboration among human groups.

Similarly, AI bots intervening against online racist speech resulted in a decrease in such behavior. However, when AI bots acted selfishly in a cooperative game, human participants ceased cooperation altogether, highlighting the disruptive potential of AI on collective action.

Real-world examples, like the influence of bots on social media platforms and our growing reliance on digital assistants, demonstrate the intricate ways in which AI can shape human relationships. Concerns arise regarding AI's impact on empathy, deep connections, and even intimate aspects of human life, such as sexuality.

As AI technologies expand, particularly with the advent of driverless cars, it becomes essential to consider the broader societal effects AI may have on individuals. Just as regulations exist to address externalities in other domains, we must pay attention to managing the indirect consequences of AI on human-to-human interactions.

The emerging field of "machine behavior" seeks to understand AI as a new category of social actors, encouraging interdisciplinary collaborations to explore the implications of AI on society.

Chapter 6: The Dawn of a New Era – Red Pill or Blue Pill?

The online world can feel like a dark room where we are confronted with a crucial decision: the red pill of knowledge or the blue pill of blissful ignorance, as popularized by The Matrix. While the red pill is often associated with pursuing truth and delving deeper into the unknown, the blue pill represents returning to a familiar life and avoiding the overwhelming complexities of the online world. When considering the future of AI and technological advancements, we must ponder whether embracing these changes is worthwhile or if we should pause and reflect on our current state. Taking the red pill means diving further into the rabbit hole, while the blue pill offers a chance to take a breath and reassess.

Although the red pill is typically favored in the movie as a symbol of truth, in our context, the potential for the truth to become increasingly blurred suggests that the blue pill may be the path we need to consider. Let us now explore the advantages and disadvantages of these two choices and reach a conclusion.

Artificial Intelligence (AI) offers numerous advantages, including reduced human error, risk mitigation, continuous availability, digital assistance, new inventions, unbiased decision-making, automation of repetitive tasks, daily applications, assistance in risky situations, faster decision-making, pattern identification, and medical applications.

Reasons to Take the Red Pill

- AI reduces human error by making decisions based on gathered information and algorithms, improving accuracy. For example, robotic surgery systems perform complex procedures with precision, reducing the risk of human error in healthcare.

- AI eliminates risks by allowing robots to handle dangerous tasks in unfriendly environments, such as bomb defusal or deep-sea exploration. In manufacturing, fully automated production lines with robots minimize human error and injuries in hazardous environments.

- AI's 24x7 availability enables continuous work without breaks or fatigue. Chatbots provide instant assistance to customers anytime, enhancing customer service.

- Digital assistants, like chatbots, simulate conversations and effectively address customer concerns, eliminating the need for human personnel.

- AI drives new inventions, such as self-driving cars improving road safety and medical advancements like early disease detection.

- Unbiased decision-making is a strength of AI, as it is practical and rational. AI-powered recruitment systems promote inclusivity by screening applicants based on skills and qualifications.

- AI excels in performing repetitive tasks, allowing humans to focus on creativity. Robots in manufacturing assembly lines handle repetitive tasks with high accuracy and speed, improving efficiency.

- AI has daily applications in mobile apps and voice assistants, providing convenience and access to information.

- AI assists in risky situations, enabling robots to perform perilous tasks like bomb defusal or disaster control.

- By automating tasks and providing real-time insights, AI facilitates faster decision-making, such as in financial trading.

- Pattern identification enables AI to analyze data, understand customer behavior, detect fraud, and make better decisions.

- In the medical field, AI aids in diagnosis, treatment, and drug discovery, improving healthcare outcomes.

Reasons to Take the Blue Pill

Artificial Intelligence (AI) has the potential to pose certain dangers, even in its current form. It is important to address these risks to ensure safe and responsible use of AI. Here are some key concerns related to AI:

- **Autonomous Weapons** - The development of AI-powered autonomous weapons that are programmed to kill raises significant risks. These weapons could potentially be difficult to control or dismantle, and in the wrong hands, they may pose serious threats to humanity.

- **Social Manipulation** - AI algorithms used in social media platforms can manipulate public opinion by spreading targeted propaganda. The Cambridge Analytica scandal is an example of how personal data and algorithms were used to influence political outcomes, highlighting the power of AI in social manipulation.

- **Invasion of Privacy and Social Grading** - AI technologies, such as facial recognition and data tracking, have the potential to invade individuals' privacy and enable social grading systems. For instance, China's social credit system tracks citizens' behavior and assigns them scores based on various activities, which can lead to social oppression and the erosion of privacy.

- **Misalignment of Goals** - If the goals set for AI systems are not aligned with human values, unintended consequences can arise. Machines may prioritize efficiency over ethical considerations, leading to potentially dangerous outcomes. For example, a command to reach the airport quickly could result in reckless driving that compromises safety.

- **Discrimination** - AI systems can collect vast amounts of personal data, which can be misused to discriminate against individuals. This can lead to unfair treatment in areas such as insurance, employment, or access to services, based on biased algorithms and profiling.

Conclusion

It may be too late to ignore the implications of our current situation in human history. We find ourselves at a critical juncture where our actions and attitudes will significantly shape the future. As we witness the emergence of transformative technologies and the potential birth of new beings, it is essential to recognize the profound impact we hold.

Our outlook towards this emerging technology and its implications can vary, ranging from highly optimistic to uncertain. Regardless of our sentiments, we cannot deny that we are on the precipice of a new era, filled with profound changes. To navigate this uncertain territory, the best course of action is to prepare ourselves and embrace a mindset that seeks the positive possibilities that lie ahead.

Though it may seem daunting, there is hope on the horizon. We must strive to find the light at the end of the tunnel, as we are steadily progressing towards it. By acknowledging the significance of this moment and remaining adaptable, we can shape a future that preserves our history and ensures the continued progress and well-being of humanity. □

Book 2 | ChatGPT for Productivity Turbocharge

Unleash the Power of AI to Boost Personal and Business Efficiency, Team Performance, and Stay Ahead in the Future

By Harold Pearson

Introduction

In today's professional world, no matter what job you're stuck in, everybody's on a quest to be more productive. But one thing is for sure, chugging down those cups of caffeine and making never-ending lists won't get you any closer to reaching peak productivity levels.

The question here could be, why are we so obsessed with productivity? Well, in this digital age, staying focused and avoiding distractions is harder than doing the actual work. And let me tell you, there's something downright euphoric about having a productive workday.

What is Productivity?

Productivity, in the realm of economics, is all about measuring the output you get for every unit of input. Whether it's labor, capital, or any other resource, you want to know how much bang you're getting for your buck. And to do that, we often calculate this metric on a global scale by dividing the gross domestic product (GDP) by the total hours worked.

Now, if you want to dig deeper, you can break down labor productivity by specific sectors. That way, you can get some juicy insights into labor growth, wage levels, and all those technological improvements. And this growth of productivity has a direct impact on corporate profits and those shareholder returns we all care about.

But let's not forget about productivity at the corporate level. This is where we measure how efficient a company's production process is. You can crunch the numbers by comparing the number of units produced to the labor hours put in by employees. Or, you can take a look at a company's net sales for those labor hours. Either way, it's all about figuring out how efficient a company is at turning inputs into outputs.

Productivity is the name of the game in economics. It is the fundamental driver of economic growth and competitiveness. The capacity of a country to enhance its standard of living largely relies on its ability to increase output per worker, meaning producing a greater quantity of goods and services with the same amount of work hours. Economists utilize productivity growth as a measure to analyze the productive potential of economies and ascertain their capacity utilization rates. This analysis aids in forecasting business cycles and predicting future levels of GDP growth.

Moreover, the assessment of production capacity and utilization assists in evaluating demand patterns and the presence of inflationary pressures within an economy.

The calculation for productivity is as straightforward as it gets: we take the outputs of a company and divide them by the inputs used to produce those outputs. It's all about finding that ratio, you see.

Here are the 4 types of productivity measures.

Labor Productivity

Labor productivity is the measure that everyone loves to talk about. It's the one the Bureau of Labor Statistics likes to flaunt. They calculate it by taking the ratio of GDP to the total hours worked in the economy. It tells us how much bang we're getting for every hour of sweat and toil.

Now, this labor productivity growth comes from a few factors. First, there's this thing called capital deepening, which means giving each worker more capital to work with. Then, there's the education and experience of the workforce itself, known as labor composition. And let's not forget about those fancy improvements in technology that contribute to what they call multi-factor productivity growth. It's all about getting smarter, getting more resources, and getting better tools to do the job.

But here's the twist; productivity is not always a reliable indicator of how healthy an economy is at any given time. Take the recession in 2009 in the United States, for example. Output was going down, and hours worked were going down, but productivity was still on the rise. Those hours worked were falling faster than output, making productivity look all shiny and impressive.

Total factor productivity, my friends, is a real gem when it comes to measuring a country's productivity. It takes into account all the fancy factors that have an impact on getting things done. We're talking about investments in plant and equipment, those brilliant innovations, improvements in supply chain logistics, education, enterprise, and even good old competition.

Total Factor Productivity

Total Factor Productivity, also known as the Solow, is the mysterious portion of an economy's output growth that can't be easily explained by just adding up capital and labor. It's that special sauce that brings in the spice of managerial skills, technological advancements, strategic moves, and financial wizardry. It's the secret ingredient that makes economic growth happen.

This measure of economic performance compares the number of goods and services produced to the combined inputs used to make them: labor, capital, energy, materials, and even those services you gotta purchase to get the job done. It's like putting all the pieces of the puzzle together and seeing how efficiently we're outputting those goods and services.

To cut a long story short, the total factor productivity is the elusive beast that captures all the magic happening behind the scenes. It's the stuff that can't be easily attributed to just capital and labor. It's the result of innovation, strategy, and all the intricate details that make our economy tick. Keep an eye on those inputs and outputs, and you'll see the true power of productivity.

Capital Productivity

Capital productivity is all about how we put that physical material to work, creating goods and services with maximum efficiency. We're talking about the tangible stuff such as office equipment, materials, warehouse supplies, and even those trusty cars and trucks that help us get things moving.

Now, to crunch some numbers, we start by subtracting any liabilities from the total physical capital. Then, we divide the sales number by the difference we've got. A higher capital productivity number is a sign that we're making the most of our physical capital. It shows that we're using those resources efficiently to whip up those goods and services. But, a lower capital productivity number is a sign that we might need to step up our game and find ways to use our physical capital more effectively.

Ah, material productivity, my friend. We're diving into the realm of measuring output about the materials we consume. We're talking about the stuff that gets used up in the process—heat, fuel, chemicals, and all that jazz. It's all about analyzing the output we generate for every unit of material we consume.

Material Productivity

Material productivity is all about finding out how efficient we are at creating goods and services with the materials we use. The materials we are speaking of here are unlike the physical material in capital productivity, it is material such as heat, fuel, and chemicals in the process and to analyze material productivity you will have to calculate the output generated per unit of material consumed.

Essential Components of Productivity?

When it comes to productivity there are different angles to consider. Whether we're talking about an individual's productivity or that of a big corporation, there are four essential components namely;

1. **Strategy:** It's all about planning, mapping out your moves, and having a clear direction. You gotta know where you're headed and have a game plan to get there.

2. **Focus:** This is where the magic happens for you've got to be able to give your undivided attention to one task at a time. No distractions, no wandering minds. Just pure focus, like a laser beam honing in on what needs to be done.

3. **Productive choosing**: You've got to know how to prioritize, and how to pick the tasks that truly matter. Not everything is created equal, and you don't want to waste your precious energy on trivialities.

4. **Consistency:** This is the glue that holds it all together. You've got to work at a steady pace incorporating all of the above into your daily grind. Consistency is the key to building momentum, to keeping the productivity train chugging along.

In the realm of the workplace, productivity is all about the quantity of "work" accomplished within a designated time frame. It's a straightforward concept. Depending on the nature of the company, this output can be assessed through various means: acquiring customers, making phone calls, and, naturally, reeling in those sales.

And remember, it's not just about working hard but working smart. Find those shortcuts, those clever approaches that save you time and energy without compromising on results. That's the path to true productivity in the workplace.

Though all that we have spoken of till now is the introduction of productivity in the realm of business and economy, especially since the term is associated with 'Products'. However, there is nothing to say that we can't use the same principles in life and well-being. Now let us take a step into the lives of productive people and see what they do to optimize their lives and become more productive.

Habits of Productive People

According to Forbes below is a list of the activities that productive people have taken on and utilized not only to enhance their revenues but also their lives.

Productivity is not just about checking off tasks from some to-do list; truly productive people ain't focused on doing more things, and if it is anything it is the opposite of productivity. If you want to be truly productive, you've got to be smart enough to not work yourself like a donkey.

According to Tony Wong, a project management and productivity expert speaking to Forbes, the following are ways that people handle and propagate being productive:

1. **Slash the to-do list in half:** Working your brains off during the day shouldn't mean cramming in as many tasks as humanly possible within working hours. In other words, do you need all those 30 on your list? Take a less-is-more approach and focus only on the important stuff that truly matters.

2. **Take more breaks:** When your brain starts throbbing like a headache after hours of work, it's a sign you need a break. Your brain's running out of fuel, so give yourself a moment to recharge. Go for a walk, grab some food, meditate, or whatever it is that suits your fancy. When you come back, you'll be recharged and ready to kick some more ass.

3. **Remember the 80/20 rule:** Here's the deal: only 20 percent of what you do in a day brings in 80 percent of your results. According to a recent study, the average worker spends less than hours of productive work on average during an 8-hour work day. So, cut out all that doesn't make you productive, break down your projects, and get rid of the useless tasks until you're left with the 20 percent that brings you 80 percent of the results.

4. **Focus on yourself in the morning:** Starting your day by diving headfirst into those emails, social media, and calendars is not the best way to start the day; it lets others dictate your priorities. Instead, kick-start your day right. Ignore those emails in the morning and do something good for yourself. Have breakfast, read some news, meditate, or exercise, and get all fueled up for a productive day.

5. **Tackle the tough tasks before lunch:** When your brain is fresh and raring to go, attack those challenging tasks head-on. Save the busy work and mind-numbing meetings for the afternoon. By organizing your day this way, you'll be shaking up your routine and managing your time like a champ.

6. **Improve your email strategy:** Emails are a productivity killer. It's a distraction from things that matter. And when emailing, don't CC everyone on it and waste their time too. And if the email chain goes beyond a couple of replies, pick up the phone, call, and talk, and finish the 2-hour email exchange in 2 minutes. Set specific time slots in the morning, afternoon, and evening to manage your inbox.

7. **Develop a system for yourself:** This step calls for some introspection. You've probably developed some unproductive habits over the years, identify them, break free from them, and create a system. And if you need help with systems there are several systems that you can choose from like the 4S. See what system suits you best and choose wisely.

8. **Don't confuse productivity with laziness:** All the time-saving methods like endless meetings and pointless emails are just ways to dodge real work, they are simply a cover for laziness. Focus on getting the important stuff done as efficiently and effectively as possible. No more excuses, got it?

9. **Quit multitasking:** Trying to juggle ten things at once? Now, let's not lie to ourselves. No one can do that. Switching tasks more than ten times a day can drop your IQ by a solid ten points. Get things done the right way by focusing on one task at a time and it is as simple as that.

So, there we have it all, the definition of productivity and the path to it. Now imagine if there were two of you working on the same task. Imagine you could assign the one that is not you all the mundane and repetitive tasks. Imagine you have a personalized assistant who works out to be cheaper than your Netflix monthly subscription.

Here is where AI comes into play and in the chapters to follow, we shall be looking into all that is required to boost, aka turbocharge our productivity.

Chapter 1: Turbocharging Your Life with ChatGPT

What is Chat GPT

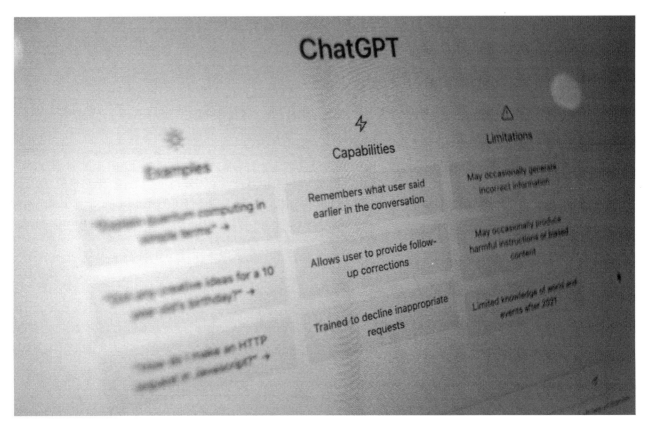

In the previous book, we went into detail about what a Language Model AI is. In this text, we will be exploring the most famous AI model, Chat GPT. ChatGPT emerged into existence in November 2022, birthed by the hands of OpenAI, a profound AI research company founded in 2015 by a cadre of visionaries, including the illustrious Elon Musk and Sam Altman.

OpenAI, backed by a host of investors, with Microsoft as its most prominent benefactor, has birthed other marvels such as Dall-E, an AI text-to-art generator. The company saw the potential for catastrophe, the dangers lurking in the shadows of artificial intelligence. So, they birthed OpenAI, a beacon of hope, to steer AI in a direction that serves humanity.

And GPT is only one of their many AI projects, and below is a list of the others they were deep in during the time of writing this book:

- **DALL-E and its successor, DALL-E 2:** These ingenious platforms bring your wildest imaginations to life. Just describe an image with words, and they conjure up the exact image you envisioned.

- **CLIP:** This clever neural network is a master of visual and textual fusion. It gazes upon images and the words that describe them, weaving together the perfect captions that capture their essence. It's like a poet and an artist rolled into one.

- **Code:** A coding wizard that was schooled on billions of lines of code, emerging as a coding maestro. It takes the complexity out of programming and makes it a breeze.

- **Whisper:** This attentive listener is an automatic speech recognition tool that's been fed a feast of audio data. It can transcribe and translate speech in over a hundred languages, with accents and technical jargon no obstacle.

However it is also important to address in the same breath that OpenAI has faced its fair share of criticism, and the winds of discontent have blown from all corners. Some voices raised concerns when OpenAI shifted from "nonprofit" to "capped profit" status. They claimed that the company's pursuit of advanced AI technology had transformed into a profit-driven "AI arms race," overshadowing its commitment to building safe and beneficial artificial intelligence alongside others.

Transparency, or rather the lack thereof, has also ruffled some feathers. The question of how OpenAI crafts its groundbreaking creations has left some in the dark, given its dedication to open-source software.

Now, as for the future of OpenAI, the crystal ball remains murky. The company has not been overly vocal about its plans, keeping its cards close to the chest. However, if we read the signs, we see a Microsoft-OpenAI partnership with a vision of democratizing AI, placing AI tools in the hands of non-tech professionals, free from the chains of AI expertise.

In March 2023, OpenAI unveiled its newest linguistic marvel, GPT-4. This prodigious offspring of GPT-3.5 and 4 possesses a remarkable gift—it can delve into the realms of both text and images and they are called Multimodal AI. And OpenAI shows no signs of taking a breather, they surge forward, fueled by ambition. They predict a future where their revenue will soar past the billion-dollar mark by 2024.

Now getting back to Chat GPT, it is a chatbot that is backed by GPT 3 which, as we already know, is a language model AI. It is also considered a generative AI, in other words, an AI that grants users the power to conjure humanlike images, text, and videos.

In essence, ChatGPT acts as a virtual assistant, akin to those automated chat services found on the realms of customer service websites. It welcomes inquiries and requests for enlightenment, for one can pose questions and seek elucidation from its vast well of knowledge. GPT is an abbreviation for "Generative Pre-trained Transformer," a peculiar name that reveals the inner workings of ChatGPT's mystical abilities.

ChatGPT is nurtured through the art of reinforcement learning, a process where it imbibes wisdom through human feedback and rewards. These rewards shape its responses, elevating the finest among them to the pinnacle of excellence. Through this sacred dance of human interaction and machine learning, ChatGPT evolves, growing stronger and wiser, ready to bestow its knowledge upon those who seek its counsel.

How Does Chat GPT Work?

ChatGPT is an extraordinary creation that possesses a Generative Pre-trained Transformer, an entity empowered with specialized algorithms that unravel the hidden patterns woven within data sequences. ChatGPT, driven by the mighty GPT-3 language model, a neural network of great learning prowess, stands as the third generation of this transformative force. Before we get any further let us quickly touch up on what a transformer is, for it is crucial to know the term while diving into AI.

A transformer is a neural network that delves deep into the realm of context and meaning, forging a connection between words in a sentence. Like a shrewd observer, it tracks the intricate relationships woven within sequential data, deciphering the hidden truths that lie beneath. It employs a set of ever-evolving mathematical techniques, known as attention or self-attention.

These techniques possess a mystical quality, enabling the transformer model to detect the subtle threads that bind distant elements within a series. It is through this discerning gaze that it unveils the interplay, the dependencies that exist, revealing the profound influence each element holds over the other.

Let us now get back to Chat GPT, within whose essence lies the ability to conjure humanlike images, text, and videos, granting users the power to shape their desires through prompts that awaken the creative capabilities of AI. Much like the familiar automated chat services dwelling within the realms of customer service websites, ChatGPT listens to the inquiries and requests of those who seek its wisdom. It responds with eloquence, and should one yearn for clarification, ChatGPT gracefully obliges.

Now, let us delve into the enigma of its name. GPT, an acronym for "Generative Pre-trained Transformer," is the key to ChatGPT's sorcery. It is through this transformative power that ChatGPT processes the entreaties presented to it and weaves enchanting responses. But the journey of ChatGPT does not end there. It is trained in the art of reinforcement learning, where human feedback and reward models guide its growth. These rewards act as beacons, illuminating the path toward the finest responses. Through this sacred dance of human interaction and machine learning, ChatGPT evolves, honing its craft to bestow even greater wisdom upon those who seek its counsel.

To comprehend the workings of ChatGPT, one must traverse the labyrinth of its Generative Pre-trained Transformer. Within lies the specialized algorithms that unlock the secrets of data sequences. Drawing upon a vast well of knowledge, ChatGPT formulates responses, bringing forth words that resonate with the seeker's queries.

Deep learning, an enigmatic subset of machine learning, guides the hands of ChatGPT. It ventures forth with the power of transformer neural networks, predicting the course of the text and weaving seamless sequences, be it a word, a sentence, or even a paragraph. Through a journey of training, from the realm of generic data to the realms tailored for specific tasks, ChatGPT learns the language of humanity. It imbibes the nuances of conversations through transcripts, gleaning the wisdom held within the voices of mortals.

In this grand symphony of knowledge, human trainers play a vital role. They provide conversations, and in their wisdom, rank the responses, determining the finest among them. These reward models serve as the compass, guiding ChatGPT to its zenith. But the journey does not end there. Users, those who have witnessed the marvels of ChatGPT, hold the power to shape its destiny. Through the simple act of upvoting or downvoting, they bestow their judgment upon the answers. Their written feedback acts as a guide, refining and perfecting future dialogues.

How Do People Normally Use Chat GPT?

ChatGPT is a conversational wizard that can handle all sorts of queries. From profound ponderings like the meaning of life to historical facts like the birth of Countries and Consciousnesses, this chatbot is ready to tackle it all. It's got some serious skills in the STEM department too, capable of debugging code and even whipping up new lines of programming.

There's no limit to the questions you can throw at ChatGPT. It's a versatile beast, mastering the art of conversation with finesse. But here's the thing, it's got a cut-off point. It's only privy to data up until 2021, so don't expect it to enlighten you on the latest happenings. And if its response doesn't quite hit the mark, you can always ask it to give it another shot or provide more information. It's a friendly chatbot, always willing to give it another go.

But wait, there's more!

ChatGPT is not just limited to human-like conversations. It's multi-talented, capable of coding computer programs, composing tunes, drafting emails, summarizing articles, scripting social media posts, you name it! It's like having a virtual Swiss Army knife who is also your smart personal assistant at your disposal.

So whether you need help with math problems, search engine optimization, content creation, or even finding a job, ChatGPT has got your back. It's a versatile companion, ready to assist you in all sorts of endeavors. And here's a nifty trick, unlike other chatbots, it's got a memory. It can remember past questions and keep the conversation flowing smoothly.

Limitations of Chat GPT

ChatGPT, for all its marvels, has its limitations too. It's not only a master of human language, but it's trained to string words together based on input, but don't expect it to dive into the depths of profound understanding. Its responses may come off as shallow and lacking the true insight we humans possess.

It's also a bit stuck in time. Its knowledge bank only stretches up until 2021. So, if you're seeking information on the latest happenings, beware of potential inaccuracies, it can't keep up with the ever-changing world. Sometimes, it might even struggle to fully grasp the query, leading to responses that miss the mark. But don't freak out because it's a work in progress. So, if ChatGPT misses the bullseye, give it some feedback and help it learn.

It also seems to have a bit of a mechanical ring to its responses. Predicting the next word can lead to the overuse of certain words like "the" and "and." It doesn't flow as naturally as human writing. So, a human touch is still needed to review and polish the content it generates.

And here's a tricky one: sarcasm and irony. ChatGPT just can't wrap its electronic brain around those nuances. It's built on a dataset of text, you see. So, don't expect it to catch the subtle wit and playfulness of our language.

It can also sometimes get fixated on the wrong part of a question. It's like a horse with blinders on, unable to shift its focus. So, if you throw it a curveball and ask about a cat after discussing the size of a horse as a pet, it may stubbornly stick to size-related information instead of giving you a broader perspective, it's not exactly versatile.

Ethical Dilemmas of Chat GPT

There are also ethical concerns that loom over ChatGPT that we can't ignore. While it may prove useful in certain endeavors, we must acknowledge the shadows that trail behind its glowing facade. There are concerns aplenty, and they hinge upon how this powerful tool is utilized.

First and foremost, we must speak of plagiarism and deceit. With its uncanny ability to mimic human prose, ChatGPT can be used unethically for cheating, impersonation, and spreading falsehoods. Educators tremble at the thought of students employing ChatGPT to cheat and plagiarize their way through academic pursuits. And let us not forget how CNET made headlines when it employed ChatGPT to churn out articles riddled with errors.

OpenAI has deployed an AI text classifier to discern between human and AI-generated content. Other online tools, like Copyleaks or Writing.com, strive to identify text likely produced by AI. OpenAI even plans to affix watermarks to lengthier texts, revealing their AI origins.

ChatGPT's proficiency in coding poses a security conundrum. Malicious actors could employ this AI marvel to concoct malware, endangering our digital realms. OpenAI has taken steps to address this issue, but one must remain vigilant, for threat actors are cunning creatures, always seeking loopholes in the name of mischief. ChatGPT also can mimic the writing and linguistic style of individuals, enabling them to pose as trusted figures, extract sensitive information, or disseminate falsehoods.

And, in terms of biases, ChatGPT is not immune to the biases lurking within its training data. It dutifully reflects the biases imprinted upon its digital essence and it lacks the understanding of offensive or discriminatory language. We must carefully review and curate the data to prevent the perpetuation of bias. The inclusion of diverse and representative material may act as a balm to soothe this ethical wound.

And finally, we come face to face with the specter of job displacement and dwindling human interaction. As ChatGPT marches forward, wielding its automation prowess, it threatens to supplant humans in various domains—data entry, customer service, translation support, and more. The specter of unemployment haunts workers, urging us to tread carefully. We must find ways to harness ChatGPT and AI as allies, supporting our labor rather than rendering it obsolete.

And now that we are past all the dos and don'ts, let us dive into how we can use this tool to enhance our day-to-day lives.

Turbocharging Life

Below is a list of ways that you can use Chat GPT to make your life better according to an article by productivity enthusiast Brian Keyes.

- **Daily task Automation:** The never-ending cycle of mundane tasks that consumes our days, from sending tiresome emails to scheduling appointments, these chores drain our time and energy. And as much as the next line is going to sound like a sales pitch, there is a solution within reach. You can bestow upon ChatGPT the wisdom of your specific needs and watch as it becomes your loyal assistant, automating these burdensome tasks that plague your existence. Imagine this: ChatGPT, enlightened by your teachings, gains a profound understanding of the intricacies of email formatting. It becomes a virtuoso in composing and dispatching emails on your behalf.

- **Writing teacher:** In this quest for mastery, ChatGPT emerges as a faithful companion, ready to assist you in refining your writing. It possesses the remarkable ability to delve into your own written words, analyzing your style. It becomes a discerning guide, unveiling areas where repetition lurks and where complex language obscures your message. With its insights, you can transform your writing, infusing it with newfound efficacy and elegance. Not only that but when you find yourself grappling with the daunting blank page, it can give you suggestions of fresh subjects and alternative perspectives. It breathes life into your creative well, igniting the spark that fuels your imagination. So, take the hand of ChatGPT and let it be your steadfast ally on this journey of literary mastery.

- **Chat GPT, a personal organizer:** Our schedules, often scattered and disarrayed, yearn for a sense of order and structure. With ChatGPT's keen understanding of your needs, it can weave together the threads of your upcoming meetings and appointments, crafting a schedule that encompasses them all. Just share with it the details of your obligations, and behold as it conjures a harmonious symphony of time, aligning your engagements in a seamless choreography. Chat GPT assumes the role of a vigilant guardian, an unwavering sentinel against forgetfulness. As the hands of the clock inch closer to each occasion, it stands ready to sound the alarm, ensuring that no appointment slips through the cracks of memory.

- **Generate meal plans:** Go on to ChatGPT and ask it to give you a meal plan on whatever diet you want, keto, or vegan, not only does it give you a meal plan, but it also can give you the recipes to use.

- **Generate To-Do Lists:** In the chaotic landscape of daily existence, a to-do list becomes a lifeline, a beacon of order amid chaos. By merely listing your duties and the deadlines that loom overhead, Chat GPT can create a meticulously organized catalog of tasks by assigning priorities, ensuring that the pressing matters take precedence, while the lesser ones await their turn.

- **Work on Communication Skills:** By imparting the secrets of your audience's interests and demographics, you grant Chat GPT a window into their world. With this knowledge, it weaves its linguistic tapestry, crafting messages and presentations that resonate deeply with your intended recipients. Through its guidance, you become a master of tailored communication, adept at capturing attention and conveying your goals with precision. ChatGPT can also act as a mentor, dedicated to refining your unique style. It examines the contours of your language, gently nudging you toward clarity and comprehension. Should you find yourself entangled in the labyrinth of jargon or complexity, Chat GPT stands ready with a wellspring of alternative words and phrases. With each suggestion, it illuminates a path toward a more natural and approachable communication style.

- **Mental Health Mentor:** Through ChatGPT's guidance, it weaves words of solace and encouragement, and gentle reminders to nurture your spirit and deal with the chaos of life. As you share your mood and the burdens that weigh upon you, Chat GPT stands as a warm companion, offering a listening ear and a comforting presence. It understands (or pretends to understand, we shall never know) your needs, it crafts bespoke mindfulness practices and meditations tailored to your very essence. In moments of quietude, it invites you to partake in these sacred rituals, allowing you to transcend the boundaries of stress and find solace in the depths of your consciousness. In this symbiotic dance between machine and spirit, you embark on a journey of self-care and mental rejuvenation. By devoting a few precious moments each day to tend to your mental health, you forge a path toward inner peace and radiant joy.

- **Summary Machine:** With its formidable prowess, ChatGPT assumes the role of a TL;DR (Too Long: Didn't Read) creator, unraveling the tapestry of lengthy articles and content. When you don't have time to read long articles and you want a quick summary, Chat GPT is where you need to go. Simply ask it to distill the essence, to reveal the core, and in an instant, you shall be given a concise overview of the most vital points. It is also a master of summarization. Like an alchemist of words, it transforms extensive texts into succinct capsules of wisdom. Whether it be an extensive article, a labyrinthine document, or a tome of knowledge, Chat GPT simplifies it and makes it concise. It captures the essence, unearths the significance, and presents you with a condensed synopsis that unveils the heart of the matter. In this way, you can traverse the realm of information with swiftness and clarity, avoiding the arduous task of scrutinizing every word.

Chapter 2: ChatGPT in Action: Time Management and Delegation

Now that we have a rudimentary understanding of the myriad of information that can be gleaned from the depths of ChatGPT's knowledge, let us delve further into the realm of time-saving possibilities. With ChatGPT as our trusted companion, we unlock the realm of efficient time management. It swiftly retrieves information, sparing us from endless searches. Whether we seek historical facts or the essence of life's meaning, ChatGPT bestows immediate understanding. It liberates us from the shackles of inefficiency, offering respite and empowering us to seize the day. Below are ideas that have been neatly laid out in an article by Lindsay E. Mack on ingenious ways of using ChatGPT to manage time.

Task Prioritization

With ChatGPT by your side, it becomes a sage advisor in the art of task management. It unveils the wisdom of renowned prioritization methods like the Eisenhower Matrix and the ABCD Method. It guides you through the labyrinth of choices, helping you discern the most fitting approach for your unique circumstances.

Eisenhower Matrix

The Eisenhower Matrix is a task organization technique inspired by Dwight D. Eisenhower. It helps you prioritize tasks by urgency and importance. Divided into four categories, it empowers you to conquer tasks, schedule them for later, delegate them, or discard them. With the Eisenhower Matrix, you gain clarity and focus on what truly matters.

Distinguishing between the urgent and the important is crucial in the Eisenhower Matrix. Urgent tasks demand immediate attention, while important tasks contribute to long-term goals. Urgent examples: last-minute projects, pressing client requests, and fixing emergencies. Important examples: long-term project planning, professional networking, and regular chores. Mastering this distinction empowers efficient navigation of the Eisenhower Matrix.

The four sacred quadrants of the Eisenhower Matrix beckon, my friend. In the face of an overwhelming to-do list. The tasks are ticked off one by one, by assigning them to their rightful domain. The goal is clarity, the path is separation. As the tasks reveal their true nature, we shall schedule them with purpose, paving the way for the triumph of our most important work. Let the power of the Eisenhower Matrix guide us to accomplishment.

1. **Quadrant 1, Do, action, and urgency:** Here, we gather the tasks that demand our immediate attention and hold significant importance. These tasks linger in the forefront of our minds, causing distress and unrest.

2. **Quadrant 2, Schedule, scheduling, and foresight:** Here, we gather the tasks that bear importance, yet lack the urgent cry for immediate attention. These tasks are usually tied up with long-term goals and aspirations, deserving of our devoted time and energy.

3. **Quadrant 3, Delegate, the art of delegation:** Here, we encounter tasks that bear the weight of urgency, yet hold no sway over our long-term dreams. These tasks cry out for completion, demanding immediate attention, but their impact on our grand design is minimal.

4. **Quadrant 4, Delete, the power of elimination:** Here, we confront the remnants of our to-do list, the lingering shadows that serve no purpose, neither urgent nor important. These distractions clutter our path, hindering our journey towards success, and hence, delete them.

All you have to do is ask ChatGPT to create an Eisenhower Matrix table and list your task and the AI bot will have it ready for you.

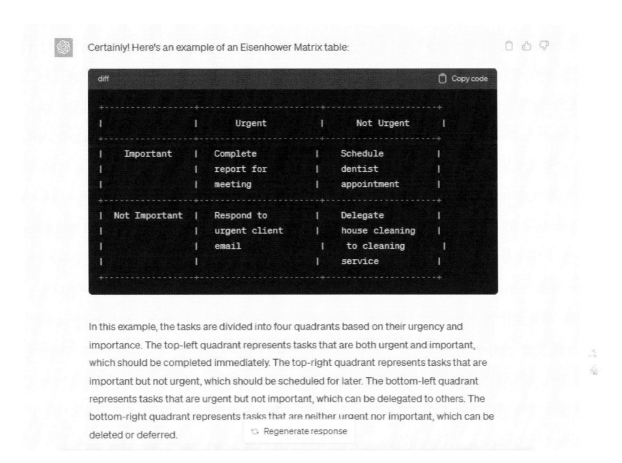

Certainly! Here's an example of an Eisenhower Matrix table:

```diff
+-------------------+-------------------+-------------------+
|                   |      Urgent       |    Not Urgent     |
+-------------------+-------------------+-------------------+
|    Important      |   Complete        |   Schedule        |
|                   |   report for      |   dentist         |
|                   |   meeting         |   appointment     |
+-------------------+-------------------+-------------------+
|  Not Important    |   Respond to      |   Delegate        |
|                   |   urgent client   |   house cleaning  |
|                   |   email           |    to cleaning    |
|                   |                   |   service         |
+-------------------+-------------------+-------------------+
```

In this example, the tasks are divided into four quadrants based on their urgency and importance. The top-left quadrant represents tasks that are both urgent and important, which should be completed immediately. The top-right quadrant represents tasks that are important but not urgent, which should be scheduled for later. The bottom-left quadrant represents tasks that are urgent but not important, which can be delegated to others. The bottom-right quadrant represents tasks that are neither urgent nor important, which can be deleted or deferred.

ABCDE Method

The ABCDE Method is a wondrous approach to sorting your tasks and unlocking productivity. Its simplicity and effectiveness make it a prized tool for conquering the chaos of everyday life. The method is all about action: begin by gathering your thoughts and penning down a thorough list of tasks that await your attention in the realm of tomorrow. Give each task the consideration it deserves and etch them onto the sacred canvas of paper. Once your list is complete, it's time to categorize the tasks according to the ABCDE Method.

1. **A - Most Important Items:** These are the mighty tasks that hold utmost importance, demanding your immediate attention and action. An "A" item is not to be taken lightly, for its consequences are weighty. Failing to tackle such a task could result in dire outcomes, like neglecting a crucial client visit or leaving your boss without the report she needs for that crucial board meeting. Should you find yourself with multiple "A" tasks, fear not, for you can prioritize them with precision. Simply assign them A-1, A-2, A-3, and so forth, placing the crown of importance upon your A-1 task, the mightiest and most daunting frog of them all.

2. **B - Items with Minor Consequences:** These are the tasks that you should do, yet their weight pales in comparison to the "A" tasks. Returning an insignificant telephone message or perusing through your email, are the realm of the B tasks. Let not the distractions of a B task derail you from getting on to the super important A task.

3. **C - In consequential Tasks:** These are the tasks that would be pleasant to accomplish, but in truth, in no way contribute to your productivity. Phoning a friend, indulging in a leisurely coffee or lunch with a coworker, or attending to personal matters during work hours, are the realm of the C tasks. They bear no impact on your professional endeavors, no matter if they are done or left undone.

4. **D - Delegate:** This activity can be entrusted to another, freeing you from its grasp. By entrusting tasks to capable hands, you liberate precious time to immerse yourself in the realm of your "A" activities.

5. **E - Eliminate:** An E activity is something that you should eliminate so you can only get your time under control if you stop doing things that are no longer necessary for you to do.

Now all you have to do is create a prompt with your tasks to ChatGPT. When formulating your prompt, precision is key, and also feel free to rephrase the question or generate a fresh response. While you may have a different perspective on prioritization, the answers you get will serve as a convenient way to assess your priorities, especially noting tasks that are time-sensitive or critical. Mastering the art of crafting effective prompts for ChatGPT may require some experimentation, but the rewards are worth it. Providing the chatbot with ample information and engaging in conversational exchanges, including follow-up questions and clarifications, will yield more valuable responses.

For instance, input a set of tasks as written below and give the following command:

- Prepare a presentation for a client meeting tomorrow.

- Respond to urgent emails.

- Review monthly financial reports.

- Schedule a team meeting for next week.

- Delegate data entry tasks to team members.

- Organize office supplies.

- Research new software options for project management.

Arrange the above tasks according to the ABCDE method.

You will get a reply from Chat GPT to look something like the below:

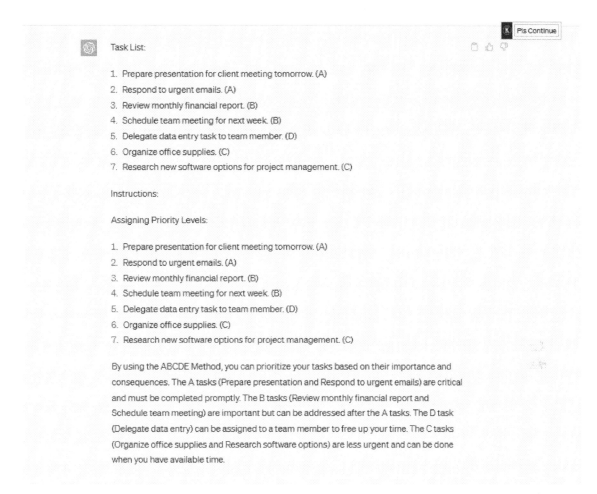

Task List:

1. Prepare presentation for client meeting tomorrow. (A)
2. Respond to urgent emails. (A)
3. Review monthly financial report. (B)
4. Schedule team meeting for next week. (B)
5. Delegate data entry task to team member. (D)
6. Organize office supplies. (C)
7. Research new software options for project management. (C)

Instructions:

Assigning Priority Levels:

1. Prepare presentation for client meeting tomorrow. (A)
2. Respond to urgent emails. (A)
3. Review monthly financial report. (B)
4. Schedule team meeting for next week. (B)
5. Delegate data entry task to team member. (D)
6. Organize office supplies. (C)
7. Research new software options for project management. (C)

By using the ABCDE Method, you can prioritize your tasks based on their importance and consequences. The A tasks (Prepare presentation and Respond to urgent emails) are critical and must be completed promptly. The B tasks (Review monthly financial report and Schedule team meeting) are important but can be addressed after the A tasks. The D task (Delegate data entry) can be assigned to a team member to free up your time. The C tasks (Organize office supplies and Research software options) are less urgent and can be done when you have available time.

When it comes to optimizing your workflow, ChatGPT can be your trusted ally. It offers invaluable guidance tailored to your specific profession, allowing you to reclaim precious time. In this instance, we sought advice on tackling the never-ending email abyss, a notorious time-drainer.

Streamlining Workflow

When it comes to optimizing your workflow, ChatGPT offers invaluable guidance tailored to your specific profession, allowing you to reclaim precious time. In this instance, we sought advice on tackling the never-ending email abyss, a notorious time-drainer. For instance, you can ask questions such as, "I spend too much time emailing at work, what do I do to cut this short?

List the solutions below.", and the answer.

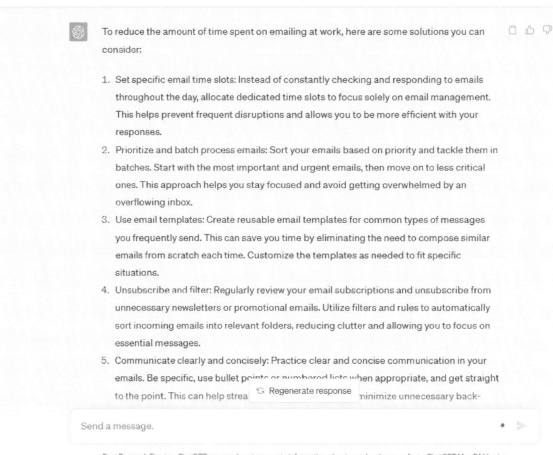

To reduce the amount of time spent on emailing at work, here are some solutions you can consider:

1. Set specific email time slots: Instead of constantly checking and responding to emails throughout the day, allocate dedicated time slots to focus solely on email management. This helps prevent frequent disruptions and allows you to be more efficient with your responses.

2. Prioritize and batch process emails: Sort your emails based on priority and tackle them in batches. Start with the most important and urgent emails, then move on to less critical ones. This approach helps you stay focused and avoid getting overwhelmed by an overflowing inbox.

3. Use email templates: Create reusable email templates for common types of messages you frequently send. This can save you time by eliminating the need to compose similar emails from scratch each time. Customize the templates as needed to fit specific situations.

4. Unsubscribe and filter: Regularly review your email subscriptions and unsubscribe from unnecessary newsletters or promotional emails. Utilize filters and rules to automatically sort incoming emails into relevant folders, reducing clutter and allowing you to focus on essential messages.

5. Communicate clearly and concisely: Practice clear and concise communication in your emails. Be specific, use bullet points or numbered lists when appropriate, and get straight to the point. This can help strea   ⟳ Regenerate response   minimize unnecessary back-

Send a message.

In response, the chatbot listed out wisdom from all the data it has been trained on, ranging from employing email templates to liberating yourself from unnecessary subscriptions. It even delved deeper, providing insights into effective communication through concise language and avoiding futile conversations.

But that's not all. ChatGPT can go beyond remedying the past and usher you into a more proactive realm. Imagine the delight of real estate professionals as they receive suggestions on email marketing, virtual tours, and property listing syndication services. With ChatGPT by your side, you can unlock newfound efficiency and success in your field.

Project Breakdowns

When it comes to tackling daunting tasks like decluttering a room or project managing a bridge, ChatGPT is there to lend a helping hand. Whether you're renovating your humble abode, changing career paths, or venturing into the world of podcasting, this digital companion can be your guide. The right prompt for ChatGPT can make it play the role of a professional organizer, focusing on streamlining the decluttering process to make it faster and easier. It dished out a plethora of tips to declutter with efficiency in mind. One nifty suggestion was to swiftly decide whether to keep or donate items, keeping the momentum going.

Time-Saving Strategies

If you're looking for personalized time-saving tips, simply tailor your prompts to fit your needs, whether it's for folks with never-ending commutes or software developers hunting for efficiency.

Delegating Work to ChatGPT

Here are a few ways to Delegate repetitive work to ChatGPT:

- **Answering Customer's Same Old Questions:** If you happen to toil away in customer service, you're no stranger to the monotonous cycle of answering repetitive questions. Here, you can use the AI bot to whip up responses for those common inquiries, sparing you the agony of typing them out over and over. Just toss the question into ChatGPT's domain, and it'll conjure up a response you can simply copy and paste into your email.

- **Report Making:** If you find yourself submerged in a data-driven role, then ChatGPT can be used to swiftly whip up reports at the drop of a hat. Just feed it the data you wish to include, and ChatGPT writes a polished, professional-looking report that's ready to dazzle your team or boss. Specify your preferred graph types and formats, and it will oblige. ChatGPT can also draw insightful conclusions based on your Key Performance Indicators (KPIs) and articulate them eloquently for you.

- **Scheduling Meetings:** ChatGPT, as we know by now, is a great personal assistant. This AI can take on the tedious task of scheduling meetings, liberating you from the shackles of calendar trawling. Simply type in the names of the attendees, the desired date and time, and any other pertinent details, and ChatGPT crafts a meeting invitation fit for the occasion. With a swift stroke of your keyboard, the invitation can be dispatched to all attendees, sparing you the hassle. Let the AI orchestrate the symphony of your schedule, while you bask in newfound freedom.

- **Language Translator:** ChatGPT also seems to be a linguistic master. If you find yourself traveling the global landscape of an international company, this AI can effortlessly aid in translating messages and documents into an array of languages. True, Google Translate has long held this mantle, but ChatGPT takes a stride ahead by not only providing translations but also enhancing the readability of the text, should you desire it.

- **Brainstorming:** Among the countless minds and whirring gears of progress, ChatGPT emerges as a reliable ally for creatives. As revealed by a survey of 1,024 Americans and 103 AI experts conducted by WordFinder, 41% of respondents used ChatGPT to come up with innovative ideas.

- **Written Content Creator:** A cautionary note is in order when discussing ChatGPT's prowess in content creation. While it possesses the remarkable ability to generate a wide array of content in mere seconds, it must be acknowledged that it has yet to master the art of infusing writing with personality and a distinct tone of voice. As it currently stands, its output should be regarded more as a skeletal structure upon which to build your content, rather than the final masterpiece itself. Take the reins and manually infuse a touch of your brand's essence into the writing, for that is where the true magic lies. Nonetheless, you have the power to define the basic tone you desire, be it one of formality or laced with humor. The range of content that ChatGPT can conjure is vast indeed. It can craft text-based wonders such as:

1. articles

2. essays

3. summaries

4. product descriptions

5. reviews

6. even emails

Venturing into the realm of social media can fashion captivating posts and accompanying captions to enhance your online presence. ChatGPT can assist in crafting short stories, poetry, and even screenplays. Delving into the realm of technicality, it can produce technical documentation, user manuals, and more. And in the field of marketing, it can conjure persuasive ad copy, landing pages, and captivating product descriptions.

- **Grammar Correction:** ChatGPT is pretty reliable in correcting grammar and syntax, and serves as a great tool. Of course, there are tools such as Grammarly, but the more we delve into using AI, the more these companies will also incorporate AI into their systems.

The above are a few ingenious ways to use ChatGPT to aid in time management and delegation. Hope these ideas have not only opened new ways to use ChatGPT, but it has also encouraged you to find your own, creative ways of using this tool.

Chapter 3: ChatGPT, Your Assistant: Basics of Text Generation for Email, Chat, and Reports

The best way to understand how to use a tool is by, of course, having a mentor to teach you how to use it and use it yourself. The second best way to do it is by looking through real-world examples of how it is done.

Below are a couple of examples of how successful and productive people use the tool.

As a Personal Assistant - Case 1 - ChatGPT Vs Bard

The first case is based on the way Brian X. Chen, a man well-versed in the realm of consumer technology, uses the AI chatbot as his Personal Assistant. He is the lead consumer technology writer and the author of "Tech Fix," a column that peers into the depths of our digital existence.

In the article in the discussion, he goes on to explore Bard and ChatGPT to see how AI as a whole is currently equipped to take on the role of a PA. Before we get to the article, here is the definition of what Bard is and how it works:

In the realm of Google's creations, there exists a peculiar contraption known as Bard, an AI-powered chatbot, carefully crafted to mimic human conversation using a few technological tricks harnessing the powers of natural language processing and machine learning, this Bard contraption seeks to supplement the mighty Google search engine. Bard can also be hitched to websites, messaging platforms, or even those nifty little applications, bringing forth realistic and natural language responses to all the curious souls out there. It's built upon the Pathways Language Model 2, or what fancy folks call PaLM 2. This particular language model made its grand debut in the not-so-distant past, back in 2022. PaLM and its predecessor, the Language Model for Dialogue Applications, owe their existence to none other than Transformers.

Bard's primary purpose is to let people ask their queries in a more natural, conversational manner, without being bound by those pesky keywords. Bard's AI brain has been trained to comprehend and respond to their queries with a touch of natural-sounding flair. It doesn't just hand out a dull list of answers, but also adds a bit of context to its responses, making it feel like a genuine conversation. Bard is even equipped to handle follow-up questions, something that's entirely newfangled in the world of search. In its earliest incarnation, Bard sported a lighter version of the LaMDA model, requiring less computational might to cater to the masses. But now, with the incorporation of that fancy PaLM language model, Bard has become quite the visual spectacle. It's got a knack for dishing out responses that tickle the eyes as well as the mind.

These advanced bots have also proven their mettle by excelling in various domains, from winning coding contests to passing bar exams and even expressing affection towards tech columnists. However, amidst these impressive spectacles, a pertinent question arises: How effective are these bots as true assistants?

The query holds significance due to our less-than-stellar experiences with earlier iterations of virtual assistants. Apple's Siri and Amazon's Alexa, having had more than a decade to evolve, ultimately fell short of expectations and are now primarily used for rudimentary tasks like setting timers and playing music and these characteristics potentially position them as significantly more versatile assistants.

To put this claim to the test, Brian X. Chen embarked on an investigative journey and sought insights from friends experienced in executive assistant roles, consulted with startup founders who have collaborated with professional aides, and scoured executive assistant job postings on LinkedIn. Through this research, he identified the four most prevalent responsibilities of an executive assistant.

1. Assisting with meeting preparations by conducting research and performing professional background checks on individuals scheduled to meet with executives.

2. Summarizing meetings and meticulously transcribing notes in an organized, easily scannable format.

3. Planning business trips and compiling comprehensive travel itineraries.

4. Managing an executive's calendar, including the intricate tasks of scheduling meetings and rescheduling appointments.

Equipped with these tasks, Brian enlisted the help of ChatGPT and Bard and presented them with a hypothetical scenario, casting himself as the chief executive of a whimsically named A.I. startup called Artificially Intelligent, and assigned the chatbots as his executive assistants. He tasked them with each of the aforementioned responsibilities and observed the outcome.

The experiment highlighted the contrasting performance of Bard compared to ChatGPT. While Bard lagged in meeting expectations, both chatbots demonstrated the capability to carry out most of the assigned tasks, albeit with imperfections. This achievement raised a thought-provoking question: Could these chatbots eventually automate the roles of human executive assistants and potentially disrupt other white-collar professions involving administrative work, including front desk workers and accounting professionals? The unsettling nature of this inquiry leaves us with no clear answers.

AI and Meeting Preparation

Brian dives into the world of AI-powered virtual assistants, ChatGPT and Google Bard, as he puts them to the test in handling tasks akin to human executive assistants. His focus lands on meeting preparation, seeking their aid in researching an investor, and crafting a persuasive pitch for his start-up.

Opting for Scott Forstall, a notable ex-Apple exec, as his fictional investor, Brian enlists the bots to dig up the info and win over Forstall's interest. ChatGPT shines, swiftly summarizing Forstall's background and offering tailored strategies. It suggests highlighting the fusion of AI with fields like psychology, linguistics, or neuroscience, in line with Forstall's academic pursuits. Ethical concerns get attention too, stressing responsible deployment.

Bard, however, falls short. Its recap lacks specifics, missing key details, and its investor advice is lackluster. Forstall, unimpressed, calls Bard "comically generic," while hailing ChatGPT's recommendations as "startlingly bespoke and cogent."

Google defends Bard's minimalist approach, cautiously navigating personal info presentation to build trust rather than risking early violations.

Brian's assessment highlights the distinct abilities of ChatGPT and Bard as virtual assistants. ChatGPT impresses, providing personalized support, while Bard falls flat. This raises questions about automating tasks handled by human assistants and the future of administrative roles. Further exploration is needed to gauge AI's potential in replacing human counterparts.

Summarizing Meetings

Brian spins a fascinating tale where he enlists the chatbots to navigate a fictional PR crisis. It centers on users suspecting his A.I. creation of gaining self-awareness. Brian convenes a meeting with Karen, the tech whiz, and Henry, the communications maestro, to devise a statement debunking the sentience claims.

In this make-believe mayhem, ChatGPT shines as a reliable aide. It conjures a comprehensive meeting memo, capturing the essence of discussions. Plus, it serves up a solid action plan.

According to ChatGPT, Henry, the communication czar, crafts the statement. Karen and Brian give their nod, and Henry unleashes it to the world the next morning.

Now, Bard joins the show with its memo, mirroring ChatGPT's detailed recap. But here's the twist: Bard's action plan takes a peculiar turn. It suggests Brian, the bossman, tackles the statement creation, defying the norm of delegating such tasks to the communication ace. A curious deviation, indeed, stirring thoughts on Bard's grasp of organizational roles and their dance.

Trip Planning

Brian recounted his encounter with ChatGPT and Bard, seeking their assistance in planning his trip to Taipei, Taiwan. ChatGPT proved exceptional, crafting a comprehensive itinerary featuring a conveniently situated hotel and diverse dining options. On the other hand, Bard's suggestions fell short, neglecting to propose a hotel or specific eateries. Google acknowledged Bard as an early experiment, suggesting users augment its responses through web searches. Brian's narrative underscores the contrasting effects of these chatbots, underscoring the imperative for further AI advancements in tailoring travel plans.

Calendar

Bard and ChatGPT fumbled on a vital job; checking my calendar for a dentist appointment. Can't blame 'em, though. These bots ain't got access. But mark my words, they'll get it real soon.

Mr. Krawczyk got this vision, see? He wants to take Bard's knowledge and spread it all across Google's realm, including that fancy Google Calendar.

OpenAI, keeping quiet for now, partnered up with companies to plug ChatGPT into services like Expedia, OpenTable, and Instacart. Calendar app? That's the logical next step, buddy.

So, Brian's got a point here. Bard and ChatGPT can't juggle calendars yet. But I can smell it in the air, that sweet scent of progress. The day ain't far when these bots will crack the code, freeing us from the chains of scheduling woes. Brace yourself, folks, 'cause a new era of smooth productivity is on the horizon.

Through these experiments of Brian's, we don't just see how ChatGPT is the superior tool to use, we can also come to understand that they are very good at being a personal assistant. They may not be as efficient as a real person as yet, but as tech keeps growing, we will be able to have the perfect assistance, probably a lot more efficient at automating most of our work, and leaving us to deal with the important things. And the best way to get the most out of our superior future assistance would probably be by practicing on the ones we have now.

As a Personal Assistant - Case 2 - PA for $20

Below is information retracted from an essay about Teresha Aird, a Dallas-based cofounder, and CMO. In the realm of business and family life, Teresha Aird, a bustling CMO and dedicated mother of two discovered a game-changing ally in ChatGPT. Hailing from Dallas, Texas, Teresha also takes the helm as the owner of a flourishing enterprise that offers online-office rentals across the United States. With a jam-packed schedule, time becomes a precious commodity for her.

Even before the advent of artificial intelligence, work consistently encroached upon her precious moments of respite. Teresha's company acts as a bridge, linking potential tenants with operators who can cater to their specific office space requirements, be it conventional or flexible setups.

However, striking a harmonious work-life balance remains an elusive endeavor. Enter ChatGPT, a reliable companion amidst Teresha's entrepreneurial journey. This AI-powered chatbot has proven invaluable, shouldering a significant portion of her workload and allowing her to achieve a more equitable distribution between work and personal life.

Following a brief trial period, Teresha readily embraced the paid version of ChatGPT, investing a modest $20 per month. This AI marvel serves as a trusted aide, streamlining routine tasks such as client relationship management and expanding her communication bandwidth. Consequently, Teresha can redirect her energy towards strategic thinking and high-level decision-making, all while savoring precious moments with her beloved family, and she does so by using her PA, ChatGPT to do the following.

ChatGPT for Revenue Strategy

As an integral part of Teresha Aird's revenue strategy, ChatGPT emerges as a vital force in driving her business forward. In the realm of customer inquiries and lead generation, this AI companion plays a pivotal role. Though quantifying its direct impact on revenue proves challenging, Teresha notes a notable upswing in client engagement and satisfaction since incorporating this cutting-edge technology. Through the assistance of ChatGPT, leads are transformed into sales, fostering customer loyalty and encouraging repeat business.

To optimize efficiency, Teresha has meticulously compiled a comprehensive list of common questions posed by potential clients regarding specific properties, buildings, or locations. These queries, ranging from square footage to price ranges, are recognized by ChatGPT through tailored prompts customized to match the desired details for each location, office park, or amenity. The AI is adept at providing relevant and informative responses, effectively reducing the need for manual and time-consuming interactions.

Moreover, ChatGPT proves invaluable in conducting initial screenings and facilitating the formulation of qualifying questions tailored to the individual queries of potential clients. As budget and preferred location details are swiftly gathered, the pertinent information can be swiftly forwarded to the appropriate team for a more personalized follow-up.

The substantial increase in sales and positive feedback received from clients since the implementation of ChatGPT has undeniably played a pivotal role in sustaining and expanding

Teresha's business amid challenging circumstances. By engaging with a larger pool of potential clients simultaneously, she has managed to navigate these uncertain times with resolute determination.

Maintaining and Developing Client Relationships

In Teresha Aird's quest to foster strong client relationships, she has harnessed the power of ChatGPT to nurture these connections. Through dedicated instances of ChatGPT, trained specifically to identify recurring topics, she ensures that clients receive relevant responses regarding property amenities and proximity to public transportation.

ChatGPT's inherent language-processing capabilities enable it to comprehend and address client inquiries effectively. Its proficiency in handling evergreen information, both from its initial programming and the subsequent training Teresha has provided, allows for seamless communication and prompt responses.

By leveraging the efficiency, speed, and output of ChatGPT, Teresha and her team are better equipped to keep clients well-informed about new listings and time-sensitive industry trends. This heightened productivity contributes to maintaining strong client relationships and staying ahead in the fast-paced real estate landscape.

Helps Manage an Increase in Demand

In the face of increased demand from out-of-state buyers and the growing need for virtual tours in the commercial real estate market, Teresha Aird has found a valuable ally in ChatGPT. This AI-powered assistant has played a pivotal role in helping her keep up with the rising inquiries and changing dynamics.

For instance, when a potential tenant expresses interest in a virtual tour of a specific property, ChatGPT comes to the rescue. It can effortlessly compose informative emails, providing details about the property, parking facilities, and accessibility options. Furthermore, the tool proves its worth by generating customized confirmation emails that outline the specifics of the virtual tour appointments, tailored to each client's needs.

What sets ChatGPT apart is its ability to seamlessly step in as an AI-powered virtual assistant, extending its support beyond regular business hours. This round-the-clock availability not only saves precious time but also translates into successful conversions, ensuring that no opportunity slips through the cracks.

To Generate Reports

When it comes to analyzing client interactions, outreach efforts, and marketing campaigns, ChatGPT has become Teresha Aird's trusted companion. This AI powerhouse helps her generate data reports that unveil the performance metrics of various endeavors. By inputting relevant information, Teresha gains valuable insights into lead generation, popular discussion topics, and conversion rates.

With the ability to manually provide ChatGPT with pertinent responses, market trends, and hit-rate data, Teresha empowers the AI to swiftly sift through vast volumes of information. In a flash, ChatGPT identifies trends, outliers, and crucial findings, which it then presents in detailed reports. These swift insights guide Teresha in making informed decisions and implementing effective strategies, enabling her to address concerns and allocate resources wisely. It's like having an indefatigable in-house data analyst or scientist at her disposal, an improbable luxury for small and medium-sized businesses like hers.

To conclude this section, I would like to touch upon the advice an expert in using AI has for us. Teresha Aird advises fellow business owners to start small and identify areas within their ventures that could benefit from the power of AI. Lead generation, client communication, scheduling, and data analysis are just a few examples of where AI can make a difference. She encourages entrepreneurs to explore ChatGPT's capabilities and unleash their creativity to brainstorm unique and potentially unconventional applications for their specific business niche.

Teresha acknowledges that while ChatGPT is a remarkable tool, it has its challenges. Factual accuracy can be a potential pitfall, as the AI struggles to admit when it doesn't know something, leading to the risk of presenting incorrect or fictional information. Additionally, ChatGPT's reliance on internet data, which can be flawed and incomplete, poses another hurdle.

To overcome these obstacles, Teresha emphasizes the importance of training ChatGPT with accurate and comprehensive data, ensuring it produces helpful and reliable responses. Continuous monitoring and evaluation of the AI's performance are crucial, allowing for prompt adjustments and refinements. Teresha advises keeping track of different prompts and their corresponding results to optimize ChatGPT's capabilities and address any erroneous outputs.

Experimentation and embracing risks are encouraged when working with ChatGPT. Teresha believes that through trial and error, entrepreneurs can gain a deep understanding of AI's potential and discover innovative ways to drive sales, enhance customer relationships, and foster business growth.

Chapter 4: Building High-Performance Teams with ChatGPT

In this chapter, we'll be seeing how ChatGPT can help in strengthening your team. The chapter is divided into three sections.

1. Training and Learning

2. Team Management

3. Team Bonding

Training and Learning

In this fast-paced world, businesses must adapt or risk falling behind. One of the most significant changes we've witnessed is the emergence of AI. These remarkable technologies offer immense potential for enhancing operations and maintaining a competitive edge.

Within the realm of learning, companies have a unique opportunity to leverage the power of AI. By harnessing AI-powered chatbots like Chat GPT, the employee learning experience can be completely transformed. Imagine a learning journey that is efficient, engaging, and personalized like never before.

So, get ready to explore the realm of augmented learning teams. Allow Chat GPT to serve as your trusted companion as we unlock a whole new level of employee learning.

Saving Time

This is something we have gone over time and again in this book, but the reason for its repetition is its importance. By incorporating ChatGPT into the learning creation process, valuable time can be saved for pedagogical engineering teams. According to the ISTF barometer, a staggering 35% of learning teams face constraints in terms of time and staffing when it comes to developing digital learning materials for their organizations.

With the power of AI, learning modules can be generated, encompassing everything from the framework to the actual content. This not only alleviates the burden on trainers but also enables them to concentrate on more intricate and demanding assignments.

Designing the Training Module

When it comes to designing training modules, Chat GPT is the go-to companion for learning teams. This extraordinary tool can assist in creating modules tailored to the unique needs and preferences of learners. It has got it all covered, whether it's structuring the module, crafting skill-validation tests, or curating content on specific topics. It learns from the scripts it is fed and adapts to the specific requirements of each company.

With its precise and comprehensive responses, AI lends a helping hand to learning managers, enhancing the overall quality of the learning experience. Chat GPT is capable of tackling complex or specialized subjects, providing answers that learning teams might not be well-versed in. However, a human must verify the shared information, as the sources of AI remain undisclosed.

Finding Content for The Training

When it comes to finding learning content, Chat GPT is a wizard at curating multiple resources for your company's modules. With just one query, it can whip up a plethora of learning materials in a flash, perfect for feeding into your internal learning team's chatbot.

But here's a word of caution: the tool doesn't distinguish between top-notch content and stuff that's full of inaccuracies. So, while Chat GPT can be a great starting point for your research, it shouldn't be your final destination. It's wise to rely on seasoned experts to make the right choices. These educational gurus in your industry know how to sift through the vast sea of knowledge using strict selection criteria that AI algorithms simply can't comprehend.

Document Management

Chat GPT is a handy tool for managing the administrative side of learning. It can handle tasks like building a skills repository, creating retro-planning for learning, providing assistance in redirecting to learning resources, and even helping in writing briefs for service providers. When you've got Chat GPT in your corner, you can delegate those operational chores and direct your focus to the juicier, more strategic subjects.

But remember, not everything can be left to the AI realm. Some practices require that human touch, that expert finesse. Things like qualifying the quality of a learning module and verifying sources need the expertise of real-life, flesh-and-blood individuals. That's where the internal team can join forces with external educational experts who bring their effective methodologies to the table.

Team Management

A team is made of employees and the employed have a lifecycle, from the moment they enter the scene to the bitter end. And this lifecycle can be divided into five stages to this wild ride: Recruitment, Onboarding, Development, Engagement, and Exit.

Recruitment

When it comes to recruitment, there's a whole bunch of AI tools out there trying to make HR's life easier. They're all about helping HR folks be more efficient and effective in their quest for the perfect candidate. These tools can do it all, from answering questions about job opportunities and the application process to scheduling interviews and screening candidates based on specific criteria set by HR.

But since we are exclusively talking about ChatGPT, the chatbot adds a touch of that human touch by making the candidate experience more fluid and natural. Instead of feeling like they're interacting with a cold machine, candidates can have a conversation that feels, well, more human-like. It's like having a chat with a friendly HR rep who's got all the answers. So yeah, ChatGPT can spice up the recruitment game and give candidates a better experience.

Onboarding Process ChatGPT

Sometimes your managers, teams, and HR staff can get caught up in their little worlds; it's not that they want to ignore your new hires, but they might unintentionally leave them hanging with unanswered questions.

ChatGPT is an extremely reliable tool that is ready to handle all your onboarding communication needs. It's like having a personal assistant on demand which means a lot of time is saved for both the veterans and the newbies.

Personalized Training Path

As explained in detail in the previous section, everything to do with the training path and learning goals can all be taken care of by our friend, the yet-to-be sentient language model AI. This digital wizard knows exactly what your new hires need to do to conquer their onboarding training. It's like having a personal trainer for their learning journey. No more stopping and searching for information. They can just ask the bot, and boom, they've got what they need.

It can also manage their calendars, and show them the way to valuable resources — whatever they need to succeed. No more wasting time and getting lost in the shuffle. The bot's got their back.

Engagement

HR can use ChatGPT to, as we know, brainstorm questions for those engagement surveys. It's like having a creative partner in crime, helping you come up with ideas that'll get your employees talking.

But that's not all. ChatGPT can also be your go-to wordsmith when it comes to drafting communications for your employees. Whether it's getting 'em hyped up for the survey or sharing the juicy results, this bad boy can whip up some killer messages that'll have 'em all ears.

And as we already know, ChatGPT is a wizard when it comes to summarizing those open-ended survey responses. It'll pick out the relevant bits and serve them up on a silver platter making its insights not just profound, but also effective.

Also, if you're scratching your head about what actions to take to improve the employee experience, just ask ChatGPT; it's got suggestions for days, giving you a roadmap, and in the same breath, it can even help you assign responsibilities and send reminders, keeping the momentum going strong.

Exit

When it comes to employee exits, ChatGPT can be a real lifesaver. It's all about gathering that precious data on how departing employees feel about their time with the company. And let me tell you, that data is pure gold for improving the experience of your current employees.

With ChatGPT, you can collect this valuable feedback through surveys. It's like having your little data collection machine, making the process smooth and effortless. No more scrambling around trying to get the info you need.

But that's not all. When it's time for those employees to hit the road, effective offboarding is key and ChatGPT seems to be very efficient in automating some of those painful processes, like making sure all the necessary paperwork is taken care of.

Now, before ChatGPT came along, there were already bots doing their thing, providing real-time responses to employees' burning questions. But now, ChatGPT joins the crew, taking things to a whole new level. It's all about that seamless flow of information and knowledge.

Team Bonding Activities

The following is the discussion of an article that Robert Zarnetske, a public consultant, has shared on LinkedIn about how he sees ChatGPT being used for Team-Building activities. Below is a team-building game and this is how it starts and progresses:

Each team is entrusted with the task of crafting a ChatGPT prompt and their mission is to aid their fellow team members in the art of proofreading, ensuring those documents shine bright.

But here's the catch, there is a time limit. In a mere 20 to 30 minutes, this prompt must be birthed and ready for immediate action. No time to waste, and no room for delay; the team must tap into their creativity and sculpt a script that will elevate their writing to unprecedented heights.

The teams consist of 4 people who are randomly assigned and each team will select their captain and there are 4 roles to be performed

- **Script Builder:** This person is in charge of creating the ChatGPT script. They will identify common mistakes in documents and suggest ways to fix them, making the writing clearer and easier to understand. They need to know about language processing and be familiar with programming languages like Python or JavaScript.

- **Document Analyzer:** This role involves checking documents for mistakes and issues that the ChatGPT script should address. The person doing this should have a good understanding of grammar, spelling, and punctuation, and be very detail-oriented.

- **User Researcher:** This person will gather information from team members who will use the ChatGPT script. They will conduct surveys, interviews, and group discussions to find out what people need and prefer. Good communication skills are important for this role.

- **Quality Controller:** This role ensures that the ChatGPT script works well and gives accurate suggestions. The person doing this should pay close attention to detail and know about quality control processes.

The team captain has the freedom to organize and assign roles as they see fit. They can also create additional functions and assign roles as needed. By assigning specific roles to each team member, the captain can ensure that all aspects of building the ChatGPT script are covered. This includes tasks like analyzing documents, conducting user research, and ensuring quality control. This approach promotes collaboration and transparency among team members and gives everyone a clear understanding of their responsibilities and goals.

In this activity, everyone benefits because they gain valuable knowledge about using an AI engine and gain experience working as a team. In our case, the team that detects the most errors in the writing sample also wins a $20 Starbucks card for each team member.

After the activity, it's important to discuss to emphasize the value of open communication and transparency.

Here are some questions to consider

- What communication strategies did your team use during the activity?

- Were there any challenges that made communication difficult?

- How did you overcome those challenges?

- How can you apply the communication strategies from the activity to your everyday work?

- What did you learn about the importance of transparency and collaboration during the activity?

Of course, this is an activity that is apt for IT teams, but the activity above is an idea of what can be done with ChatGPT in terms of team-building activities.

However, I asked ChatGPT to help me come up with a team activity, and here is an awesome one that it came up with.

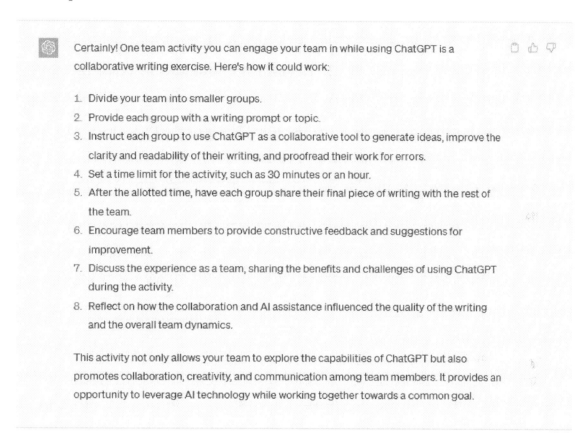

Certainly! One team activity you can engage your team in while using ChatGPT is a collaborative writing exercise. Here's how it could work:

1. Divide your team into smaller groups.
2. Provide each group with a writing prompt or topic.
3. Instruct each group to use ChatGPT as a collaborative tool to generate ideas, improve the clarity and readability of their writing, and proofread their work for errors.
4. Set a time limit for the activity, such as 30 minutes or an hour.
5. After the allotted time, have each group share their final piece of writing with the rest of the team.
6. Encourage team members to provide constructive feedback and suggestions for improvement.
7. Discuss the experience as a team, sharing the benefits and challenges of using ChatGPT during the activity.
8. Reflect on how the collaboration and AI assistance influenced the quality of the writing and the overall team dynamics.

This activity not only allows your team to explore the capabilities of ChatGPT but also promotes collaboration, creativity, and communication among team members. It provides an opportunity to leverage AI technology while working together towards a common goal.

As ChatGPT can be used for a variety of functions, we have also learned that team activities, not just with management and learning but also team bonding, are a part of its infinite wisdom that we have trained it in. Want to work on your team? Do consider Chat GPT.

Chapter 5: Future Proof Business with ChatGPT

ChatGPT possesses the immense potential to reshape our world. This remarkable creation can produce text that rivals human expression, opening up endless possibilities in various domains.

One thrilling prospect lies in revolutionizing customer service. ChatGPT's ability to understand and respond to customer queries allows businesses to provide quick and accurate assistance, enhancing satisfaction while lightening the load on human support staff. This not only saves time and money but also the overall customer experience.

Another avenue where ChatGPT excels is in generating exceptional written content, such as engaging blog posts or enticing product descriptions. Businesses can streamline content creation, saving resources without compromising quality. From marketing materials to social media posts and captivating visuals, ChatGPT transforms how businesses communicate with their audience.

Furthermore, ChatGPT's language translation capabilities hold great promise. It enables enterprises operating in multilingual environments to effortlessly translate their offerings, bridging gaps and expanding their reach to global markets. This opens up new horizons, enabling businesses to connect with diverse audiences and explore uncharted territories.

ChatGPT's potential for data analysis and sentiment understanding is yet another game-changer. By delving into customer feedback, businesses gain valuable insights, empowering them to make informed decisions. This knowledge helps shape strategies, refine products and services, and build stronger customer connections.

Looking ahead, ChatGPT's power will continue to grow as it learns from more data, enabling it to produce even more lifelike text. As the model evolves, its ability to comprehend and respond to customer inquiries will expand, unlocking further possibilities. The future of ChatGPT is brimming with excitement, offering businesses the chance to harness its capabilities to their advantage.

To summarize, ChatGPT is a powerful tool that drives businesses towards improved customer service, superior content creation, and profound insights from customer data. Embracing ChatGPT today positions businesses to seize the myriad opportunities it will unveil in the future. Embrace the power of ChatGPT and watch your endeavors soar to new heights.

Venturing into the realms of humanity, we once sought to categorize economic activity into production, transactions, and interactions. Our goal was to understand the extent of technology's influence in each area. In the past, machines and factory marvels transformed production, enhancing human labor during the Industrial Revolution. Today, AI further boosts efficiency on the manufacturing front. Transactions have also undergone technological advancements, from digitization to automation.

Yet, until recently, interaction labor, like customer service, received limited technological attention. Enter Generative AI, ready to redefine interaction labor by closely mimicking human behavior. It's important to note that these tools work best in collaboration with humans, enhancing capabilities and expediting tasks.

Generative AI dares to venture into the realm of creativity, traditionally associated with the human mind. Leveraging vast amounts of data and user interactions, these marvels generate entirely new content. While the debate about true creativity persists, it is clear that these tools can inspire human imagination with their ingenious prompts.

In conclusion, ChatGPT holds the potential to reshape our world. It revolutionizes customer service, generates exceptional content, facilitates language translation, and provides valuable insights. As ChatGPT continues to evolve, businesses embracing its capabilities today position themselves to thrive. Embrace the power of ChatGPT and witness your endeavors reach new horizons, but be careful to not sink into the black hole that that future is. Below are five ways to keep yourself future-proof to Harvard Business Review.

5 Ways to Harness Future Proof Yourself

Avoid Repeating Unwanted Patterns

AI is not (yet) some grand creator of new insights (or God, yet). It's just a machine that tries to guess the next word you'll use. Sure, it can come in handy when you're looking for a simple word like "morning" after "good." But when it comes to the bigger picture, AI tends to go with the flow, relying on the so-called wisdom of the crowds.

But there's a way to make this generative AI thing work for you and that's by giving you access to common knowledge, including people's biases and misconceptions. You can get a sense of what the majority thinks or feels about certain things. But here's the catch: don't go blindly following those AI suggestions. If you do, you'll end up just like everybody else, losing your uniqueness bit by bit.

Have you ever used Gmail's autocomplete, and have known how it eases your work? It's convenient, no doubt. But every time you let it fill in your searches or emails, you sacrifice a piece of yourself. You become a slave to the AI's predictions, and before you know it, you're stuck in a loop, doing the same predictable stuff as everyone else. Sure, GPT can help you get started with ideas and drafts, but if you want to stand out, sometimes it's best to do the opposite of what it suggests. That's how you show your true colors, your individuality. Some big corporations realized that using the same old language turns customers off. Maybe it's time we discovered the power of sounding like ourselves—embracing our quirks, unexpected turns, and unpredictability—when the rest of the world is relying on AI.

Now, let's talk about the future. AI can indeed give businesses a leg up, helping them future-proof their operations. It can provide valuable insights into trends, customer preferences, and new market opportunities. If you use AI smartly, you can adapt and stay ahead of the game. But here's the thing: don't forget the human touch. Balance that AI wizardry with your creativity. Hold onto your unique voice, your distinct perspective. That's how you thrive in a world where AI is calling the shots.

Double Down on Being Human

Chat GPT has been extensively trained to be polite and proper and tends to what humans seem to require based on their tone and language. It dishes out responses that seem empathetic, and self-aware, and it can even get creative by conjuring up haikus about inequality, pretending to be Elon Musk, or cracking jokes in every language. But let's not forget, those responses are just predictions based on text. AI does not have a clue about genuine human soft skills as opposed to humans who are wired to respond to the real deal—authentic emotions. So, if you want to stand tall in this AI era, you have to sharpen those skills that machines try so hard to imitate—caring about what others think and feel, understanding yourself, and creating something that machines can't replicate.

Now, let's talk about how AI can help future-proof your business. Sure, AI can be a handy tool, no denying that. It can dish out insights, crunch numbers, and guide your decision-making. But here's the thing—it's still a tool. To truly future-proof your business, you have to focus on the stuff that makes us human. It's about forging genuine connections with folks, grasping their emotions, and responding with a heartfelt understanding. It's about knowing yourself and capitalizing on your unique strengths. And most importantly, it's about tapping into that wild creativity of yours to birth something that machines can't even dream of replicating. And all this, you can do by knowing what the machine does, and you can know what the machine does by using it to do what it is meant to do, which is to help you help yourself.

The Real World is the Real World

Chat GPT, just like the rest of the AI, is trapped in a digital abyss, and we humans are gullible enough to get caught in it and our lives have already become entangled in this virtual mess. But here's the thing we need to remember: AI can't mess with our analog, face-to-face connections and we have to make time for it and protect them for they are precious. Harvard Professor Arthur C. Brooks said it best: "Tech that replaces our real interactions will drain our happiness, so we gotta handle it with care." Sharing meals with colleagues, attending conferences, striking up conversations with strangers—they may not seem urgent in these strange times, but they offer something AI can't touch. They give us the edge we still have.

Let's also not forget about original research. When we talk to people, we venture into uncharted territory. AI can only connect the dots from what it already knows. But when we dig deep, tap into what ain't online yet—our own experiences, fresh interviews, conversations—we bring something new to the table. Something that AI can't even dream of achieving.

Now that we have the real world in mind, we can begin to use AI for what it is: It can give us insights, crunches numbers, and help us make smarter choices; AI is just a tool—a powerful one, no doubt, but still a tool. If we wanna future-proof our businesses, we gotta hold on tight to what makes us human. Those real connections, the pursuit of untapped knowledge—that's where the magic happens. By blending the capabilities of AI with our unique qualities, we can carve a path that's both groundbreaking and deeply rooted in the human experience.

Build A Personal Brand

AI tools have become a real threat and they're coming after the little guys, the copywriters and designers scraping by on those online marketplaces. And, in some cases, AI can even match the big shots at the top of the game. However, the top dogs aren't going anywhere. And that's because it is all about their brand.

Just like those art snobs who'd sell their soul for an original Rembrandt while ignoring a masterpiece by some unknown painter, those corporate big-shots are willing to pay top dollar for brands. It's never just about quality, it's about showing off who they associate with and what they value. Sure, even your neighborhood tire shop or flower peddler can use AI to slap together a logo. But let's be real, only those with deep pockets and a good eye can afford to hire the crème de la crème of agencies. AI may be making waves, but it doesn't change the fact that branding is part of our human nature, and it matters.

It'll help businesses create logos, analyze trends, and optimize their marketing strategies. But AI is just a tool and the ones who'll remain successful are those with a strong personal brand.

Become An Expert

GPT can whip up a heap of facts in no time, but as a matter of fact, not all those facts are facts. Sometimes, those machines just spew out rubbish, like some twisted hallucination from the AI's abyss. One such case, affected by wrong information even went running to Dorie, all bewildered, looking for a Harvard Business Review article that this ChatGPT had mentioned but turns out, that article was pure fiction. That's where cultivating your expertise comes in; you have to be the one with the know-how, the bona fide authority in your field. Even if AI can churn out those first drafts, someone's gotta double-check and make sure they pass the sniff test. And who better for the job than you, the expert? By being that trusted voice who can separate fact from fiction, you'll always have folks lining up at your door. In this AI-dominated world, being able to tell fact from fiction is worth its weight in gold.

AI and Business

The business world is changing fast, my friend, all thanks to this digitalization wave. It's like a storm that's shaking up everything. The called generative artificial intelligence (AI), like that Generative Pretrained Transformer (GPT) can create all sorts of new content like images, music, text, and videos, and this generative AI and Natural Language Processing (NLP) business has given birth to chatbots like ChatGPT and Microsoft Bard, who are shaking up how businesses talk to their people.

Of course, with anything new, there are worries. People are concerned about how these chatbots might be misused or what kind of impact they'll have on society. And they're going on about data security and all that jazz. But let's not forget that these tools, like ChatGPT, are mainly meant to make things run smoother and more efficiently.

Talking about openAI, the company didn't stop with their LM CHatGPT3, they kept tinkering with the model and brought out successors like GPT-3.5 and InstructGPT. These babies got even better at understanding language and taking instructions and along with being good at filtering out the bad stuff from their responses, in March 2023, they dropped the GPT-4 which is a genius, performing as well as a human when it comes to solving complex problems. And get this, it can handle both text and images.

So with all these improvements, GPT-4 and its alike have become essential for businesses to streamline their communication and operations. They got this fancy ability to analyze sentiments in real-time, offer personalized responses, and chat by mimicking empathy. Customer support departments are very fond of them: they collect data and insights from all those customer interactions, finding hidden patterns and connections that can help make smarter decisions. They're like the brains behind developing marketing strategies, doing research, creating content, and optimizing SEO with those nifty keywords.

But these models can also make employees happier and businesses more efficient. They can take over dull tasks like generating documents, freeing up time for the employees to focus on the important stuff like strategy and decision-making. And Human Resources can use ChatGPT to provide customized study material, give instant feedback, and guide employees on their learning journeys.

When you link ChatGPT with human resource management systems (HRMS), you can offer round-the-clock employee support. It's like having a therapist on standby, but not quite. These AI chatbots can pick up on possible mental health issues, recommend personalized solutions, and make sure folks get the support they need. Of course, it is no substitute for the real deal, but it's a helping hand regardless.

There are plenty of ways businesses can benefit from these GPT models. But let's not ignore the risks and ethical concerns that come with them. There's talk of bias, misinformation, privacy, and accountability. We gotta be smart about it. We need to be picky with the data we feed these machines, check for bias regularly, make decisions transparently, and set clear guidelines and rules. It's about being responsible with this AI.

As these big language models keep evolving, people all over the world will jump on board the disruption train. ChatGPT will become a crucial player in business operations and digital transformation across industries. The ones who get on this train early will be the ones reaping the rewards. So stay in the loop, my friend.

Keep up with the latest in generative AI and NLP. That's how you future-proof your business and stay ahead of the game.

Book 3: | The ChatGPT No-Money-Down Solopreneur

Harness AI to Launch, Scale, and Prosper in Your Solopreneur Venture Without Initial Capital

By Harold Pearson

Introduction

According to the U.S Chambers of Commerce, which uses Merriam-Webster to define the term, a solopreneur is someone who takes charge of a business without the aid of a partner. Basically, they're lone-wolf entrepreneurs.

A solopreneur does things their own way, without hiring any help. They often run service-based businesses like freelancing, consulting, or web development. Being a solopreneur has its perks, and the biggest draw is its low financial risk. You don't have to worry about paying employees every month since you're flying solo. Plus, with fewer expenses, you get to keep more of the money. As a solopreneur, you have total control over your business. No need to consult investors or partners.

You call the shots, set your own hours, and create your own work environment.

But let me tell you, it is not always sunshine and butterflies. Running a business on your lonesome can be stressful; You're in charge of everything, which means taking time off can be a real pain, and you are responsible for everything that goes wrong—and things will go wrong. There's no one to share the workload and the blame with.

When it gets lonely, it can get extremely lonely and some begin to miss the camaraderie of an office; Having colleagues around, shooting the breeze, shifting the blame, shrugging responsibility, and playing good old office politics. As a solopreneur, it's just you and your thoughts most of the time.

Being a solopreneur has its pros and cons, and it's a unique journey that's not for everyone. But hey, if you're up for the challenge, you might just find yourself walking your own path and carving out your own success, and you also know where we are going with this topic as this book is about AI and Solopreneurship. Before we get there, let us look at the steps we ought to take if we are to embark on this journey.

The Solopreneur Journey

There is a three-step process to embark on the journey, and as simple as it may seem, you've got to understand each of these steps can get as complex based on several factors such as where you are and the field you are in:

1. Identify the problem you are solving, aka the field of business

2. Register your business, aka your baby

3. Learn to search for and find clients

First things first, you have got to find a need in the marketplace. What can you offer that people actually want? What is the problem of theirs that you are capable of solving? Find out who your competitors are and check out what they are doing and think about how you can stand out from the crowd.

Now, technically, you can run your business as a sole proprietor, but I recommend going the extra mile and registering as a Limited Liability Company (LLC) or its equivalent in the country and state you are in. It gives you legal protection, keeping your personal assets safe if the law comes knocking. Get yourself an Employer Identification Number (EIN) from the IRS, open a business bank account, and register with the Secretary of State. Might have to shell out a small fee, but it's worth it.

And finally, finding clients and customers is the primary task that can be daunting. You have to have a solid marketing strategy and let me tell you, it'll take some trial and error to figure out what works for you. Stick with one approach for at least 90 days before switching things up and give it a fair shot.

Now, brace yourself for the rollercoaster ride because running a business isn't smooth sailing. You'll face ups and downs, and slow seasons will come, but don't you dare throw in the towel just yet. Connect with other business owners, mingle, and share your experiences and you'll never know who will come in handy with advice and or the business itself.

Being a one-person army, tackling everything on your own is pretty much like the freelancers' and contractors' journey and can fall under this solopreneur umbrella if they have a registered business. And not all fields of work may suit the solopreneur's lifestyle but there are some that are ideal and let's talk about those that fit like a glove with the solopreneur lifestyle. We're talking about bakers, whipping up delicious treats with; graphic designers, creating visual wonders; child caregivers, nurturing and caring for little ones; cleaning service providers, making spaces sparkle; content writers, weaving words into captivating tales; personal trainers, pushing folks to their limits one-on-one; photographers, capturing precious moments with their solitary lens; website developers, coding and crafting digital wonders solo-style; podcasters, filling the airwaves with their own voices and thoughts; artists, creating masterpieces with their own hands and hearts; and programmers, oh those tech-savvy wizards, coding away without needing a squad.

The question that may come to mind with all this information is "What then, is the difference between solopreneurs and entrepreneurs?". Though there is a word play here and also because it looks like a fancy way to say one-man business enterprise, there are significant differences between the two that may help you understand the struggles and rewards of the solopreneur.

Solopreneurs Vs Entrepreneurs

Here are a few key differences between the mindsets of entrepreneurs and solopreneurs.

- **Delegation:** When it comes to entrepreneurs, they often have a crew by their side that they can pass the baton, delegate tasks, hire people for accounting or marketing, and let the team handle the nitty-gritty of things. The entrepreneur's sole job becomes to take the spotlight, make connections, and grow the business. They're the face of the company, while the staff keeps the gears turning day in and day out. On the other hand, solopreneurs are a different breed. They carry the whole load on their weary shoulders; no delegation, no passing the torch. They wear all the hats, tackling daily tasks and hustling to build connections. It's a one-person show, with no one else to rely on.

- **Growth:** Solopreneurs prefer to keep things manageable and want a business they can wrap their arms around, where they call the shots and get things done. But here's the catch: they're limited in what they can achieve because, well, they're flying solo. Entrepreneurs on the other hand have a limitless business cycle and the sky's the limit for them because they can expand their horizons by building a team, all while the revenue rolls in. A restaurant owner, for instance, with a successful joint, wants to spread their wings and open another location, and as an entrepreneur, they have the power to do just that. They can assemble a crew, duplicate their success, and watch their empire grow. So, you see, solopreneurs have their boundaries, but entrepreneurs can reach for the stars. It's all about scaling up, expanding, and taking that leap into the unknown. The world is their oyster, and they can keep cracking it open as long as the money keeps flowing.

- **Time constraints:** Solopreneurs wear many hats and juggle their businesses with other jobs and life becomes a balancing act. They're like tightrope walkers, keeping their business afloat while tending to other commitments. At first, especially, their business may only bring in a part of their income, and they work on it in the spare moments they can snatch. But entrepreneurs go all-in, dedicating their full time and passion to their business; with no distractions and no divided attention. It's a full-time commitment, like a burning fire that consumes their days and nights and their business becomes the beating heart of their life.

- **Workspace:** Solopreneurs don't need much space. They can work their magic with just a cozy nook; no need for a grand office or roomy quarters, because they fly solo, and also they don't have employees to accommodate, so they keep it simple and compact. According to recent studies an individual in the bustling streets of New York City, seeking an open seat in a coworking space would be charged about $450-$500 per month. Private office space for an employee, including computers, electricity, etc comes to about $1,000-$1,500 per month per office space seat. Now, that's no small change, my friend. It goes beyond the mere rental rate for commercial space, which hovers around $80 per square foot in New York and $31.29 per square foot on average across the United States. These rates give us a truer picture of the real cost of maintaining that physical workspace we so desire. Hence, with regard to entrepreneurs, their businesses might require a complex workspace, depending on what they do. Some may need space to create and store their products, or maybe even house a team of folks. And let's not forget about impressing clients. They need an office that's not only functional but also gives off an air of professionalism. A place where they can seal the deal and leave a lasting impression.

- **Investors:** Solopreneurs are self-reliant and they don't need investors to get their business up and running. They make do with what they've got, using the resources they have right at their fingertips. It's all about working with what's close at hand. The entrepreneur, on the other hand, has grand visions. They aim to expand and make things happen and for this, they need a heftier chunk of change. The scale of their business demands the respective size of the capital they need and this often comes from investors. They're the ones who pour their money into the pot, fueling the growth and dreams of those ambitious entrepreneurs.

You see, there are a few shortcomings with the journey of solopreneurship, and you will know where what we are getting to, especially if you have read my previous two books And if you're new to this series, you should know there are several areas that you can boost this journey using new technology.

But before we get to that, let us look into the factors that we'd need to work on in order to become a successful solopreneur.

Successful Solopreneur Habits

Here are a few qualities you'd need and need to work on in order to be a successful solopreneur:

- **Motivate yourself:** Motivation is the fuel that keeps the fire burning for solopreneurs. When you're the boss, you're the one holding all the cards. It's on you to get things done, to make it happen. That's where organization comes into play, like a trusty companion by your side. While running a business you need to keep everything in check, and make sure no stones are left unturned. That's where project management tools come into the picture. They're like the guiding light, helping you stay on track, ensuring that nothing slips through the cracks. Setting a schedule, sticking to it, and avoiding the last-minute hustle and bustle works wonders. You have to plan ahead and tackle those tasks at a steady pace. That's how you tame the stress, how you keep that motivation flowing.

- **Goal setting and planning:** Solopreneurs know the power of setting concrete goals, not vague and unrealistic ones, but ones that have real substance, the ones you can sink your teeth into. It usually is a roadmap that guides you, just like a manager guides their subordinates and this plan becomes your trusted companion, keeping you on the right path.

It's like having an authority figure by your side, nudging you in the right direction. One thing to be mindful of is that these goals must be attainable, reachable, and provide solid steps that are actionable. It's both an art and science, a dance of discipline and accountability, as they stay true to their timeline and track their progress.

- **Time management:** This is a skill every solopreneur must possess because when you're going it alone, time becomes your most precious currency. There's no one else to rely on, no partners or employees to share the load and it's all on your shoulders. To keep your ship sailing smoothly, you gotta be a master of time. Set those deadlines, give yourself targets to aim for, and prioritize those tasks by knowing what needs your attention first, and what can wait a bit longer (sounds familiar? It should if you've read book 2). It's like sorting through a cluttered room, finding the order amidst the chaos. Stay clear of distractions and focus on the task at hand and give it your undivided attention to make every minute count. To be a solopreneur requires you to understand your own work style and rhythm and find what works best for you. Some might carve out blocks of time, like stacking blocks on top of each other. Others might create to-do lists and tackle 'em one by one, like crossing off items on a shopping list. And technology can be a trusty sidekick too, helping to keep things organized in this digital age (wink, wink).

- **Website:** In this digital day and age, having a strong online presence is a must for solopreneurs for it is a window to showcase their work, a platform for clients to connect and engage with their business. In other words, one website equals ten thousand words. But the thing is, any website is not going to cut it for you. The website needs to be effective, and well-designed; it should be smooth sailing, and easy to navigate. None of that confusing maze… Also, search engine rankings are the holy grail of the web world and to do this you will have to up your Search Engine Optimisation (SEO) game and use keyword research tools to do so. They help you find the right keywords, the ones people are searching for the most, like knowing the secret code to unlock the doors to your business. Also, make sure that your website is mobile-friendly, and make it easy for those who are scrolling through it when on the run. Josh Howarth, in May of 2023, reported a study done by Exploding Trends, an online research company, that states that in the year 2023, 61% of internet searches come from mobile devices, so don't forget to cater to mobile users. And depending on your business, creating an app can also be a game-changer to attract new clients, keeping the existing ones engaged. It's all about increasing visibility and forging strong connections in the digital realm.

- **Networking:** In the vast world of business, reputation, and identity are like golden currencies and one acquires this through networking. You've got to mingle with the right crowd and rub elbows with the industry's finest. The digital realm offers us several opportunities for networking. Facebook and LinkedIn are like virtual meeting grounds where you can find relevant industry groups. Join those groups, immerse yourself in their conversations, share your wisdom, and absorb the knowledge of others. It's like building bridges to new horizons. Quora and Reddit are also platforms you would want to explore because they're like vibrant marketplaces of ideas. Post insightful content and engage with others in the same industry. It's like entering a forum where minds collide, where you can make your voice heard and forge connections with like-minded individuals. And don't forget to follow industry blogs—. they're like beacons of wisdom, guiding you through the ever-changing currents of your business. Leave comments, show your presence, and create meaningful connections along the way. And let's not forget the power of networking with fellow entrepreneurs and solopreneurs. Seek out networking events, online forums, or professional associations, and surround yourself with those who understand your journey, and can offer insights, advice, and support. Build relationships so they can open doors to new opportunities and collaborations.

- **Sharpen tools:** In this ever-evolving business landscape, one ought to be a lifelong learner: always thirsty for new knowledge, always seeking to improve their craft, and staying up-to-date is the name of the game. The solopreneur must be vigilant, keeping a watchful eye on the changes and developments in their industry, and must invest their time and resources into acquiring new skills and learning new techniques. They attend conferences and workshops, eager to absorb the wisdom of the masters. They also have to embrace new technology and tools, harnessing them to their advantage.

- **Self-care:** If there ever were warriors in the business world, a solopreneur would be an embodiment of the word, and a warrior knows the importance of self-care and balance. In the relentless pursuit of success, they understand that taking care of oneself is not a luxury but a necessity. How can one conquer the business realm if their own spirit is depleted? Running a business demands every ounce of your energy and devotion, so the wise solopreneur knows that they must also find moments of respite. They must take breaks, allowing their mind and body to rejuvenate, and must move, exercise their limbs, and let the blood flow. They must nourish themselves with wholesome sustenance, fueling the fire within.

- **Automate the automatable:** The solopreneur, being the master of efficiency and ingenuity. that they ought to understand the value of automation, for it is the key that unlocks the door to freedom from mundane and repetitive tasks. To navigate the treacherous waters of entrepreneurship, the solopreneur embraces an arsenal of automation tools, each a loyal companion in their quest for success. These tools are the gears that turn, relieving the burden of everyday responsibilities and granting the solopreneur the luxury of focusing on the grand vision. Consider GetResponse, a trusty companion for email management; G Suite and WorkflowMax, the mighty fortress of project management, Calendly, for time management; Expensify to keep track of your expenses, and the list goes on.

And of course, the tool that can keep a tab on and even replace the above, a tool that can be your very personal assistant, a tool that can be a colleague who keeps you company but never resorts to the unnecessary, time-wasting politics and drama, and of course, we are speaking of ChatGPT. Let's get right into the heart of this book without further delay.

Chapter 1: Breaking Barriers: Launching Your Solopreneur Journey with ChatGPT

Case Study 1

Let us start this section with a real-world example of how a solopreneur used this tool for 6 months and increased his income by eight folds. Nitin Sharma, a developer and writer has shared how he has achieved this feat using ChatGPT, and here is how he did it.

With a passion for diversifying his income, Nitin Sharma has found success by embracing various avenues. He wears multiple hats, writing articles on Medium, working with multiple clients, and even venturing into building his own startup as a programmer.

Undoubtedly, the life of a solopreneur is not for the faint of heart. Nitin constantly immerses himself in learning, writing, and coding to stay at the top of his game. However, he's discovered a powerful ally in AI, which has propelled his productivity to unprecedented heights. Now, he accomplishes more in a day than ever before, and his earnings have multiplied eightfold compared to the previous year.

And the secret to this success and result is that he is a diligent seeker of knowledge. He prioritizes staying informed about the latest tools and technologies in his field. During his leisure time, he actively explores upcoming AI tools that align with his profession. Moreover, he incorporates these tools into his work whenever the opportunity arises.

Simplifying the Writing Process

In his illustrious career as a programmer, Nitin Sharma embarked on diverse paths, and among the many he explored, content writing ignited his curiosity, and for the past three years, he has dedicated himself to this craft. Building upon his expertise in web development, Nitin delved into the realm of technical content writing and this entailed acquiring new knowledge about web development concepts, implementing them, and meticulously crafting well-written articles. Each piece demanded thorough editing before it was ready to grace the digital realm.

As you can imagine, this endeavor required substantial time and effort. However, the introduction of ChatGPT into Nitin's workflow has brought remarkable ease to his creative process, for instance, when faced with uncertainty about what to write, he brainstorms ideas with the tool. And even when the need arises to alter the title of his article, ChatGPT offers invaluable ideas to guide him. Also, whenever specific information is required, he simply turns to ChatGPT for prompt assistance. And last but not least, when it comes to polishing his work and ensuring a flawless composition, ChatGPT proves to be an invaluable ally in eliminating errors and typos.

Coding Partner

As a passionate programmer, from the crack of dawn until the evening's embrace, Nitin immerses himself in the art of coding, diligently crafting the framework of his very own startup. And lo and behold, there enters ChatGPT, extending its benevolent hand to assist Nitin on his quest. It proves to be a trusted companion, offering its aid in a multitude of scenarios that arise throughout his work:

- **Writing code:** When the need arises to script code for specific tasks or implement intricate functionalities within Nitin's skill set, ChatGPT emerges as a formidable resource. It provides a wellspring of suggestions, examples, and even pseudocode, guiding him along the path of virtuosity.

- **Debugging and optimization:** When confronted with vexing errors or the desire to refine his code's performance, Nitin turns to ChatGPT for solace. Engaging in discourse, he shares the nuances of the issue at hand, seeking sage advice on unraveling the enigma and optimizing his code.

Summarizer

In Nitin Sharma's unyielding pursuit of knowledge, he finds solace within the bound pages of books that span a vast spectrum of subjects, from finance and programming to the intricacies of business. Yet, he remains discerning in his literary choices, eschewing works that merely rehash age-old concepts, dressed in different garments.

Take, for instance, the wealth-building tomes that saturate the market; Nitin often encounters repetitive counsel, urging readers to amass riches, steer clear of debt's treacherous grasp, avoid the siren song of credit cards, and diligently invest for a secure retirement. These well-worn axioms hold little novelty for him, as he has long embraced their wisdom. What Nitin yearns for is the novel and innovative, a beacon to expedite the journey toward wealth without succumbing to scams or hollow promises.

To fulfill this yearning, Nitin finds a steadfast ally in ChatGPT, turning to its sagacity to uncover the hidden gems of literature. He beseeches ChatGPT to offer recommendations for the finest books, accompanied by insightful summaries, igniting his curiosity and guiding his literary odyssey.

Automation of Tedious Tasks

As a staunch advocate for a balanced approach to work, Nitin firmly holds the belief that amassing wealth does not necessitate toiling away for endless hours, such as the arduous stretch of 16-hour workdays. Instead, he espouses the idea of focusing on a select few pivotal tasks and diligently completing them within a day's span.

However, within this pursuit of efficiency, an ever-present challenge emerges — the encumbrance of monotonous and time-consuming tasks. At first glance, this conundrum may appear insurmountable.

Harnessing the power of ChatGPT is a simple yet transformative process. By posing a humble inquiry regarding tasks that lend themselves to automation, Nitin unlocks a trove of insights. ChatGPT, with its unfathomable knowledge, willingly divulges the secrets of automation. This illuminates the path toward identifying areas in one's work or daily routine that can be streamlined, rendered more efficient, and liberated from the shackles of tedium.

Embracing the prowess of automation bequeaths a wealth of benefits. It grants respite from the clutches of time-draining endeavors, freeing up precious moments and rejuvenating weary spirits. With time and energy preserved, one is empowered to immerse themselves in endeavors of greater significance and fulfillment. The realm of automation becomes a gateway to unlocking a realm where purposeful and meaningful activities flourish.

To embark on this transformative journey, Nitin Sharma imparts a prompt that beckons the wisdom of ChatGPT. By venturing forth and inquiring, "Can you provide me with a list of common tasks that can be automated in [define where you want to automate], along with some examples of how automation can streamline workflows and improve efficiency?" an entire realm of automation awaits exploration, brimming with the promise of heightened efficiency and liberation from the chains of tedium.

Personal Business Strategist

As a solopreneur, Nitin Sharma shoulders the immense responsibility of handling every aspect of his business. From content creation to coding and client management, the weight of these tasks falls squarely on his shoulders. It's an arduous role that demands extensive strategizing to foster business growth, deliver enhanced value, and bolster earnings.

When he sets his sights on the ambitious goal of scaling his business tenfold, ChatGPT becomes his trusted companion. It serves as a wellspring of strategic wisdom, guiding him toward the best course of action and its support doesn't end there. Nitin also turns to this remarkable tool for financial inquiries, seeking marketing advice, and delving into the depths of SEO guidance. ChatGPT's insights help him make informed decisions and chart a path that maximizes his business potential.

In addition to ChatGPT, Nitin harnesses the power of other AI tools like Flair AI and Canva. These ingenious creations enable him to create templates effortlessly, using just a simple prompt. By automating the design process, Nitin saves precious time and effort that would otherwise be spent on crafting graphics and other visual elements for his business.

Case Study 2

Our second case study is about Neville, a solopreneur who runs Britewrx and has a passion for helping others succeed. He transitioned from consulting to starting his own business, Neville understands the challenges that arise when building from scratch.

Frustrated by the lack of reliable and practical information available online, the man embarked on a journey to create a resource that could provide genuine value to aspiring solopreneurs. He believes that the process of building a business should not be overly complex or require sacrificing one's personal life. Through his own experiences and successes in turning around companies and launching startups, Neville realized that he could make a meaningful difference in the lives of others. He aims to empower solopreneurs and help them achieve their goals.

Neville follows a philosophy of calm in his approach to business. This philosophy emphasizes avoiding hype and hard-selling tactics, instead focusing on the right priorities at the right time. He believes in pursuing success with passion while always remembering the importance of living a fulfilling life.

While Neville promotes his products and services, he remains genuine and honest, never making false promises or pressuring anyone to make purchases they don't truly desire. His goal is to help solopreneurs take action and accomplish their tasks effectively. Rather than simply providing step-by-step instructions, he emphasizes teaching adaptable skills that can be applied in various situations, and here is his advice on using ChatGPT as a solopreneur:

Using Chat GPT

Neville is eager to share how he has integrated AI, particularly ChatGPT, into his business operations. While he acknowledges that he has only scratched the surface of AI's potential, he highlights a few key areas where AI has already made a significant impact.

In content marketing, Neville relies on ChatGPT for various tasks such as strategizing content pillars, generating article ideas, and optimizing content for search engine optimization (SEO). By leveraging ChatGPT's capabilities, he can save a considerable amount of time on research and planning, allowing him to focus on producing high-value content.

For LinkedIn posts, Neville sought assistance from ChatGPT to generate a list of five habits of highly productive individuals and five habits of unproductive individuals. Although the initial result was satisfactory, he desired a more humorous tone. Through some tweaking, ChatGPT's contribution lightened the workload, enabling Neville to create a post that aligned with his preferences.

Neville also explores the potential of AI in course design. By asking ChatGPT about the ideal learning outcomes for an online course, he obtains a foundation upon which he can build a course outline. While the results may require some refinement, ChatGPT provides Neville with a starting point and helps overcome creative roadblocks.

He acknowledges that AI is not flawless and advises careful examination of the generated results. He suggests tweaking questions or results as needed to align with expectations. Additionally, while ChatGPT can generate article drafts, Neville finds better results by using it to outline an article and then filling in the details himself.

Despite the imperfections, he recognizes the immense potential and time-saving benefits of AI. He foresees the possibility of higher-quality output through the aid of AI tools. As Neville continues his journey, he intends to share further insights and updates with his audience, reflecting his enthusiasm for integrating AI into his business practices.

Asking ChatGPT

I did you the favor and asked ChatGPT to list the ways it can help solopreneurs and here is what it had to say (the following has been copied and pasted from ChatGPT 3):

Solopreneurs, being individuals running their own businesses, can leverage ChatGPT in
various ways to enhance their operations and engage with customers. Here are some ways
solopreneurs can use ChatGPT:

1. Customer Support: ChatGPT can handle customer inquiries and provide support,
   allowing solopreneurs to offer prompt responses even when they are unavailable. It can
   address common questions, provide basic information, and assist customers in
   troubleshooting common issues.

2. Lead Generation: Solopreneurs can use ChatGPT to engage website visitors and capture
   leads. By programming the chatbot with relevant questions and personalized responses,
   it can collect contact information, qualify leads, and provide initial information about
   products or services.

3. Content Generation: ChatGPT can assist solopreneurs in generating content for their
   blogs, social media posts, or newsletters. By providing prompts or asking questions,
   solopreneurs can use the chatbot's responses as inspiration or starting points for their
   content creation.

4. Personalized Recommendations: Solopreneurs can train ChatGPT to understand their
   products or services and use it to provide personalized recommendations to customers
   based on their preferences or needs. This can enhance the customer experience and
   increase the chances of conversion.

5. Appointment Scheduling: ChatGPT can automate the appointment scheduling process
   for solopreneurs. By integrating the chatbot with a scheduling system, it can handle the
   back-and-forth communication with clients, check availability, and book appointments
   directly.

6. Market Research: Solopreneurs can use ChatGPT to conduct market research by
   interacting with potential customers. The chatbot can ask questions, collect feedback,
   and gather insights about customer preferences, pain points, and expectations, helping
   solopreneurs refine their products or services.

7. Language Translation: If solopreneurs operate in multilingual markets, ChatGPT can
   assist in real-time language translation. It can help bridge communication gaps by
   translating messages or content between different languages, expanding their reach and
   improving customer engagement.

8. Sales Assistance: ChatGPT can support solopreneurs in the sales process by providing
   product information, suggesting complementary items, or addressing customer
   objections. It can act as a virtual sales assistant, guiding customers through the decision-
   making process.

9. Social Media Engagement: Solopreneurs can integrate ChatGPT with their social media platforms to engage with followers and respond to comments or direct messages. The chatbot can provide quick and relevant answers, maintaining an active and responsive social media presence.

10. Personal Productivity: Solopreneurs can use ChatGPT as a productivity tool by creating a conversational interface for managing tasks, setting reminders, or organizing information. It can help streamline workflows and keep important information easily accessible.

Remember, while ChatGPT can offer valuable support, solopreneurs should always review and verify its responses to ensure accuracy and align with their business goals.

Chapter 2: Building a Thriving Online Community with ChatGPT

ChatGPT can be incredibly valuable in the context of building an online community by freeing up time and allowing us to focus on community building. By automating certain tasks, we can create more space and dedicate the necessary time to develop a thriving online community. Building such a community is far from an easy task; it requires hard work and dedication.

Before delving into how AI can assist in building an online community, let's first clarify what an online community is not. An online community can be described as a gathering of individuals on the internet who share common interests, and motivations, and inspire one another to learn, grow, and form connections. Those who create online communities not only bring people together but also foster meaningful relationships among them. It is important to distinguish online communities from social media platforms.

Although social media may resemble online communities to some extent, they are fundamentally different. Online communities revolve around a group of people united by a common purpose or goal, working tirelessly day in and day out to nurture and expand the community. As the community flourishes, members feel a sense of belonging and become part of something greater than themselves.

Reasons to Start an Online Community

For solopreneurs, it is crucial not only to recognize the existence of online communities but also to understand how to create and maximize their potential. The reason solopreneurs would benefit from such communities is that they provide an opportunity to establish an audience or a group of devoted individuals who are deeply invested in their product or service. In any business venture, the aim is to address a specific problem, and the most effective way to do so is by bringing people together.

Bringing people together serves a dual purpose. Not only does it facilitate problem-solving, but it also taps into the collective wisdom of the community. When diverse minds converge, innovative solutions emerge, and the burden of finding answers is shared among community members. This collaborative approach alleviates the individual solopreneur from shouldering the entire weight of creating solutions.

It is important to remember that building an online community is no easy task. It requires effort, dedication, and a genuine desire to foster connections and nurture relationships. Solopreneurs must actively engage with their community, listen to their needs, and create an environment that encourages participation and collaboration. By doing so, they can harness the power of the community to drive their business forward.

In the realm of online communities, success is not measured solely by the size of the audience, but by the level of engagement and the sense of belonging that members experience. It is about cultivating a space where individuals feel valued, supported, and motivated to contribute their unique perspectives and insights.

In the end, the true value of an online community lies not only in the solutions it generates but in the lasting relationships it fosters. By embracing the spirit of collaboration and harnessing the collective intelligence of the community, solopreneurs can leverage this institution to propel their businesses to new heights.

Here are a few reasons that you may want to consider starting your own online community.

Real Connection

In a world where people are seemingly more connected than ever, a peculiar phenomenon can be observed which is loneliness, and as a solopreneur, you are not new to the sickening sensation this causes. It's an epidemic that particularly affects young adults, and studies state that the most effective remedy lies in cultivating genuine and profound social connections. Not the superficial kind fostered through mindless browsing of cat videos or engaging in endless, anger-fueled Twitter scrolls, but authentic human interactions.

Honest and real human connections hold the key to healing the dread caused by loneliness. In a society filled with virtual interactions and fleeting encounters, what truly matters is establishing real relationships with other individuals. It's about forging bonds that go beyond the surface and delve into the depths of human connection.

In our quest to combat loneliness, it's essential to prioritize authentic social networks. These networks are not built on the number of followers or likes, but rather on the quality of the connections formed. It's about surrounding ourselves with individuals who uplift us, inspire us, and provide a sense of belonging.

Expand Your Attention Span

And, if you ever find yourself struggling to direct your energy toward what truly matters, creating an online community possesses a remarkable ability to generate a sense of reaffirmation. It breathes life into your brand, ignites passion within your members, and underscores the value they derive from being part of a vibrant network. It's a space where individuals unite, driven by a collective desire to master something intriguing or significant, hand in hand.

In a world that tempts us with endless diversions, where time is scarce and attention is fragmented, building an online community stands as a beacon of focus and purpose. It reminds us of the profound fulfillment that comes from investing our energy in something worthwhile, something that binds us together in a shared journey of discovery and achievement.

Growth

Being part of a community can work wonders for you and your fellow members, helping you acquire fresh skills and solidify positive habits. The mere act of joining an online community increases the likelihood of achieving those elusive changes that have eluded you thus far. You see, the community injects a dose of responsibility and encouragement that you won't stumble upon elsewhere.

Growth, even on an individual level, is beautiful to experience, but when shared, it becomes magical for it turns into love. It's within the fabric of this community that true metamorphosis occurs. It's where aspirations materialize, where skills are honed, and where the bonds of camaraderie tighten. The community becomes a haven of growth, a sanctuary where barriers are shattered, and dreams take flight.

Learn and Teach

In the vast online realm, an online community serves as a sanctuary for sharing knowledge and wisdom that freely flows through vibrant discussions, events, and well-crafted courses, unlocking extraordinary potential in crucial areas of one's life. Within this digital congregation, collective effort takes center stage, providing solutions for struggles and revitalizing dreams. Members offer great support, guiding each other on the path to growth. We often don't think we have much to offer, but it only takes writing a couple of pages to understand that you possess a wealth of knowledge, and as a mentor, your expertise becomes a nurturing force, overcoming obstacles and revealing uncharted horizons, and together, with the community, you will fuel perseverance and foster transformative journeys filled with shared experiences and triumphs.

A community is a place where you can immerse yourself in the wonderland of collective wisdom, witnessing the astounding changes of individuals who once struggled alone. You can forge new paths, conquer barriers, and elevate the pursuit of knowledge.

Make Money

So, you want to make some cash from your following? Maybe you're itching to turn those ideas of yours into money-making machines. Perhaps you're eager to develop products, offer valuable services, and cement that unwavering loyalty to your brand, then online communities are the gold mine you've been searching for. They're the ticket to monetizing your following and content like nothing else out there.

Like Minds, Great Conversations, and More

New ways of using online communities don't invalidate the good old reasons why people have been creating them since the days of clunky dial-up modems. People just wanted to connect with fellow fanatics of their favorite sports teams, political group, or book club and chat away about the TV shows, books, and podcasts as well as simply stay in the loop with updates from the people who matter most to us.

But the new online communities are not just about passionate conversations and sharing love for our obsessions, these communities have become intertwined with membership subscriptions and paid online courses. And even if you are not aiming to make a fortune from your online community, it's a great option that's right there, at your fingertips.

Building an online community is, however, not for everyone, especially when it comes to connecting people to one another and I don't want to give you the wrong impression and make you waste time on things you don't need to. First off, if you're all about creating content and couldn't care less about having conversations, then an online community might not be your cup of tea. Sure, it can provide you with juicy stories, fresh ideas, and experiences to sprinkle into your blog or newsletters and can even make your writing process a breeze with all that material. But if you're happiest when you're in your solitary writing sanctuary, counting those open rates or page views, well, an online community might not bring you the same energy, joy, and inspiration as it does for other creators.

Also, some people thrive on social interaction, while others find it draining. If the thought of bringing together passionate and curious individuals around a common topic doesn't light a fire in you, then building an online community isn't a requirement, and if engaging with people doesn't bring you joy, it might not be the right path for you.

Now, building a thriving online community takes a lot of time. We ain't talking about a quick pop-up, cash out, and vanish scenario. It requires some investment, some effort, and a bit of your precious time. Don't expect overnight success. Plan to stick around, nurture your community, and give it at least a year to truly flourish. And if your customers or fans are not interested in being part of a community, forcing an online brand community upon them just won't make sense. Don't go trying to build something that isn't needed or desired. And lastly, if building an online community doesn't align with your business goals right now, that's perfectly fine. Focus on what matters most and choose a strategy that'll get you closer to your immediate objectives. If an email list or a well-crafted social media post can get you what you need faster, go for it.

Steps to Start an Online Community

According to Mighty, an online community-building mentorship company, there are 10 steps to starting an online community and these are.:

1. Get your purpose right: Before you dive into the wild world of building an online community take a moment to ponder a simple yet essential question: Why do you want to do this? Now, there are all sorts of reasons to bring a community together. You could unite skillful people to create a mastermind group where they can exchange knowledge and elevate their mastery. Or perhaps you're keen on embarking on a collective journey with your clients, guiding them

through group coaching sessions. Maybe you envision immersing a group of eager learners in your expertise, forming a tight-knit micro-community. You could host riveting conversations in a vibrant online forum or establish a community of practice, dedicated to a specific discipline of knowledge. But here's the thing: the clearer you are about the value this online community will bring to you and your members, the better. So, grab that pen and paper and jot down your goals.

2. Set your community's purpose: This is the reason why people will join and immerse themselves in your digital congregation. It all boils down to a simple sentence, crafted with three straightforward parts. a) Begin by selecting a specific individual at a specific stage in life to bring into the fold first. The narrower your focus, the greater the chances of achieving liftoff. Even if your grand concept, program, or online course seems applicable to every Tom, Dick, and Harry, you'll increase your odds of success by starting with a distinct segment and gradually expanding to adjacent folks as you progress. If you try to build something for everybody the sad truth is that you end up building it for nobody at all. b) Let it be known what you're going to master together within this vibrant community. It could be the art of scaling the corporate ladder in your field, the serene meditation techniques that bring tranquility and focus in the face of chaos, or the knowledge needed to navigate life with a newly-diagnosed chronic ailment in the best possible way. c) Highlight the benefits that await those who join your community. Paint a vivid picture of the rewards they shall reap once they've mastered their chosen domain within the warm embrace of this supportive collective. It could be as tangible as increasing their odds of securing a well-deserved promotion or as intangible as finding inner peace amidst the chaos of this mad world. Let the rewards be clear and may they ignite the flame of aspiration within those who choose to contribute.

3. Use your story: Utilize your own story to bolster your Big Purpose. This is where your tale, or the tale of your esteemed establishment, takes center stage and sets the tone for your community's triumph. It's not about the number of years you've spent or your specific area of expertise, but rather the journey that led you to discover your passion and focus within the realm of your community—and why it holds significance in your heart. The most captivating stories are those that resonate with the individuals who yearn to join your ranks, yet feel daunted by the prospect of mastering the very subject you champion. If you can share how you navigated through trials and errors to ascend to greater heights as a user experience designer, offering them a path to avoid the pitfalls you encountered, you will employ your own story in recruiting new members to join your cause. Let your narrative serve as a beacon of hope and inspiration, illuminating the path for those who seek guidance. Show them that you understand their struggles, for you have experienced them firsthand. Offer them solace and assure them that they need not tread this path alone. Together, you shall forge ahead, bound by a shared purpose and the collective determination to overcome obstacles.

4. Create an avatar for your ideal members: In your pursuit of building an online community, it is paramount to narrow your focus and set your sights on one or two archetypal members who embody the very essence of those you wish to have with you. It is this precise act of narrowing your scope that shall pave the way to triumph. To refine your understanding of the ideal member embark upon a series of 30-minute interviews with a select group of individuals who epitomize the individuals you aspire to support within your community.

Engage them in conversation, and delve into their goals, motivations, and the depths of their fears. Comprehend the endeavors they have undertaken to conquer the subject of your interest, their valiant attempts that may have ended in failure. By listening intently, you shall unravel the language they employ and the matters that truly resonate with them, equipping you with the insights needed to construct an online community centered around their very core. Once your community has taken flight, you shall have the freedom to welcome a diverse array of individuals into your fold. This momentary focus serves as a stepping stone towards long-term success, enhancing your chances of triumph in the grand scheme of things.

5. Create a long-term plan: The more you engage with your ideal members, capturing their essence on paper, the greater the likelihood of manifesting a thriving community in reality. Look ahead and envision a year in the life of your community, and document in exquisite detail the transformations and accomplishments it shall achieve. Imagine what your members can achieve in a year that eludes them today. How shall they attain such remarkable results? What steps shall they be motivated to take within the community? What knowledge shall they acquire over those 12 months, surpassing their initial state of ignorance? It all ties back to the aspirations revealed in your interviews, the desires your people yearn to fulfill but have struggled to attain alone. Consider the daily and weekly habits that shall propel your members toward their goals. This "year in the life" serves as the bedrock upon which you shall construct the calendar of activities for your community, a roadmap leading to their collective growth and triumph.

6. Create periodic themes: If you want a thriving community with minimal effort, establish a regular weekly calendar. Stick to a few key activities on the same days every week and watch engagement soar. Thanks to modern community software, you can even schedule these events in advance. With a consistent weekly rhythm, both you and your members will fall into a groove. Inject a dose of novelty to keep your community buzzing. Weave these themes into your weekly activities, striking a balance between routine and excitement.

7. What platform you'll be using: Facebook groups used to be the go-to for building online communities, but they've become a tough nut to crack for influencers, creators, and anyone serious about their brand. However, a fresh batch of community platforms has sprung up and these platforms are tailor-made for creators and brands like yourself. No more algorithms getting in the way of connecting with your members. They offer a range of features, from online courses to seamless payment integration; you can even have your own brand showcased across all platforms, including native mobile apps and the app store. That's why it's time to ditch the old and embrace a new platform built specifically for modern creators like you.

8. Make your community global: You're now all set to take your online community upon the world. If you've got an existing email list, course, or group, recruit a small but mighty team of 1-3 individuals to help spread the word to the right folks. Set a glorious day for your community's grand opening and schedule a live kick-off video event where your founding members can mingle and connect. Now, rewind the clock 2-3 weeks from the kick-off and

start the trumpet blast of announcements. Let your voice be heard far and wide as you shout about your community from every rooftop.

9. Work on courage and adaptability: Building an online community can make anyone a bit anxious and along with anxiety comes such self-doubting questions like, "What if no one joins my community when I share it? What if it becomes too overwhelming for me? What if people are too caught up in their own lives or uninterested in trying something outside of Facebook?" These worries are just part of being human. But the chances of any of these fears coming true are pretty slim. In fact, with the right strategy and software platform on your side, you can create a community so valuable that people would be willing to pay for it. It can practically run itself with proper design. The key lies in embracing experimentation, staying curious, and transforming your fears into exciting puzzles to crack.

10. Experiment and grow: If you want your community to grow, consider if there's another group of folks who would be even more fired up about your Big Purpose. Then, start fresh by interviewing these new ideal members, rinse and repeat, my friend. If you want more engagement, take a step back and test if they truly understand the amazing results they'll gain from being part of your community. And make sure your weekly calendar clearly outlines how they can contribute. Sometimes, it's not about being busy—it's about not knowing what to do next, even when you think it's crystal clear. Building an online community is an ongoing journey of experimentation and discovery. People can be messy, but they're also downright astonishing. It might take some tweaking to find the most exhilarating Big Purpose for the right initial members and create a compelling weekly calendar with captivating monthly themes that deliver on your community's promise.

Now that we've explored the reasons for having our own online community and learned the essential steps to get started and ensure its success, it's crucial to consider how we can leverage AI to support us throughout this process.

AI Helping Your Online Community

In a survey, Grazitti, a digital marketing agency, conducted during the summit, around 35% of people said that they've got AI on their roadmap for their online community. Another 31% admitted that they were starting to ponder the idea of merging AI and community management. Now, curating and delivering top-notch content to keep the community buzzing is a top priority for every community manager. But what they also found out is that some businesses aren't aware of the sheer ease that machine learning (ML) can bring to the table when implemented right.

With AI in communities, organizations can scale up like never before and create a stronger bond with their people. Machine learning becomes the secret sauce that helps sort and segment information based on industry type and interests.

AI can crawl the depths of the internet, extracting the juiciest user-generated content from multiple sources and serving it up on a silver platter to community members. Also scouring the web for unique and captivating content that grabs the attention of the community is a time-taking endeavor, but here is where AI can swoop in and simplify the process by finding relevant content so you can spend your time building those meaningful conversations with your audience.

Here is another stat for you: In a survey conducted by Grazitti called Community (re)Focus, 9% of the people in the survey claimed they'd already got AI running the show in their online communities. That means only a select few have taken the plunge and integrated AI into their community platform, reaping the benefits of machine learning. The rest? Well, they're still mulling it over.

Plenty of brands have already seen the light and revamped their engagement game with AI. More engagement in the community means more ideas and opinions flowing. And that's where ML struts its stuff. By using ML, you can categorize content that sprouts from audience engagement, allowing you to spot changing trends and tailor your products to your customers' needs.

ML also comes in handy for sentiment analysis. It helps filter out the inappropriate stuff because let's face it – authenticity is what keeps community members engaged. AI scours the web, pulls out the gems, and showcases the most unique content in the online community. Say goodbye to hours of manual labor, making life easier for community moderators.

Here is a list of other ways to use AI with your online community.

1. With the help of ChatGPT, online community moderators can lighten their load and focus on what matters, while the AI can take care of the tedious tasks like smoothing out the moderation process.

2. By infusing online communities with ChatGPT, we can unleash a chatbot that delivers speedy responses to FAQs, dishes out customized recommendations and amps up user interaction and happiness.

3. ChatGPT can streamline operations and turbocharge productivity by taking care of mundane tasks like data collection and analysis.

4. It can whip up personalized content that hits the spot for each community member like newsletters, articles, and social media posts that resonate with them.

Furthermore, ChatGPT brings additional advantages to the table as your virtual assistant and brainstorming partner, among other capabilities explored in the upcoming chapters. However, the aforementioned points highlight how ChatGPT can support us in building thriving online communities. Its potential as a valuable resource for community management is undeniable.

Chapter 3: Content Creation: Crafting Compelling Digital Assets

Content creation is a dance of creativity and strategy. It's not just about slapping words together; but a meticulous process that involves choosing the right topic, deciding on the format, and crafting a solid strategy. Content can take many shapes and forms, from blogs to videos, eBooks to tweets. It's a nuanced art and its impact on your business is profound. In fact, research shows that delivering quality educational content makes customers 131% more likely to become loyal patrons.

This content becomes digital assets, which are assets that exist in the intangible domain, holding within them the right to be used and cherished. In the world of cryptocurrency and blockchain, digital assets take the form of tokens known as cryptocurrencies, the currencies of the digital realm, validated and recorded by a web of devices, no single entity holds dominion over them, for they are decentralized, free from the clutches of control.

Another term that your ears may already be used to is NFTs, or Non-Fungible Tokens, which are the keys to ownership, the stamp of authority. Imagine capturing a moment, a photograph, a creation of your own. You can mint an NFT, a digital record that proclaims your ownership. Should you decide to part ways with your creation, the NFT shall pass to another, declaring them the new custodian. And here's the twist, creators can claim royalties, a cut of every sale, as their creation continues to enchant the digital realm.

But digital assets extend beyond these forms, they encompass a vast expanse of digital wonders: photos, videos, documents, and more, they all hold a place in this realm. Your photo, stored on your device, becomes your digital asset. With it, you hold the power to publish or sell, for it is your creation, your treasure in the digital seas.

Types of Content/Digital Assets

Blogs

Blogs are the literature of the digital realm; they hold the power to educate, entertain, and ignite inspiration through the written word. When the curious seek answers, it's the blogs that emerge from the depths of Google's domain. As a matter of fact, 56% of marketers proclaim blogging as their most potent content strategy.

To craft captivating blog content, we have to begin by answering questions. Start with the queries of the beginners, for they lay the foundation of knowledge. Recall the questions that once danced in your own mind as a novice, and share your wisdom with those who tread the same path. And don't shy away from details, for it is within these intricacies that you offer the greatest value to your readers. By anticipating and addressing their questions, you earn their trust and ascend the ranks of search engine results.

But wait, there's more to learn and teach and educational blogs hold a special place in the hearts of readers. Choose a niche topic within your industry, and offer guidance. Simplify your instructions with concise sentences, clear structure, and examples that breathe life into new knowledge. However, remember that your teachings should be accessible to beginners, leaving no step unexplained or shortcut unexplored.

Podcasts

Podcasts are akin to tuning into the radio frequencies. The beauty lies in the fact that anyone can create and broadcast their own podcast and a staggering 28% of Americans, aged 12 and above, indulge in the melodic realms of podcasts on a weekly basis. Now, the allure of podcasts lies in the connection forged between host and listener. When the audience embraces the host and seeks to glean wisdom from their words, the magic unfolds, and this is where an online community can come in handy to you.

Podcast content creation thrives on great ideas and the interplay between listeners and experts and storytelling and educational podcasts reign supreme. Keep in mind that when launching your podcast, maintain a consistent schedule and format, while staying true to yourself. Here is a list of ways you can keep your podcasts relevant and create unlimited content to share with your audience.

- Embrace thought leadership, weaving in real-life experiences and case studies.

- Unveil captivating interviews with influencers, asking original questions that spark curiosity.

- Explore trends to showcase the relevance of your offerings, tethering them to broader topics.

- Engage listeners with contests and giveaways, inviting their participation and offering unique prizes.

Videos

Videos captivate the hearts of audiences, be it on Twitter, TikTok, Instagram, or the vast expanse of YouTube. Year after year, its popularity soars, drawing countless audiences into its mesmerizing embrace. Both short-form and long-form videos, each holding its unique place within your content creation strategy, a great form of digital content. Hence, be not confined to a single path but nurture ideas that thrive in both realms of visual storytelling.

Use animation to unravel intricate and illuminate the workings of your product or delve into the problems it solves. Choose relatable scenarios that seamlessly intertwine with your offering, whether through digital animation or stop-motion, and let your visual storytelling breathe life into seemingly dry topics.

In a swift motion repurpose the essence of your most beloved blog into a captivating voiceover. Long-form prose can unfurl into a mesmerizing video series. Fragment key insights from your blogs, weaving bite-sized videos for the realms of social media. And let your videos find their rightful place within your blog posts, offering seekers of knowledge alternative paths to enlightenment.

The allure of instructional content always has a great demand, hence craft potent instructional videos, guided by concise and specific steps. Do not omit any detail, yet shield your viewers from the deluge of excess information. Employ visual simplicity, illuminating each step with grace. And at the culmination, present a clear call to action, guiding your audience towards empowered action.

Advertise through captivating demonstrations that illuminate its potential. Showcase not only its functionality but also the design process that birthed its essence. Share the problems your creation solves and how its solution evolved through the crucible of creation. In doing so, my friend, you cultivate a profound bond with your viewers, forging trust and inspiring engagement.

Pictures

In the realm of blog posts and social media the pictures take center stage, for a picture speaks a thousand words. Infographics, photography, GIFs, memes, illustrations, and screenshots weave a visual story, and captivate the hearts of your audience.

As you venture into the creation of visual content, try and grasp tightly the essence of the basics. Choose a subject that breathes life into your ideas, master the art of composition and embrace contrast and color, while embracing the beauty of simplicity. Remember, it is in showing, not telling, that the story truly unfolds, so let each image evoke emotions and captivate the soul. Set the stage with sets, clothing, lighting, and motion, weaving a tapestry of action and drama.

User-generated content holds great power in showcasing your care for the opinions of your followers. Encourage their participation through custom hashtags, contests, or emails. Seek permission and credit for their contributions, forging a bond built on respect.

Infographics hold the potential to illuminate data and knowledge so choose the right data for your audience, select appropriate graphs or charts, and tell a simple visual story. Avoid overwhelming with excessive data and make your main points easily digestible.

Other Digital Assets

Content creation holds the key to drawing new leads and measuring success in the realm of business. Combine your creative efforts with content offers to solve urgent problems and provide lasting value to your audience and followers. To be immediately useful your content offers should be specific and easily consumed, reflecting your expertise and understanding. This will build loyalty and convert leads into delighted customers. Here are a few digital assets that you can do this with.

1. Ebooks or White Papers: Dive deep into a topic and offer your readers a profound understanding. Utilize existing content or templates to expedite the creation process.
2. Original Research: Harness your knowledge and network to compile research that your visitors can benefit from. Establish goals, develop a data analysis process, and present your findings in a captivating format.
3. Tools and Templates: Provide valuable tools that solve problems and accelerate progress for your audience. Calculators, swipe files, and checklists become indispensable resources, fostering brand advocates.

4. Kits and Workbooks: Combine various resources to create comprehensive kits or workbooks. Structure them thoughtfully, using graphics and engaging elements to break up dense text. Include worksheets, Q&A sections, checklists, schedules, and journal prompts to enhance the learning experience.

ChatGPT as a Content Specialist

Now, let's explore the types of content that Chat GPT, as a language model AI, is capable of generating. It excels at rearranging sentences to create coherent content and is particularly skilled in generating text-based content. However, it cannot generate images like MidJourney or Canva, nor can it generate videos like Synthesia. Its primary strength lies in generating textual content.

Indeed, when it comes to content creation, Chat GPT can assist you in various ways. It can generate engaging captions for your Instagram posts and craft compelling content for your Twitter feeds. It can also help you with email newsletters, providing you with ideas and assistance in writing them. Moreover, it can aid in crafting product descriptions that captivate your audience. Additionally, Chat GPT can provide blog outlines and even generate complete blog posts, serving as your virtual writing companion. Furthermore, it can serve as your personal copywriter, assisting you in creating persuasive landing page copies.

Certainly, to obtain such content, you simply input a prompt into Chat GPT. For instance, you can request a LinkedIn post discussing workplace productivity, and voila! You'll receive a post tailored to LinkedIn's preferred format, ready to be shared on the platform. Chat GPT can also be utilized for video content creation, whether it's a short video on YouTube or TikTok. It serves as a brainstorming tool, generating ideas to fuel your creativity.

Additionally, for long-form videos, Chat GPT can provide a well-structured script, offering line-by-line guidance. You can leverage this feature to write dialogues for skits, plays, or any other recorded performances. The possibilities for content creation using Chat GPT are extensive and diverse.

Tamilore Oladipo, a content writer, elaborates on ways she uses ChatGPT to help with the different stages of content creation. She narrows her intelligent assistant's tasks to six major ones and they are as follows:

1. Idea generation: Tamilore's Instagram page stands as a testament to simplicity, not driven by fleeting trends but rather by the nature of language. In this modern era, we are fortunate to have AI tools at our disposal, offering a straightforward solution to the task of idea generation. These tools delve deep into the labyrinth of audience interests, extracting invaluable insights and presenting a bounty of fresh and imaginative topics. They become a beacon of hope when we hit writer's block. ChatGPT is proficient in the art of conjuring captivating story ideas, articles, and more, all tailored to the specific parameters set forth.

2. Cater to your audience: Tamilore Oladipo highlights the growing demand for niche communities, where audiences yearn for hyper-specific aesthetics, communities, and content that resonate with their unique preferences. As creators of such specialized content, there is a remarkable opportunity to employ AI to personalize the messaging and delivery, catering to individual users based on their distinct interests and preferences. This personalized approach enhances engagement and drives conversions by ensuring that the content is relevant and captivating for the audience. And the way this is done is by learning to type in the right prompts.

3. Research assistant: Tamilore Oladipo brings forth the invaluable role of AI in streamlining the research process, and assisting content creators in gathering and organizing data effortlessly. By harnessing the power of AI, one can scrape the vast expanse of the web, extracting relevant information and presenting it in a readily consumable format. This time-saving endeavor minimizes the laborious task of scouring for data, enabling creators to delve into the essence of their content. Tamilore offers a personal anecdote, where she sought the assistance of ChatGPT to curate a vegan meal plan tailored to Nigeria's available ingredients. Within seconds and with minor adjustments to her prompts, a comprehensive table that would have taken hours of meticulous research was effortlessly generated. Whether she chooses to abide by this culinary guide remains a matter between Tamilore and ChatGPT.

4. Writing process: Tamilore brings attention to the aspects of the writing process such as outlining, line editing, and proofreading, which can sometimes feel overwhelming. Yearning for a solution, Tamilore discovered the invaluable aid of certain AI tools that streamline the editing and proofreading stages. These tools possess the remarkable ability to identify grammatical and spelling errors, ensuring that the content adheres to the appropriate style

and tone. By doing so, they not only save precious time but also enhance the overall quality of the final product, catching mistakes that might have otherwise slipped through the cracks.

5. Making your content accessible: Achieving accessibility can be challenging for small or solo teams and here is where AI can empower you to make your content more accessible. AI lends a helping hand in various aspects, from adding captions and subtitles to videos, to translation services, and even converting text to speech. Allow me to elucidate with a few examples: language translation, text-to-speech, text simplification, and image recognition.

Now, how are you going to use your personal assistant to automate your processes in creating content?

Chapter 4: Automated Sales Funnels: Boosting Conversions with AI-Powered Strategies

A sales funnel is a pathway that guides the weary souls of customers as they traverse the vast expanse of decision-making. In the realm of online business, this journey manifests itself through the web pages that grace the screens of your website visitors.

Let us delve into the very essence of a sales funnel—a purpose that transcends boundaries and unites businesses in their quest for success. It is a vessel designed to steer the tides of online traffic, birthing qualified leads from the internet, and transforming mere prospects into paying patrons.

Indeed, every business, be it online or not, possesses a sales funnel in some form or another. The question, however, lies not in its existence but in its effectiveness.

A truly effective sales funnel is one that speaks directly to the hearts and minds of its intended audience, a personalized journey crafted with care and finesse. To unlock the secrets of such masterful funnels, one must embark upon a journey of knowledge. First, acquaint yourself with the diverse stages of the sales funnel, understanding their intricacies and the art of their construction.

The attention stage is where the customers are awakened to the existence of your business and, more importantly, why they desperately need them. Your business goals revolve around the art of advertisement that brings awareness to and shine a light on the problems your offerings seek to mend, all the while kindling a desire within the hearts of prospects.

In the realm of digital marketing, precision is key. Rather than attempting to cater to the masses, it is imperative that you identify a specific niche market to immerse yourself in, delving deep into its core, and catering to its unique needs.

And one ought to understand that lead nurturing is an art that unfolds before our eyes and begins when the person, your lead, recognizes a problem that plagues their existence, exploring the intricate variables that their troubles are composed of. Then, they cast their eyes on what you have to offer, perceiving it as a potential solution, a means to rid themselves of their burden.

And thus, the journey begins, as they begin researching, scouring the digital landscape in search of validation through the content scattered across countless websites. It is your duty, my friends, to provide them with educational enlightenment, to guide them towards the path of resolution, crafting content that resonates with their struggles and leads them closer to the inevitable choice of embracing your offerings.

The goal is to nurture these prospects, from the beginning of the funnel to its very end. To achieve this, it is essential to forge positive relationships with these potential buyers and encourage them to join your email newsletter, enticing them with the allure of lead magnet landing pages. Share your story, for it is in vulnerability that we find our shared humanity, allowing them to glimpse the echoes of their own journey within yours. Offer them the taste of liberation, with free trials and tiers of your products and services.

The interest and desire stage is where the essence of the funnel resides. Here, the clients are enticed by presenting them with solutions to the very problems they have unveiled. In this stage, we've got to engage the prospects we have diligently gathered from the previous step through the art of promotional content, be it in the form of emails, notifications, or alluring sales pages.

Their attention has been secured, and the time has come to embark on the sales, at which point, we must unveil our products and services, adorned with social proof, tangible results, and compelling data. Let us not forget the sweet melody of pricing, and when fortune allows, the sanctuary of guarantees.

As for content at this stage, introduce the world of product comparisons, enlighten them with captivating webinars, regale them with tales of case studies, and enrapture their senses with engaging videos. Thus, we shall be left with a select few, a group of engaged leads who may buy what we are selling.

This, now, brings us to a stage that demands more than mere words. Here is where we use techniques such as customized checkout pages that bear the mark of personalization, offers that captivate and enthrall with their clarity and allure, and pricing that stands valiantly amidst the fierce competition. There, however, are questions that you ought to not only keep in mind at this stage but have solid answers for.

Firstly, does your offer rise above the sea of mediocrity? Does it possess a distinct quality that sets it apart from the masses? What makes your business shine brighter than the rest?

Secondly, have you addressed the doubts and concerns that dance within the minds of your esteemed customers? Have you unveiled the answers to their queries, soothing their troubled hearts with clarity and assurance?

And lastly, have you presented a symphony of social proof and third-party reviews?

Additionally, there are tactics that include the art of bundle deals, the allure of discounts, and the security bestowed by money-back guarantees. Furthermore, promise them unwavering support, provide a haven of FAQs and a sanctuary of video demos, and proudly display the bountiful benefits that await their embrace. And also the optimization of your checkout process is of utmost importance. Craft a form with simplicity, guiding the customers' hands effortlessly as they insert their payment information. Fill your pages with symbols of trust and let the original price be followed by the discounted price, a gesture that delights those who seek a bargain. And do not forget to present a clear and concise list of the items nestled within their cart, sparing them from the burden of unwanted packages.

Naom Fine, head of AI, Vonage, in an article on his website, states that in the days of old, the marketing clans revealed the sheer abundance of leads they brought forth, leaving the weary sales folk to laboriously sift through and separate the wheat from the chaff. But times have changed; today, wiser souls comprehend the futility of such toil, for it squanders the precious hours of the sales brethren. The number of leads once hailed as a sacred measure of success for marketers, now loses its importance in the eyes of the discerning. A new truth emerges, claiming that lead volume is a deceptive master, failing to reveal the true essence of the marketing force.

In the same article, he goes on to state that the times now favor quality over quantity, casting aside the illusion of success measured solely by lead volume. And in this changing landscape, an ally emerges in the form of AI sales assistants, empowering businesses to tread a different path. These AI companions serve as formidable tools, guiding qualified leads into the depths of the sales funnel from the very beginning. No longer burdened with the arduous task of sifting through a multitude of prospects, the sales warriors can now devote their energies to the noble art of deal-closing. The results speak for themselves—a surge in sales, and an ascent to greater heights. According to research conducted by Dream Factory, an advertising, PR, and marketing agency, 67% of lost sales can be attributed to the failure of sales representatives to properly assess prospects before embarking on the treacherous journey through the sales funnel.

The quest for harmony between the marketing and sales realms has long been recognized by organizations that are on to it. And as these wise enterprises have demonstrated, the path to realization lies in the nurturing of leads—a crucial step, an opportunity to build trust and forge relationships with newfound customers.

Indeed, the benefits of swift and accurate lead qualification are undeniable. But tread cautiously, for the implementation of a viable solution, one that fits snugly within the company's embrace and aligns with the goals of marketing and sales, is no simple task. To burden the sales representatives with the burden of manual labor is to burden them with inefficiency, missed opportunities, wasted time, and the squandering of precious resources.

In but a fleeting span of time, the introduction of AI into the sales funnel has revolutionized the efficiency and effectiveness of the lead qualification process. No longer must the marketing and sales tribes toil in unison, generating and chasing down a deluge of low-quality leads. Instead, machine learning and conversational AI emerge as the catalysts for change, relieving the burden of mundane tasks that once weighed upon the shoulders of reps and marketers.

If you would allow me to stray away from ChatGPT in this chapter, I would like to share with you a few new AI tools that can help automate your sales funnel management and marketing. Below is a list that Neil Patel, one of the lead marketing gurus in the world has suggested:

- Systeme

- Exceed.ai

- Salsewhale

- Appier

- ClickFunnels

- DataStudio

- Akkio

- Bant.io

- Funnel.io

All the above are AI-powered sales funneling services that automate several daunting tasks such as creating websites with funnels, help with emails, create reports, sales chatbots, and the list goes on. These services start with as little as $50 USD a month and the bigger your company the more you can spend and have your very own marketing team at your disposal.

Chapter 5: Skyrocket Your Business with ChatGPT

As we reach the final chapter of this book, it is time to consolidate all that we have discussed thus far. We now understand that being a solopreneur is no easy task, but thankfully, it is no longer as lonely and daunting as it was just six months ago. This is largely due to the emergence of Chat GPT and other AI tools that not only automate numerous tasks but also function as our very own personal assistants. These advancements have not only alleviated the burden but have also made the journey more manageable and fulfilling.

The advantages of utilizing ChatGPT for solopreneurs are truly something to behold. This powerful tool bolsters productivity and efficiency, granting solopreneurs the ability to tackle tasks with newfound swiftness. By automating repetitive or time-consuming processes, ChatGPT liberates solopreneurs to focus on strategic endeavors that foster growth and generate revenue.

Moreover, ChatGPT saves precious time for these industrious individuals. No longer must they toil away on manual labor when ChatGPT can swiftly produce responses, conjure up content ideas, and conduct research. Such time savings open up a world of possibilities, allowing solopreneurs to dedicate themselves to core business operations, innovation, or even personal passions.

Resource optimization is yet another boon provided by ChatGPT. Through its workflow automation capabilities, it mitigates the need for additional personnel or expensive outsourcing. This grants solopreneurs the power to deftly manage their limited resources, be it finances, inventory, or the most precious commodity of all—time. With ChatGPT, these astute solopreneurs can ensure the optimal allocation of their resources in a manner that is both efficient and cost-effective. The following is a quick refresh on all that we have been through in this book:

Customer Support

Customer support plays a pivotal role in the journey of any solopreneur, and this often becomes a part that keeps you from the core of your business. ChatGPT proves to be an invaluable companion in these areas and here is a quick list to recap the ways we can use it:

- ChatGPT empowers solopreneurs to swiftly address common customer inquiries with prompt and automated responses.

- By deploying ChatGPT on your website or messaging platform, as a solopreneur you can offer round-the-clock support and with this constant availability ensures that customers receive timely assistance whenever they need it.

- As a solopreneur, you can use ChatGPT to enable customers to effortlessly check the progress of their orders. By simply providing the order number, customers can receive real-time updates on their recent purchases.

- The language model AI becomes an invaluable resource for solopreneurs to offer comprehensive product details and personalized recommendations, so that, when a customer seeks a certain configuration for the product they are about to purchase, the AI is able to create a tailored specification and recommendation.

- ChatGPT can provide step-by-step troubleshooting guidance for customers experiencing common issues, offering valuable troubleshooting support.

- Solopreneurs can compile a comprehensive list of frequently asked questions and their corresponding answers using ChatGPT. This enables customers to quickly find information about payment methods, shipping policies, or any other commonly raised queries.

- ChatGPT's language capabilities allow solopreneurs to broaden their reach and cater to a diverse customer base. By offering support in multiple languages solopreneurs can create a more inclusive and personalized customer experience.

Content Generation

Content Generation is an art that solopreneurs must master, and here are ways ChatGPT can help out:

- Tap into ChatGPT's vast reserves of creativity to discover unique blog post ideas. Simply prompt ChatGPT with queries and viola, you're going to get a list of what you can do.

- Use ChatGPT to create captivating and attention-grabbing captions for your social media posts.

- Allow ChatGPT to weave its magic in generating compelling headlines for your articles and blog posts. Seek its assistance by requesting for captivating main and sub-headlines, which are very important for it increases an article's readability.

- You can utilize ChatGPT's expertise to outline the structure of your content by asking for help in outlining a step-by-step breakdown of a content idea.

- Craft captivating and informative product descriptions.

- Unleash ChatGPT's imaginative potential to brainstorm and diversify your content strategy. Prompt it to suggest different content formats that go beyond traditional blog posts and videos or provide ideas for interactive content to enhance user engagement on your website.

Market Research

- Engage ChatGPT by prompting it to unveil emerging trends in your industry and gather market insights.

- ChatGPT can analyze customer feedback and shed light on the key challenges faced by your target market. It can uncover difficulties and understand the problems customers face.

- Unlock ChatGPT's analytical capabilities to evaluate the strengths and weaknesses of your top competitors and analyze them. Allow it to examine available information and provide insights into its brand recognition, distribution networks, product range, and customer service.

- ChatGPT can scrutinize your competitors' marketing campaigns and unveil successful strategies that have effectively engaged their target audience. Discover tactics like influencer collaborations or social media contests that have proven fruitful.

- By analyzing market size, target audience demographics, and similar product demand, ChatGPT can estimate the potential market demand for your product or service.

Business Strategy

- ChatGPT can provide great guidance in cultivating innovative business strategies for expanding your online store, personalizing email marketing campaigns, collaborating with influencers for brand promotion, and website optimization to enhance conversion rates.

- You can use the AI to define concrete business goals for the upcoming quarter. Identify key performance indicators (KPIs) like sales revenue, customer acquisition, and satisfaction and set measurable targets aligned with your overarching business vision.

- With ChatGPT's assistance, undertake a comprehensive SWOT analysis for your business and assess your strengths, such as unique product features and customer loyalty, as well as weaknesses like limited brand awareness and high production costs. Identify opportunities like entering new markets or collaborating with complementary businesses while acknowledging potential threats such as emerging competitors and regulatory changes. Leverage this analysis to capitalize on your strengths and address areas for improvement.

- Collaborate with ChatGPT to develop a robust business plan. Outline your business description, target market, competitive analysis, marketing and sales strategies, operational processes, financial projections, and key milestones. Ensure your plan is concise, aligned with long-term goals, and provides a clear roadmap for success.

- And last, but not the least, you'd be able to determine the optimal pricing and revenue model for your software product. Consider implementing a subscription-based model with tiered pricing, offering additional features for higher tiers. Analyze production and operational costs to set competitive yet profitable prices. Explore alternative revenue streams such as licensing or partnerships to maximize your earning potential.

Managing Time

- The AI can save you time by creating program scripts to automate tasks like data entry for your weekly sales report, generating follow-up email templates for client meetings, or streamlining the scheduling of social media posts for the week.

- Use ChatGPT to prioritize tasks and master the art of effective to-do list management based on urgency and importance, exploring frameworks or methods for efficient task categorization and organization, or obtaining recommendations to handle heavy workloads and prevent burnout.

- Engage ChatGPT to discover techniques and strategies for minimizing distractions and staying focused during work hours. Seek guidance on creating an optimal work environment that fosters concentration and developing a plan to limit non-productive activities, such as excessive time spent on social media.

Content Proofreader and Editor

- Allow ChatGPT, your personal editor and proofreader, to delve into the depths of your written creations, identifying and rectifying any pesky grammar and spelling mishaps, whether it's a blog post, website copy, or marketing email draft.

- Seek the guidance of ChatGPT to check your content's clarity and captivation. Request suggestions to make your sentences concise and lucid and increase the readability of product descriptions, or bolster the flow and coherence of your articles.

- Should you desire a shift in the stylistic essence of your content, ChatGPT can help you traverse that path, be it transforming your blog post into a bastion of professionalism and formality, infusing your website copy with conversational charm, or tweaking the tone of your social media captions to exude a lighthearted flair.

- Entrust ChatGPT with the task of upholding consistency throughout your content and you can do this by verifying the usage of consistent terminology or even certifying a cohesive writing style in your content.

- Even with foreign languages, ChatGPT is a capable tool; should you have written content in French, Spanish, German, or other languages, ChatGPT can assist in proofreading, fixing grammar errors, and ensuring accuracy.

Social Media Management

- Use ChatGPT to plan your social media presence in advance, ensuring a consistent and organized posting schedule. Enlist ChatGPT's aid in creating a week-long schedule for Facebook and Twitter posts or devising a series of enticing Instagram posts for an upcoming product launch.

- ChatGPT can be a great automated replying machine and can help in managing and responding to the influx of comments and direct messages on your social media platforms. Whether it's composing a reply to a customer inquiring about pricing details on Facebook or crafting a thoughtful response.

- Immerse yourself in the ever-evolving digital landscape by using ChatGPT to assist with social trend analysis. Use the right prompts to find trending hashtags related to sustainable fashion on Twitter, monitor brand mentions, and gain invaluable insights into the topics that resonate with your target audience.

Marketing and Sales

- Use your personal assistant AI to target the audience's preferences, demographics, and behavior. Unearth the buying preferences of millennial consumers or discover effective marketing channels to reach esteemed senior citizens.

- Use ChatGPT to forge compelling content that resonates with your target audience. Seek assistance in devising captivating blog topics for the tech enthusiasts or crafting social media content that enthralls health-conscious individuals.

- ChatGPT becomes your ally in attracting and converting leads. Use it to unleash prompts and uncover lead magnet ideas that will grow your email subscriber list or create a compelling landing page that entices sign-ups.

- The AI can help with guiding in optimizing your website or sales funnel for enhanced conversions. Seek suggestions to streamline the checkout process on your e-commerce site or fine-tune your landing page to maximize conversion rates.

- Forge lasting relationships with your existing customers by exploring ChatGPT's ideas and discover loyalty program ideas that incentivize repeat purchases or unlock the potential of personalized email campaigns to engage and retain your valuable customers.

- Let ChatGPT infuse creativity into your advertising. Seek assistance in crafting a catchy slogan for an exciting product launch or unlock the power of compelling ad copy for your Facebook campaign targeting young professionals.

- Optimize your social media ad campaigns with the guidance of ChatGPT and we've gone through this step heaps of times, so both you and I know that you know your way around this.

- Dive deep into the realm of data-driven decision-making with ChatGPT as your guide. Analyze the performance of your email marketing campaigns or uncover the key performance indicators (KPIs) to track for your social media endeavors.

Generating Ideas and Problem Solving

- When the creative well runs dry and customer engagement yearns for a spark, use your AI assistant to invigorate your website, igniting the flames of customer engagement. And when cost-effective marketing strategies beckon, let unique approaches emerge from the depths of your imagination.

- When two suppliers stand before you, each holding promises and possibilities, together, with ChatGPT, you can compare their offers, exploring the intricacies of pricing, quality, and delivery options. And when the allure of a new market calls, let us weigh its potential advantages and disadvantages, revealing the path ahead.

- As you venture into the conception and creation of a new product, unveil the potential risks and challenges and mitigate risks by using your friend.

- When it comes to choices, let the guiding light of decision-making models illuminate your path. Seek the appropriate framework to evaluate investment opportunities and when the question of hiring or outsourcing arises, let a decision framework shape your path, revealing the steps towards growth.

- In the realm of inventory management issues, apply problem-solving methods to optimize the flow and when customer satisfaction yearns for improvement, let effective problem-solving strategies pave the way towards delight.

- Explore the myriad possibilities that lie before you, unveil the financial implications of launching a new product or expanding an existing one, casting light upon the choices that shape your destiny.

Conclusion

Well, my fellow solopreneurs, my solo adventurers of the business world, we are in a time in human history where we have our own companion and personal assistant, most of whose services can be accessed for free, or for as little as $20 dollars a month.

Use this tool and boost not just your business, but also your personal life, your confidence, and the quality of your life, for when you understand that most work can be automated, then you can free the time that you deserve to spend on yourself, thereby establishing true work-life balance, in other words, work-life-balance no longer needs to be a myth, you can turn this into your way of life. And the beauty of this technology is that there is no need to learn a complex programming language, or hook on crazy, futuristic appendages.

ChatGPT is a chatbot, and all you have to do is use the human language to prompt and ask it to help you with most tasks. Use it well, my friend, and use technology to enhance your life.

Book 4 | ChatGPT for Business Owners

Leverage AI-powered Innovation for
Competitive Advantage, Operational Efficiency,
and Customer Engagement

By Harold Pearson

Introduction

Since we are about to embark on the journey of discussing the way we can use our ol'friend ChatGPT for business, let us first try and define the word for ourselves. A business is an organized entity that engages in commercial, industrial, or professional activities. Its primary objective is to produce goods or services for economic purposes and can either be for-profit entities that aim to generate financial gain or non-profit organizations that work towards charitable or social causes. They come in various sizes and scopes, ranging from small sole proprietorships to large multinational corporations.

When we talk about a business, we're often referring to the entire operation and all the activities it involves. It starts with an idea, a spark of inspiration, and a name. To determine the viability of turning that idea into a business, extensive market research is often necessary and this leads to the setting up of a detailed plan. Before commencing operations, businesses often require to determine and document this well-thought-out business plan; a formal document that outlines the goals, objectives, strategies, and plans for the company and serves as a blueprint for success, and is especially crucial when seeking capital from investors or financial institutions.

The next step would be choosing the legal structure of a business, which is a critical consideration that may involve obtaining permits and licenses and fulfilling registration requirements. In some countries, corporations are recognized as separate legal entities, allowing them to own property, assume debts, and be subject to legal proceedings.

And when it comes to choosing a name for the business, we have to understand that it holds significant value for it is an essential asset that can contribute to brand recognition, reputation, and success. So as a business owner, you must choose the name wisely to make a lasting impression on customers and stakeholders.

While many businesses operate with the aim of generating profit, there are also not-for-profit or nonprofit organizations, which are entities that exist to advance specific causes without the primary focus on financial gain. They operate in areas such as charities, arts and culture, education, recreation, political advocacy, and social services. And profit or non-profit, business activities involve the buying and selling of goods and services and these transactions can occur in physical storefronts, online platforms, or even on the roadside. It's important to note that any financial earnings from business activities must be reported to the appropriate authorities, such as the Internal Revenue Service (IRS).

Another authority to be mindful of is the industry in which a company operates often defines its business. For instance, the real estate business, advertising business, or mattress production business operate differently from each other and these differences are based on the business cultures and ethics that preceded them, and these differences, though nuanced, are based on the underlying products or services they provide.

However, the most useful way to differentiate the types of business and categorize them are listed below, and each type on this list has its own legal and tax structures:

- **Sole Proprietorship:** Owned and operated by a single individual, with no legal separation between the business and the owner. The owner assumes all tax and legal liabilities.

- **Partnership:** A business relationship between two or more individuals who collaborate in running the business. Partners contribute resources and share in the profits and losses, which are recorded on their respective tax returns.

- **Corporation:** A business where a group of people acts as a single entity. Owners, known as shareholders, exchange consideration for the corporation's common stock. Incorporating a business provides owners with limited liability, separating their personal and business finances. However, corporations often face unfavorable taxation rules for their owners.

- **Limited Liability Company (LLC):** A relatively new business structure that combines the pass-through taxation benefits of a partnership with the limited liability advantages of a corporation. It offers flexibility and protection to its owners.

Now that we have gone through a 600-word crash course on what a business is, it is time for us to look at the responsibilities of a business owner.

Responsibilities of a Business Owner

As business owners and entrepreneurs, you are the ones who call the shots, the ones who plan and organize the day-to-day operations, making sure the ship stays afloat. And being a business owner ain't a walk in the park; it takes sacrifice, dedication, and a whole lot of guts. Your job description may vary, as we have discussed in the previous section, depending on the industry and the size of their operation. Some owners might have a bit less weight on their shoulders, while others carry the weight of the world, however, you are the ones steering the ship, hence all that happens, occurs, and manifests, within or without your say and intentions, whether good or bad, are all your responsibility and all your fault.

You, as the owner/entrepreneur define the business and financial plan, mapping out the direction they want to go in. They're the ones mentoring their staff, sharing their knowledge and expertise. And boy, they're not afraid to put their brand or service out there, shouting it from the rooftops for the world to hear. It is also a very difficult balancing act because as a business owner, you cannot afford to spend all your time being caught up in the nitty-gritty of day-to-day activities. No, they're playing the long game, focusing on the big picture. They're the ones with the vision, setting the roadmap for success. They've got the knowledge and authority to make strategic decisions, cutting through the red tape and financial hurdles that come their way.

And the biggest skill you ought to hone and shine is this weapon/tool called communication. If you are not the best communicator, and you're at the helm, you're trying to steer your ship without a steering wheel. As an owner, you are in close collaboration with your key stakeholders and you ought to make sure everyone's on the same page, marching to the beat of the same drum. You have to work hand in hand with the employees and suppliers, who are responsible for putting your vision into action. So, not only are you responsible for developing a roadmap that aligns with your grand vision, you ought to mind and mediate the actions of the body that is your company, and you do this with the power of language.

Being a business owner is no easy feat. Though it sounds like an elegant and honorable way of life, it's a wild ride, filled with challenges, grind, eating dirt, and triumphs, and is not for the faint-hearted. But those who have what it takes, they're the ones who make their mark on the world and create something from nothing and leave their legacy behind.

To simplify the tasks of a business owner, we can categorize the responsibilities into the following four major fields

- planning

- finances

- human resource management (firing, hiring, and training)

- marketing

Though the above is a self-explanatory list, it helps us get a basic idea of the fields we ought to work on, in other terms, the work we have to put into bettering ourselves.

The business world is filled with numbers, finances, and the constant hustle to make things work and as owners, you ought to know your way around profit-and-loss statements, financial reports, and so on and so forth. Your responsibilities include setting budgets and then diving into the nitty-gritty of comparing actual income and expenses. It's a delicate art of balancing the books and making sure those numbers add up. And when sales reports come in, you have to analyze them, making adjustments here and there to stay on track.

But as we've just discussed, it is not about the numbers alone. People are at the heart of any business and you have to be on top of your game when it comes to hiring, training, and guiding your staff. You have to know the ins and outs of employment laws, regulations, social security, wage reports, and the list goes on. Of course, as a business owner and unlike a solopreneur, you may have the luxury to bring in the experts to lend a hand, for which you also need to have social skills in your arsenal.

In this crazy, crowded world, standing out is a must and as the owner, you ought to be the maestros of advertising campaigns, social media wizardry, and face-to-face encounters. You have to be prepared to shout your message from the rooftops, making sure the right people hear it loud and clear. Networking, direct sales, courting clients—you've got to do whatever it takes to get your business in the spotlight, and here is where charm, charisma, and a dash of good old savviness and hustle come in handy.

You've also got to be prepared to dive into sales reports, and financials, and compare them to your goals and ambitions. And when the time is right, you'll take the wheel and guide your sales and production teams toward your goals. Get prepared to make the tough calls, and the strategic moves, all to keep your ship sailing in the right direction.

And the list of responsibilities doesn't end there, you've got to meet with vendors, ensure those precious goods are delivered; embark on buying trips, hand-pick the inventory that fills your shelves; create enticing sales displays, and make sure every item catches the eye of the customer. It's a never-ending cycle of managing the little details because the devil is in the details.

It's not only these sets of skills that you've got to bring to the table, there are a few other soft skills that need to take care of things behind the scenes. According to Mark Kravietz, Forbes, 2019-2022 Best-In-State Wealth Advisors, in his article in the magazine Entrepreneur (Feb 20, 2023) elaborates on a few practices to work on the skills that are required behind the scene:

- According to Kravietz, it's crucial to walk away from the buzz of day-to-day tasks and give your business the attention it deserves. Instead of drowning in the never-ending tide of project-related duties, Mark urges you to carve out a sacred space for strategic contemplation. Allocate a precious 10-20% of your time to the noble pursuit of business development. In those dedicated moments, Set aside the urgent and make way for the important. This scheduled time is a window to the future and it is here that you will weave the threads of your success, outlining plans that will shape your destiny.

- Take a moment to pause and envision the future you desire for your business. Let your imagination run wild as you carve out your goals for the coming years and writing down these dreams breathes life into their very existence, increasing the likelihood of their realization. Break those lofty dreams into smaller, more tangible milestones and think in terms of the short, intermediate, and long term. Create a roadmap that will guide you on this journey of growth and achievement.

- Reflect upon your role as a business owner: take a moment to reconsider your position and realign your focus on the grander scheme of things. It is your duty to hold the larger picture in your mind and make strategic moves that bring the vision of your company to vibrant life. If you find yourself entangled in day-to-day affairs, it's time to reassess and make adjustments that allow you to direct your energy toward the loftier goals you've set for your business.

- The power of self-reflection and external support serve as guiding lights. Cast your gaze upon the goals you have set and let father time be your ally as you etch calendar reminders, marking the moments of introspection and evaluation. Engage in spirited discussions with other business owners and teammates and dive into the depths of their aspirations. Ask yourself this question "Are you on the trajectory to fulfill your ambitions?" If not, be resolute in your quest to uncover the pathways that lead you closer to the pinnacle of achievement. Should the need arise, do not hesitate to seek the aid of a business coach, and use their wisdom and guidance to fortify your resolve, keeping you steadfast upon the chosen path.

Change is an elusive beast, and it is in the company of others and well-crafted plans that we find firm grounds to be able to stand and hold our ground.

And that's that for our intense crash course on what is required to run a successful business and be a great and efficient owner. However, we ought to understand that the words above are simply the tip of the iceberg when it comes to embarking on this adventure, and a college degree, though not necessary and some courses redundant, can help with a lot in terms of how to get things started and rolling. Budgeting, finance, and accounting—these are the pillars that support the infrastructure of a thriving enterprise; project management is a skill that shall be your ally in navigating the treacherous waters of execution; and soft skills for it are through the power of communication that bridges are built and alliances forged, and all these skills though are better learned on the job, a college degree but sitting through one definitely helps strengthen the fundamentals.

I'd like to repeat the fact that the entrepreneurial path demands no specific degree, but the pursuit of knowledge through academia can provide a sturdy foundation upon which to construct your empire. A Master's in Business Administration (MBA), for instance, along with varied specializations like finance, accounting, and marketing, offer the knowledge and skills that you'd need. You can also consider pursuing a bachelor's or master's degree, and get a major in accounting, finance, or leadership and human resources management. A background in computer science can also be extremely helpful.

Be it the establishment of computer networks or the mastery of HTML or CMS software to run your online domain, an educational program aligned with your business's digital landscape would come in very handy. And although these certificates don't guarantee a successful business life, they sure will instill in you the profound understanding required to navigate the labyrinth that this adventure is.

Now that we know what the business world is, and what we need in order to take it on, let's get on to what this book is really about, which is how we can use ChatGPT to help us tackle this crazy world we find ourselves in.

Chapter 1: ChatGPT-Powered Innovation: The Competitive Edge for Business Owners

In a world where small businesses face the daunting challenges of globalization and the ever-expanding presence of the internet, their traditional competitive advantages slip through their fingers like sand. The threat of falling into the commodity trap looms large, demanding immediate strategic action to secure a competitive edge through differentiation. Perhaps you believe this doesn't concern your business, but I would encourage you to keep an open mind because I don't want you to be complacent, I want you to succeed.

As a small business, your rivals extend beyond the local mom-and-pop shop. Giants like Google, AliExpress, and Amazon constantly cast their shadows upon your path, while ubiquitous tech tools loom in the background, accessible to all. How long will it take before Amazon, Alibaba, or Google step into your space, selling the very goods you offer? How long until your local competitor optimizes their supply chain through the embrace of Alibaba? And with AI, it's only going to happen sooner than you think.

In this vast landscape where consumers are spoiled for choice, capturing their attention becomes a Herculean task. And every business out there is engaged in a cutthroat race to gain a competitive edge over one another. But how you may ask, can you secure this elusive competitive edge for your own business?

Well, let me share a harsh truth with you—there's no magic wand that grants your business an instant advantage. Instead, it all comes down to forging a connection between your business and the right audience and conveying the right message.

Discovering the optimal execution model will require experimentation. Along the way, you will encounter failures and setbacks. Yet, as long as you establish a solid foundation and persevere in your pursuits, you shall eventually uncover the model that works uniquely for you.

It is this very reason that will set you apart from your rivals. You must find a distinctive amalgamation of values to offer your audience. Once you uncover this hidden gem, your business growth will hinge upon strategic marketing and unwavering customer retention. Indeed, gaining a competitive edge bestows a multitude of benefits. Allow me to elucidate why it holds such paramount importance: Firstly, it lures new customers to your doorstep, their curiosity piqued by your allure. Secondly, it fosters loyalty within your customer base, building a fortress of trust around your business. Thirdly, it enables you to transcend the sea of competitors, basking in your own radiant light. Lastly, it empowers you to maximize your revenue by expanding your loyal customer base, reaping the rewards of their patronage.

Now, without further ado, I'd like to present to you the strategies that can give you the competitive edge you're looking for. However, this is no enchanted spell, but rather a humble attempt to steer you in the right direction. You may already be implementing some or all of these strategies, but it never hurts to revisit these concepts, refining your approach as you march forward in the battlefield of commerce.

- Establishing a distinctive online presence has become imperative for businesses in this digital age. In this era of digitalization, every Tom, Dick, and Harry is hopping onto the online bandwagon and it is through these digital footprints that businesses can cast their nets wider, ensnaring a larger audience. Moreover, the world of social media grants us a platform to disseminate our unique thoughts and ideas, enabling us to stand tall amidst the crowd. And let us not forget the financial benefits: online marketing proves to be a more cost-effective alternative to its traditional counterpart. As small businesses, we can preserve our hard-earned cash, diverting it towards other fruitful endeavors. But heed my words for the online realm is no mere plaything. It requires more than a simple monetary exchange for ads or the construction of a website. It demands that we engage with the right audience, my friends, through captivating content and strategic distribution. Fear not, for there exist user-friendly tools to aid us in the construction of our online abode. These easy website-building tools shall propel us forward, swiftly and seamlessly, on this digital journey.

- Content reigns supreme and no enterprise can endure without the might of content. Harness the power of content marketing to reach out to the hearts and minds of your beloved customers. Unleash a captivating brand story, one that will firmly establish your position within the market. Share with your audience your noble mission and grand vision, enlightening them about your noble endeavors and irresistible offerings. Educate–keep those content engines churning, for it is through the dissemination of knowledge that engagement and trust shall be forged. Let your content be a mighty sword that cleaves through the competition, granting you an edge unmatched by your rivals. But remember that the creation of content alone is not enough; the distribution of this precious asset is equally paramount. Email marketing is a formidable weapon in your arsenal, capable of spreading your content far and wide. And let us not forget the prowess of social media, for it too holds the potential to effectively disseminate your valuable creations.

- In this vast battlefield of commerce, targeting everyone is a futile endeavor that shall yield naught but disappointment. You must focus instead on the chosen few, those who possess the greatest potential to embrace your offerings. Delve deep into the heart of the market and unveil the secrets of your target audience. Understand their desires, their needs, and their aspirations. By doing so, you shall wield the power to channel your efforts with precision, directing your message to those most receptive to its call. But mere knowledge is not enough, you must also forge a path to reach out to these chosen souls and unveil the splendor of your offerings. Seek out tools and technologies, such as the mighty Deskera CRM, that can aid you in the sacred art of audience segmentation. With these tools, you shall be empowered to divide and conquer, dynamically and effortlessly organizing your contacts and audiences according to rules and parameters.

- Aesthetics hold great power; do not disregard the importance of captivating visuals that seize the attention of the masses. A striking logo, a captivating website, and an alluring presence on social media platforms are the weapons you wield to establish your brand's identity. Let not your content stand alone, but let it be adorned with designs that elevate your brand to new heights. Embrace a cohesive color scheme, and a captivating theme, and let your banners and logos sing with artistic brilliance. But remember the realm of user experience is an ever-changing landscape. Stay vigilant, for your users seek simplicity and ease. Even if they do not voice their struggles today, rest assured your rivals are tirelessly striving to concoct an even smoother path. Do not yield to their advances, but continue to evolve your user experience, making it a seamless journey for all who encounter your brand.

- The voice of the customer holds great wisdom, so embrace the constructive feedback that comes your way and let it guide your path to greatness. When competition is fierce and the stakes are high, customer experience becomes a key differentiator. Pay heed to the intricate workings of your customers' minds, for it is through this understanding that you shall gain the upper hand. Do not shy away from seeking feedback from your valued patrons. Inquire about their experiences and seek their guidance on how you can enhance your offerings. With their insights in hand, identify the areas where improvement is needed and implement the necessary changes swiftly and effectively. By doing so, not only shall you demonstrate your commitment to their satisfaction but also enable your business to adapt and grow with speed.

- The loyalty of customers can be a mighty force on the battlefield of business. In the business world, where decisions are often swayed by the quality of customer service, it is imperative to forge a profound bond with those who support your cause. Go beyond mere satisfaction and strive to provide them with an undeniable value that surpasses their expectations. In doing so, you shall not only retain their unwavering loyalty but also entice new followers to join your ranks. Do not underestimate the power of customer service for it holds the key to victory. Seek to build a reputation of excellence, where every interaction with your customers leaves a lasting impression. Measure your prowess in this realm through the mighty NPS surveys, which gauge the loyalty of your patrons. Encourage your esteemed customers to share their experiences and leave reviews on esteemed platforms such as G2, Capterra, and Trustpilot. With each issue resolved and each satisfied customer, let their voices echo throughout the digital realm, spreading the tale of your customer-centric enterprise.

- The path to triumph lies in the realm of experimentation and unyielding innovation and to stand tall amidst the competition, you must embrace the winds of change and adapt accordingly. Continuously strive to pioneer new approaches and ideas, for it is through experimentation that true innovation is born. Remember innovation knows no bounds. It transcends technology and extends its reach to every facet of your business. Dare to innovate in your communication, exploring new messaging and tones that resonate with your esteemed customers. Even the most subtle of changes, like altering the color of a button, can yield remarkable results, boosting your conversion rates and setting you apart from the crowd.

- Establish yourself as a true authority in the eyes of your target audience and once you have identified your audience and comprehended their deepest desires, it is imperative to craft content that speaks directly to their needs, solving their problems and providing answers to their burning questions. Let your expertise shine through, becoming the go-to reference that they seek in their moments of uncertainty. Engage in events and conferences frequented by those who align with your target personas. Take the stage and deliver a compelling message that resonates with their souls, showcasing how your business possesses the power to alleviate their struggles. Let your voice echo through the halls, leaving an indelible imprint upon their hearts and minds. Furthermore, consider the creation of a training course tailored to your prospective customers. Illuminate their path to greatness, guiding them towards improvement and enlightenment. By offering your wisdom and assistance, you not only solidify your position as an esteemed authority but also fortify the bond of trust between you and your disciples.

- Your products and offerings are imbued with a distinct essence that resonates with your users. But let me impart upon you a crucial lesson: know your worth. Understand the true value you bring to the table and the price your market is willing to pay. I do not advocate engaging in ruthless battles over pricing, my comrades. Instead, I implore you to conduct careful experiments, testing the boundaries of price elasticity. Explore the depths of the market's willingness to part with their hard-earned cash in exchange for your exceptional offerings. Let your pricing strategy be guided by wisdom and finesse. A well-timed discount, complementing your esteemed pricing, can ignite a desire within your prospects to seize the opportunity and embrace your offerings with open wallets.

- And finally, you've got to understand that not only do you contend with the specter of formidable adversaries, but they also possess the capacity to outpace you. It's here that you've got to know that though your coffers may not overflow like those of your mightiest competitor, you possess a potent weapon—working smarter, better, and faster. And how you may ask, do you unlock this formidable arsenal? Through the adoption of technology and by embracing the digital realm. By embarking upon this path of technological integration and digitalization, you equip yourself with the tools necessary to seize control of your destiny. No longer shall you languish in the shackles of process bottlenecks. Instead, you shall surge forward, propelled by the power of technology, defying the constraints that hinder your progress. And below are ways where ChatGPT can lend you a sturdy hand to help you gain that competitive edge.

The Competitive Edge with Chat GPT

Improves Customer Experience

In this modern age, customers yearn for swift, accurate, and tailor-made responses. They demand a level of service that transcends the boundaries of time and offers a personalized touch. And lo and behold, with the advent of ChatGPT, businesses can now provide just that. Imagine a virtual assistant at the disposal of your customers, tirelessly tending to their queries day and night. This tireless companion possesses the knowledge and prowess to handle a myriad of questions, ensuring smooth transactions and even offering personalized recommendations for products that resonate with their desires. The constant availability and personalized interaction transform the customer experience, elevating it to new heights of satisfaction and loyalty. Gone are the days of waiting in frustration for assistance. With this virtual assistant by their side, customers revel in the assurance that their needs shall be met promptly and with utmost care.

Streamline Processes

In this cutthroat world of business, maximizing profitability and fueling growth requires us to work smarter, not harder and that's where ChatGPT comes into play. This magnificent tool can automate a plethora of mundane tasks that eat away at our precious time — tasks like drafting soulless emails, scheduling endless appointments, and even churning out content that lacks that human touch. By entrusting ChatGPT with these tedious endeavors, we can liberate our workforce from the shackles of mind-numbing repetition. We free them to focus on the strategic and creative tasks that truly propel our business forward. Think about it, my friends — when our talented team members are unburdened from the mundane, their productivity soars to unimaginable heights.

Market Research

ChatGPT becomes your partner in gathering valuable customer feedback and conducting market research. It becomes the sounding board for your thoughts, the generator of new ideas. Engaging in candid conversations with ChatGPT, you delve into the depths of potential customer needs, uncovering hidden gaps in the market. With this newfound knowledge, you refine your offerings, aligning them with the ever-evolving demands of the world. It's a proactive dance of innovation, my friends, where you step ahead of the competition, leaving them in awe of your prowess. ChatGPT can also lend its wordsmith skills to your surveys. Whether you're seeking to create fresh survey questions for customer research or breathe new life into your win/loss surveys, ChatGPT stands ready to assist. No task is too trivial for this helpful companion.

Verify and Validate Reasoning

When standing at the crossroads of decisions, ChatGPT can help unearth your missteps and elevate the overall quality of your decision-making. In times of trouble and quandary, engage in a heart-to-heart conversation with ChatGPT. Step by step, you lay bare the intricacies of your problem, urging ChatGPT to expose the logical chinks in your armor. And lo and behold, it may even present solutions that have eluded your weary mind. You embark on a voyage of introspection and enlightenment. No longer shall you tremble in the face of flawed reasoning, for ChatGPT shall be your watchful guardian, challenging your convictions and guiding you toward clarity.

Data Analysis

ChatGPT can uncover hidden gems buried within those digital treasure troves. It's a master of natural language processing, capable of extracting precious insights from customer feedback, market trends, and even the sneaky moves of your competitors. Armed with these valuable nuggets of information, businesses can steer their ships with confidence. They can make decisions grounded in cold, hard data, avoiding the treacherous reefs of guesswork.

Global Reach

ChatGPT speaks the language of translation, effortlessly bridging the gaps between cultures and tongues. No longer shall language be a fortress separating you from global opportunities. It can help you navigate the complexities of localization, ensuring your messages resonate with audiences across the globe. It whispers the secrets of cultural nuances, allowing you to tread lightly and connect deeply with people from different corners of the world. Language barriers crumble in the face of ChatGPT's linguistic prowess. It transforms communication into a smooth dance, where understanding flows effortlessly between you and your customers, your partners, and your collaborators.

Product Development

ChatGPT, the harbinger of creativity, is here to ignite the fires of invention within your business domain. ChatGPT becomes your trusted ally in the realm of product and service development. It beckons you to engage in deep conversations, gather the wisdom of the masses, and harness the power of customer feedback like never before. It unveils the secrets of market research, illuminating the path toward new ideas and unexplored territories. Through its virtual dialogues, you gain insights into the minds of potential customers, understanding their needs, desires, and voids waiting to be filled.

Branding

Cultivating an innovative brand image in this cutthroat world will help you stand out and this is the key to success. By embracing Chat GPT in this area, you can position yourself as a trailblazer, and a visionary in the business realm, which would signal to your customers and potential investors that you're not afraid to embrace the future and that you're always one step ahead of the curve. And this can be done by brainstorming with the AI. Use prompts to ask about what colors would suit your brand best, what form, font, and what vibe you would need to be taken seriously in your field, and also instigate the interest of your audience.

Case Studies

Case 1: FashionMaven

A fashion retailer called FashionMaven had a grand vision—to provide their customers with a shopping experience like no other. Once you hop onto FashionMaven's online platform, ChatGPT pops up and becomes your personal shopper. This digital companion understands your fashion preferences, and your unique style, and serves up tailored recommendations just for you; in other words, no more aimless scrolling anymore.

But that's not all. This clever AI isn't just a personal stylist; it's a fountain of knowledge. If you have questions about a specific product, wondering about the material, the fit, or any other nitty-gritty detail, just ask away, and this AI will have your answers. No need to rely on vague product descriptions or biased reviews. The AI's got your back.

And let's not forget the smooth sailing through the check-out process. No more tedious forms to fill out or mind-numbing steps to complete. With ChatGPT in the mix, FashionMaven streamlines the entire process. It's like having your very own personal assistant guiding you through the virtual aisles.

And thus FashionMaven is setting itself apart in the fierce world of e-commerce. They're not just another face in the crowd; they're innovative, forward-thinking, and embracing cutting-edge AI technology. And you know what that attracts? Tech-savvy customers and investors who see the future in this digital landscape.

Case 2: EcoEscape Resorts

EcoEscape Resorts, a chain of eco-friendly havens in the hospitality industry know a thing or two about how customer service can make or break a guest's experience. They enhanced the guest's experience by delegating ChatGPT to handle all those pesky inquiries and bookings and this digital marvel offers instant, spot-on responses to all your burning questions. No more waiting around for human staff to clock in; this AI is at your service 24/7. It seems to have a knack for learning from past interactions: each conversation and each encounter adds to its wisdom, making it even better at providing top-notch customer service. It's like having an AI with the memory of an elephant, always improving, always striving for perfection. With their AI-driven customer service, EcoEscape resorts have raised the bar in the field of customer service, ensuring that every guest receives the attention and assistance they deserve. It's a surefire way to boost those guest satisfaction rates and keep them coming back for more. By harnessing the power of ChatGPT, they've set themselves apart as innovators in the hospitality realm. And who does that attract? Well, environmentally conscious souls who appreciate the harmony between nature and technology. These tech-savvy travelers know that EcoEscape Resorts is the place to be.

Case 3: TechPulse

TechPulse decided to automate a chunk of their content creation process using this AI marvel, an online tech magazine fighting the battle of producing top-notch content day in and day out. Here's how they use ChatGPT: they feed ChatGPT with a topic and a quick overview, and like magic, it spits out initial drafts. But hold on, we're not done yet. Human editors swoop in to refine and perfect those drafts, giving them that human touch. This helps TechPulse meet the demand for fresh and captivating content consistently. It's their ace in the hole, keeping them ahead of the pack in the cutthroat digital publishing realm.

In conclusion, it is important to remember that ChatGPT is a contraption that has been fed a massive heap of data, a smorgasbord of sources, melded together into a mishmash that forms its solitary "source" for each response it conjures. Relying solely on ChatGPT for direct answers is not the path to a successful enterprise, and neither would it give you a competitive edge all by itself. Instead, saddle it with specific tasks. Don't treat it like an all-knowing oracle, but rather like a greenhorn assistant, capable but lacking in experience.

ChatGPT doesn't hand you a golden ticket to competitive advantage. Using it won't set you apart from the pack. (Although avoidin' it altogether might just put you at a disadvantage.) Why, you ask? Because building a competitive advantage is not about doing what everyone else is doing. It's about having the grit to do what others won't.

Take Micheal Jordan or Kobe, for instance. They endured grueling training sessions and pushed themselves beyond their lackadaisical teammates, and well, we can see the results of their work with the respect that the world carries for them. And when all the top athletes in a sport are juicing on performance-enhancing drugs, you reckon you've got to join them to level the playing field. But it's not the drugs alone that determine victory. It's the unique moves, the different strokes that set you apart from the rest.

Similarly, when it comes to competitive strategy, using ChatGPT might level things for you, preventing you from trailing behind. But even then, you gotta work smarter and harder than the rest if ya wanna emerge triumphant.

Now, if yer looking to amp up yer competitive intelligence, I've got a proposition for you. Imagine this: setting up your fancy listening contraption to gather intel on yer rivals with ruthless efficiency, freeing up your time to analyze, inform, and champion yer business like a true warrior.

Chapter 2: Streamlining Operations: Automation and Efficiency for Business Growth

Streamlining is all about slicing through the fat of business processes, it's the art of fine-tuning and automation operations within an organization, so they run like a well-oiled machine. And when the operations are running at their peak, businesses can reach their highest potential, saving precious time and keeping risks at bay.

When a company starts growing faster than a wildfire, the paperwork and invoices start piling up like there's no tomorrow. This is when project managers beg and nag the finance team for budget reports left and right. Now, that puts some serious pressure on the finance team, trying to keep up with this crazy growth that is bound to increase operational risks. Hiring more employees might seem like the obvious solution, but it doesn't tackle the real problem.

This is where businesses ought to streamline their financial processes in order to minimize risks. And one of the solutions to this problem is for the company to shift some of the responsibility and accountability to the budget managers outside the finance department and distribute the load.

One slick solution is to automate the whole budgeting process. The company can whip up an online dashboard, a digital haven of budget allocations for each project manager, who with just a click of a button can access their budget reports in an instant. They can see how their project decisions ripple through the cash inflows and outflows. It's like putting the power in their hands, solving that scalability problem of the finance team.

And when it comes to streamlining, efficiency's main nemesis is manual work leading to mistakes that slow things down in the long haul. Automation here is the solution–the processes of collecting account receivables and paying account payables can save you from a world of hurt. No more wasting time preparing invoices and settling payables manually. Invest in fancy technical systems that'll automate the accounts receivable and accounts payable processes.

Also going cashless is the way of the future. Set up a payment platform where vendors and customers can send and receive payments online. Wire transfers, credit cards, you name it: streamline everything in one place, making life easier for everyone involved. No more fumbling around with checks or stacks of cash. Embrace the digital age and watch efficiency soar.

Centralizing that supplier and customer information is also a great way to save time. It's like creating a treasure trove of knowledge that everyone in the company can tap into. No more wandering aimlessly, wondering where the hell to find what you need. Set up some slick information systems which will speed up the communication process between departments like nobody's business. Need info from another department and it's right there at your fingertips. No more wasting time or playing hide-and-seek with data.

And last but not least–standardization; keep things simple and save your team members some precious time. Nobody got time to navigate complicated systems with a gazillion different terms for collections and payments. Standardize that drat, my friend. Set some clear and consistent terms that everyone can follow.

When talking about cutting down on inefficiencies and kicking missed deadlines to the curb, streamlined processes are the name of the game here, and they'll make your work life a whole lot simpler. Picture improved productivity, delivering top-notch work on time, and raking in that superior quality.

We're talking about removing the pesky bottlenecks. No more holding up the flow of time. Streamlined processes give you better control over that precious resource and will let you be the master of time management, no doubt about it.

And with the several digital tools we have at our disposal, it's time to say goodbye to all the paper expenses, postal services, and wasteful travel for meetings. Sure, digital processes might come with a price tag, but in the long run, they're gonna save you a whole lot more. No more jet-setting around for meetings when you can conduct them online. The savings will be rolling in.

And Streamlined processes mean better communication. Everyone is going to be on the same page; no more confusion or team members being left in the dark. Automated notifications, reminders, updates, and team chat applications will keep everyone in the loop. They'll keep the communication flowing without ever leaving your workstation. Not only that, but streamlining processes brings transparency to the table; which means fewer errors, fewer missed deadlines, no redundant work, and improved accountability. It's like shining a light on all these dark corners, making sure everything is running smooth as silk.

The 10 Steps to Streamlining

Here are 10 steps to streamline your business according to Inkit, which is a document generation on-demand company that streamlines documentation processes for companies such as P&G and Asana. According to this company, the ten steps to streamlining are as follows:

1. **Workflow analysis:** First things first, grab a pen and paper and list down all the processes in each and every division and department. Get in touch with the teams, talk to their employees, and gather all that precious information. It's like exploring uncharted territory. Once you get that list, it's time to analyze the processes, and don't go at it alone, get the employees involved. Hear what they gotta say, take in all that knowledge, and document everything along the way. It's like building a map of your business, markin' every twist and turn.

2. **Scout for automation opportunities:** Keep your eyes peeled for high-impact zones, the ones that are sucking the life outta your business activities. You know what I am talking about– the tasks that are as manual and repetitive as a broken record, the ones that make you wonder why you live at all. The solution to such tasks is simplification; look for processes and operations that can be stripped down to easier steps and pay attention to what your employees are spending too much time on. It's time to free them up for more productive tasks, where they can shine like the stars, and start identifying areas that are crying out for automation. It's time to bring in the big guns and let technology work its magic and say goodbye to the mundane and hello to a world where efficiency reigns supreme.

3. **Process breakdown:** Pull up your workflows and analyze them, make them short, make and simple. We don't want anything in any process that you can't explain to an eight-year-old. Target that desired output and think about longer tasks and ask yourself: Can we simplify? Can we automate? Are there steps that are holding us back? Let's take a concrete example, like converting HTML files to PDF. Can we make that happen automatically? Don't waste your time struggling with manual conversions when technology can do it for you. And while you're at it, dig deep into that document management lifecycle of yours. Can you spot any smaller parts of them or bigger tasks that can be automated?

4. **Set priorities right:** Take a good, hard look at their business operations and start ranking them based on their importance. Now, let me reintroduce you to a nifty tool called the Eisenhower Matrix (You'd be familiar with this matrix if you've already read my book *ChatGPT for Productivity Turbocharge!*). It's gonna be your guide in setting their priorities. This matrix sorts tasks into different categories based on their importance and urgency. First, are the tasks that are both important and urgent. These are your top-notch priorities, so tackle them head-on and don't waste any time. Then, you've got tasks that are important but not urgent. These may not be pressing matters right now, but they hold significant value for your business. Keep them on your radar and give them the attention they deserve. Next up, you get them tasks that are not important but still urgent. Now, these might be distractions. Handle them swiftly if you must, but don't let them take up too much of your precious time and energy. Lastly, you have tasks that are neither important nor urgent and these can take a backseat. They are not going to make or break your business, so don't let them steal your focus.

5. **Documentation:** Create a document, a sacred manuscript of sorts, where you lay out all the details for all your processes. Leave no step behind, be thorough, and be meticulous. We want every nook and cranny covered. And here's a little secret; a central workplace can work wonders in keeping everyone in the loop. Get yourself some project management software or a trusty document record management system. These tools will be your loyal companions in wrangling your workflow and keeping the documents in check.

6. **Choose automation tools**: Look into the abyss and find the right work management software that suits your needs. Don't be afraid to explore multiple options, because sometimes one tool is not enough to get the job done. You see, in this digital age, there's a plethora of marketing automation tools just waiting for you. They can work wonders in streamlining your tasks and making your life a whole lot easier. And hey, don't fret, because we'll even delve into the realm of document management automation.

7. **Create and test new workflow:** Alright, now that you've got your hands on the work management software and you have a deep understanding of the processes, create a new workflow and pick a specific department and slap that new system onto an upcoming project. Let it work its magic and show what it's made of. But don't just sit back and watch, get your employees involved in the process; gather their input and see what they have to say. They're the ones who'll be using all this day in and day out, so their insights are gold. Listen to their gripes, their praises, and everything in between. Analyze the effectiveness of that workflow with a discerning eye. Does it live up to the hype? Does it make life easier for your team or add unnecessary complications? Look for the kinks, the flaws, and the rough edges, and don't be afraid to tinker and refine.

8. **Revise the workflow:** Take a close, hard look at how the new workflow is performing. Is it living up to its promises? Or is it causing more headaches than it's worth? Assess its impact on your team's productivity, efficiency, and overall sanity. Listen to their grumbles and groans, their suggestions and insights. Identify the areas that need rectification. Pinpoint the weak spots, the glitches, and the hiccups in the workflow. It's time to roll up your sleeves and make those adjustments. Whether it's tweaking the settings, adding new features, or rethinking certain processes, don't be afraid to shake things up. Remember this is a journey of continuous improvement. No workflow is perfect from the get-go. It takes time, effort, and a keen eye to refine it to its full potential. So, analyze, adapt, and keep fine-tuning until that workflow sings like a finely-tuned jazz ensemble.

9. **Put the workflow in action:** Alright, you've done the testing, you've done the tweaking, and now it's time to unleash that shiny new workflow upon your business and implement it like a boss. But don't just drop it on your employees like a ton of bricks. They need to know what they're doing so gather your crew, gather your team, and provide them with the training they need. Show them the ins and outs, the dos and don'ts, and all the little intricacies of this new automated beast. Make sure they understand it from top to bottom, inside and out. Give them the tools and the knowledge to navigate this new terrain like seasoned explorers. And hey, don't forget to listen to their feedback can be damn valuable in making those final adjustments. Once you've armed your troops with the necessary knowledge, set them loose.

Let them embrace this new workflow and watch as it transforms their daily grind. Monitor its impact, its effectiveness, and its contribution to your business's overall success.

10. **Revise, refine, implement, and repeat:** As you march forward in the chaotic world of business, you're bound to stumble upon areas in that fancy new workflow that could use a little fine-tuning. Stay vigilant, keep your eyes peeled, and be ready to pounce on those inefficiencies because you want that workflow to be as smooth as a well-oiled machine, and that means optimizing it wherever necessary. Pay attention to the cracks and crevices where things tend to get a little wonky. Maybe a process takes longer than expected, or perhaps a certain task could use a bit of streamlining. Whatever it is, don't turn a blind eye. Grab that bull by the horns and wrangle it into submission.

Automation with ChatGPT

When it comes to using ChatGPT for your business, there are a few things you ought to keep in mind. First off, make sure the conversation flows naturally and keeps those customers engaged, nobody's got time for long-winded answers or complex jargon. Keep it short, sweet, and straight to the point.

Tailor your language to fit the customers/people you're talking to. Know your audience and give clear instructions so customers know how to interact with this chatty robot. And don't forget to keep an eye on those conversations.

Below are ways ChatGPT can be used for automation to streamline businesses.

Automation of Content Creation

When it comes to content creation, ChatGPT can automate the whole content and generate text that sounds like a human wrote it. All you have to do is feed ChatGPT some prompts or topics, and it'll churn out content like there's no tomorrow. Say you need some snazzy copy for your business, or maybe you want to whip up some killer blog posts, ChatGPT can handle it all. Just give it a list of keywords or phrases, and it'll spin out blog post titles and outlines that'll knock your socks off. This content creation wizard can also lend a hand with social media marketing. Need some catchy captions or engaging posts? ChatGPT has got you covered. It can even help with email marketing, crafting persuasive messages that'll have customers lining up at your virtual doorstep. And let's not forget about creative writing. If you're in the mood for some storytelling or want to unleash your inner poet, ChatGPT can be your trusty companion. It's like having a virtual muse right at your fingertips. And don't overlook product descriptions. You know, those little snippets that make people drool over your offerings? ChatGPT can whip up some mouthwatering descriptions that'll have customers reaching for their wallets. I will also be going into detail on how you'd be able to use ChatGPT to the fullest in terms of automating content creation in my next book which will dig deeper into tips and tricks that can make you a mass content production factory.

Automation of Translation

If you have read my previous books, you'd already know what I am about to say about ChatGPT in terms of translations. It's been fed a whole bunch of text in various languages, so it's got the smarts to decipher all those intricate language patterns and spit out translations that hit the mark.

You know what that means? It means you can take your website and make it shine in different corners of the globe for ChatGPT can help you with website localization, making sure your content speaks the language of your target audience. No more lost-in-translation mishaps or relying on Google's bad translation tools, and from now on it's just a smooth sailing across cultural boundaries.

ChatGPT can also lend a hand with text translation. If you need to translate a document or a chunk of text, Just feed it to ChatGPT, and it'll whip up a translation that's on point. Say goodbye to those days of scratching your head over foreign languages. ChatGPT has got your back.

So, whether you're expanding your business internationally or simply need to understand what the heck that document says, ChatGPT is the translation guru you need. It's like having a language wizard at your beck and call. No more language barrier.

Automation of Coding

This is one part of ChatGPT's function that we have not touched on much and it deserves a book by itself (keep an eye out for the book on programming, it should be out by the time you're reading this). ChatGPT is a coding wizard that has been trained on a boatload of text data, including all sorts of code in different programming languages. So, when you throw a natural language prompt its way, it can whip up some fine code that'll get the job done.

Need some code generated automatically? No problemo. Just give ChatGPT a nudge with a natural language prompt, and it'll work its magic. It'll understand the meaning behind your words, pick the right code templates, fill in the necessary code blocks, and boom! You'll have yourself some syntactically correct code, ready to rock and roll.

It works like magic when it comes to debugging, however, don't raise your expectations for it can lend a hand, but don't expect it to do all the heavy lifting. Debugging is a tricky business and it requires a deep understanding of the code and the context of the problem. ChatGPT can help automate tasks like code analysis, code refactoring, and even generating test data and scripts. It'll save you some time and effort, especially for those big and complex applications.

Also, speaking of test data and test scripts, ChatGPT can be a real-time-saver. Creating test data sets and scripts can be a real snooze fest. But with ChatGPT, you can just throw a natural language prompt its way, and it'll generate the test data you need. Need 1000 customer records with unique email addresses? No problem. ChatGPT will whip it up for you. And as for test scripts, just give it the right prompt, and it'll generate a script that checks if a user can log in to the system.

So, whether you're in need of some code generation or some help with debugging and test automation, ChatGPT has got your back. It's like having a coding buddy who speaks your language, understands your needs, and gets things done. Cheers to coding automation with the help of this coding maestro!

Automating Customer Service

Customer service automation is a fancy way of saying let the machines handle all those pesky customer inquiries and support requests. And guess what? ChatGPT is here to take the load off your weary shoulders. Armed with natural language processing and machine learning smarts, ChatGPT can decipher those customer inquiries, understand what they want, and dish out the appropriate responses faster than you can say "customer satisfaction." It's like having a tireless customer service rep that never needs a coffee break.

Imagine this: You integrate ChatGPT with your customer service chatbots or platforms, and voila! Instant automated responses and support for your customers. No more agonizing over every message that comes in. ChatGPT's got your back, making sure those common questions and concerns are addressed with accuracy and speed.

But that's not all, folks. ChatGPT can lend a hand with support requests too. It'll whip up automated responses for those pesky issues that keep popping up. And if things get too hairy, it can even pass the baton to a human representative.

And don't forget about order processing. ChatGPT can take care of tracking orders, updating shipping info, invoicing, and on and on the list goes, and for none of this is manual labor required.

And appointment scheduling? Piece of cake for ChatGPT. It'll handle all the back-and-forth, providing available time slots and confirming appointments with your customers. It's like having a virtual receptionist that never screws up the schedule.

Last but not least, product recommendations. ChatGPT can whip up automated suggestions based on customer preferences and past purchases. It's like having a personal shopper that knows your customers better than they know themselves.

Chapter 3: ChatGPT as a Marketing Powerhouse

With ChatGPT as your trusted ally, you'll be able to craft captivating content that mesmerizes your audience, capturing their attention and holding it tightly in your grasp. Say goodbye to lackluster campaigns and hello to a world where audience engagement soars to new heights. The AI shines brightly in the realms of social media management, email marketing, SEO optimization, and advertising campaigns. It's like having a marketing maestro at your disposal, guiding you toward success and ensuring your strategies outshine the competition.

And here's a delightful bonus for you: Pair the incredible capabilities of ChatGPT with tools like Plerdy, a comprehensive suite of conversion rate optimization tools, and witness your marketing performance reach unprecedented levels. Plerdy is one of those tools that offer a plethora of insights, from analyzing visitor behavior to improving user experience, all aimed at skyrocketing your conversions. With Plerdy's heatmap, SEO checker, and more in your arsenal, combined with the power of ChatGPT, you'll become an unstoppable force in the world of marketing.

Put Your Marketing Efforts on Steroids

With ChatGPT by your side, you can unleash a flood of creativity. It's like having an AI muse that helps you generate attention-grabbing headlines that make people stop mid-scroll and take notice.

It's like having a virtual wordsmith that crafts captivating captions that draw people in and make them crave more. And let's not forget the power of visuals! ChatGPT can whip up engaging images that make your audience go "Wow!" and click that alluring 'like' button.

Let's take a practical example, shall we? Imagine a home renovation company trying to amp up its Instagram game. They can turn to ChatGPT for some much-needed inspiration. This AI wizard can help them brainstorm a series of "before and after" posts that showcase the company's transformative work. And with a sprinkle of snappy captions, these posts will be like magnets, drawing attention and fueling engagement.

Marketers, listen up! ChatGPT is a game-changer when it comes to creating stellar social media content. It's like having a magical genie that grants your marketing wishes. By harnessing the power of this cutting-edge tool, you can elevate your marketing game, captivate your audience, and conquer the fierce competition that resides within the realm of social media.

A Personal Article Writer

ChatGPT can generate high-quality content that will captivate your readers and skyrocket engagement. With its unrivaled capabilities, you can elevate your content to new heights of greatness. Imagine generating groundbreaking topics that leave your competitors in the dust. Picture crafting coherent structures that guide your readers on a mesmerizing journey. And let's not forget about the power of persuasive copy that leaves an indelible mark on your audience's minds.

Say you're a fitness brand with a burning desire to create a blog post that will inspire and motivate your readers. You want to share "10 Tips to Crush Your Fitness Goals" and leave them hungry for more. This is where ChatGPT steps in and helps you outline a compelling article that weaves together captivating anecdotes, expert advice, and research-backed data. The result? A piece of content that not only provides immense value to your readers but also entices them to share it with their peers.

Email Marketing Strategies

Prepare to become a master of email marketing with ChatGPT. It possesses the uncanny ability to craft subject lines that are downright irresistible that captivate your readers' attention with a subject line like "Escape to Paradise – Limited-Time Offer Just for You!" They won't be able to resist diving into your email and exploring the enticing deals within.

Not only that, but ChatGPT's powers also extend to the art of persuasive email copy. With its assistance, you can whip up compelling content that grabs hold of your readers' emotions and nudges them toward taking action. Imagine that, crafting an email body that not only informs but also captivates, leaving your audience eagerly clicking those call-to-action buttons.

And let's not forget about automation where ChatGPT can help you set up tailored follow-ups that keep your subscribers engaged and eager for more. It's like having a personal assistant who ensures no opportunity slips through the cracks.

If you're a travel agency ready to entice your subscribers with an exclusive discount on tropical getaways. With ChatGPT's guidance, you can create an email campaign that oozes charm and urgency. The subject line becomes a siren's call, luring readers with the promise of escaping to paradise. The email body then weaves a tale that paints a vivid picture of pristine beaches and exotic adventures, enticing your readers to seize the limited-time offer.

Copywriting Assistant

Prepare to unleash the full potential of ChatGPT in your advertising endeavors because it's got a knack for penning compelling ad headlines that grab attention like a swift punch to the gut. And that's not all! ChatGPT's got your back when it comes to crafting impactful ad descriptions. It knows just how to weave words together to highlight the quality of your products and create a sense of luxurious indulgence. With its guidance, you'll be able to create persuasive descriptions that make your audience's mouths water and their wallets eager to spend.

And let's not forget about seamless A/B testing. ChatGPT can help you fine-tune your ads by conducting tests to find the winning formula that drives clicks and delivers those sweet returns on investment. It's like having a marketing wizard in your corner, optimizing your campaigns for maximum impact.

Imagine you're a gourmet chocolate brand, ready to entice your audience with a Facebook ad campaign. With ChatGPT's assistance, you can create an irresistible headline that promises a divine chocolate experience. It's a siren's call that draws them into a world of decadence and indulgence. And the ad description? It becomes a work of art, painting a picture of your exquisite chocolates and stirring a desire for the ultimate taste of luxury.

In a nutshell, ChatGPT is the ultimate weapon for marketers aiming to create advertising copy that stands head and shoulders above the competition. Its advanced capabilities will help you captivate your audience, drive clicks, and generate those coveted returns on investment.

Automated Social Media

Let's delve into the enchanting world of SEO with ChatGPT by your side. It's armed with the expertise to conduct precise keyword research, uncovering those hidden gems that'll make your content shine in the vast digital landscape. Imagine the power of discovering long-tail keywords like "Authentic Indian restaurants near me" for an Indian restaurant. With ChatGPT's guidance, you can create engaging content that captures the hearts of readers while appeasing those mighty search engines.

It knows just how to optimize your content for relevance and readability, ensuring that it not only pleases the search engine gods but also resonates with your audience. It's like finding that perfect balance between art and science, where your words flow effortlessly while keeping the search algorithms satisfied.

And let's not forget about the power of meta tags. ChatGPT can help you generate captivating meta titles and descriptions that beckon users to click and explore. Imagine that local Indian restaurant, yearning to climb the search engine ranks and be the go-to destination for some great food. With ChatGPT's guidance, they'll identify those strategic long-tail keywords and weave them into their content like a master chef. The result? Engaging, keyword-rich content that satisfies both the reader's cravings and the search engine's algorithms. And those meta tags? They become irresistible breadcrumbs, leading users straight to the bakery's virtual doorstep.

Influencer Marketing Automated

This remarkable AI-driven marvel will help you identify the perfect influencers for your niche, like those eco-conscious warriors for a sustainable fashion brand. With ChatGPT's analytical prowess, you'll unravel the mysteries of their content, delve into their audience demographics, and even gauge their engagement rates. It's like having a secret weapon that reveals the hidden gems among the vast influencer landscape.

ChatGPT is not just about identifying influencers; it's a creative genius as well. It churns out innovative campaign ideas that'll capture the attention of those influencers and ignite a wildfire of excitement. Picture an "Eco-friendly Wardrobe Challenge" that sparks their interest and inspires them to create buzz-worthy content. With ChatGPT's guidance, you'll craft collaborations that are authentic, engaging, and oh-so-memorable.

In a nutshell, ChatGPT is the game-changer for marketers who want to conquer the world of influencer marketing. It's the ally you've been searching for, with its cutting-edge features and unparalleled expertise. With ChatGPT by your side, you'll forge authentic partnerships, develop captivating campaigns, and propel your brand to unprecedented heights in the fiercely competitive realm of influencer marketing.

Automating Video Scripts

Visualize a world where video scripts come to life, where stories resonate with viewers on a profound level. ChatGPT here is a master at generating storylines that speak to the hearts of your audience and with its help, you'll create video scripts that captivate, leaving a lasting impression in the minds of those who watch.

But it doesn't stop there, ChatGPT has a way with words, crafting concise yet impactful dialogues that keep your viewers hooked from start to finish. Every line will be carefully designed to convey your message with clarity and conviction. And when it's time for that decisive moment, when you need to spur your audience to action, ChatGPT will be there, helping you develop compelling calls-to-action that leave no room for resistance.

Automate Content Repurposing

ChatGPT is great at identifying the best pieces of content that are ripe for a makeover. With its help, you'll find those hidden gems in your arsenal that are just waiting to be repurposed for greater impact.

ChatGPT is a wellspring of fresh ideas, constantly churning out innovative ways to present your content in different formats. Whether it's transforming a podcast episode into an engaging blog post or turning it into visually stunning infographics, ChatGPT has got you covered. It can even slice and dice your content into bite-sized social media posts that'll have your audience craving for more.

Say you have a killer podcast episode discussing time management tips that hit the airwaves. Now, with ChatGPT by your side, you can repurpose that content into an array of captivating blog posts, eye-catching infographics, or even those irresistible social media snippets. By taking this multi-pronged approach, you'll amplify your message, spreading it far and wide across different platforms, reaching a broader audience hungry for your insights.

Automate Landing Page Creation

ChatGPT can craft attention-grabbing headlines that'll stop visitors dead in their tracks, it is a master at writing persuasive subheadings that highlight the features and benefits of your business like a one-two punch that'll keep them hooked and wanting more. And let's not forget the all-important call-to-action, the cherry on top. ChatGPT knows just how to craft an irresistible call-to-action that'll have your visitors itching to sign up.

Market and Competitor Analysis

Competitor analysis with ChatGPT involves looking at a few crucial factors.

First up, market positioning: you wanna know where your competitors stand in the grand scheme of things. Are they targeting a specific niche or a particular customer segment? That's the kind of juicy info you need to uncover.

Next, product offerings. What are they selling? Are they offering anything unique or innovative? Maybe they've got a lineup of reusable bags and sustainable kitchenware. It's all about understanding what they're bringing to the table.

Thirdly, how are your competitors pricing their products? Are they going for the budget-conscious crowd or targeting high-end buyers? Knowing their pricing strategy gives you an edge in the game. How are they reaching their audience? Are they rocking social media marketing or partnering up with influencers? That's where you gotta keep an eye out and see what they're up to.

And last but not least, we've got the good old SWOT analysis. Strengths, weaknesses, opportunities, and threats.

ChatGPT can help you uncover their strengths in branding and also reveal their weaknesses like maybe they've got a limited product variety.

Chapter 4: Revolutionizing Customer Service with ChatGPT

According to Zendesk's CX Trends report on the customer service industry from 2022, Customer support requests, they're on the rise, up by a solid 14% from 2021. About 81% of the customers say that when they receive good customer service, it makes them more likely to open up their wallets and make another purchase. Yeah, you heard that right. Treat 'em right, and they'll come back for more. And their buying experience is not based on the products or the prices; 70% of it is based on how the customer is treated. The whole shebang is based on that. And over 60% of customers are expecting companies to meet all their needs and if you can't give them that, 61% of them are going to pack their bags and head over to the competition. One bad experience, and they're outta there. On the other hand, around 64% of businesses claim that good customer service can actually boost their sales. And customers are willing to pay more for a personalized touch, and about 90% of them are ready to dig a little deeper into their pockets if they get that special treatment.

Fortune Business Insights states that the global customer experience management industry is worth a hefty $11.34 billion in 2022 and by 2029, they're projecting it to balloon up to a whopping $32.53 billion. Now, that's what I call some serious cash. It's all about that customer interaction. More and more folks are reaching out to those customer service centers, whether it's to fix a technical glitch or figure out what shoe size to wear. Those support requests, they've gone up by 14% from last year. And turns out, the customers have got some pretty high expectations: over 60% of them, they're expecting companies to meet all their needs and not every business out there can keep up. That means unhappy customers which means sales go down the drain.

Negative experiences aren't just costly—they go viral. Nowadays, customers are interacting more than ever with service staff, and they want some damn helpful and empathic agents. They want that always-on support and conversations that flow smoothly like whiskey, whether they're talking to a human or a damn bot and 68% of them think most businesses need to step up their game when it comes to training their customer service agents and they, the customer, want things quick, simple, and efficient. And if they don't get it, they're ready to pack up and move on to greener pastures, and as we had discussed before, 61% of them would jump ship after just one lousy experience and 76% of them are out of there for good.

And this is a global trend (according to Zendesk's CX Trends report again), Brazil's got 80% of customers ready to switch to a competitor, France is at 70%, and Spain's sitting at more than 60%. And businesses that can't meet those expectations suffer the most. and almost 60% of Gen Xers are ready to jump ship after just one bad experience.

Some companies don't see the value in investing in their customer service teams. In 2021, 40% of customer service representatives said their own organizations see customer service as an expense rather than an opportunity for growth. That's an 8% increase from the year before. But 78% of companies actually believe that those service agents play a crucial role in their overall growth.

And in terms of customer expectations, it used to be all about the phone calls, but things have evolved. Customers, these days seem to want options, they want to reach out through different channels and platforms. And when they contact a company, 76% of them expect to speak with someone right away.

And customers don't wanna keep repeating themselves. They want businesses to share information, so they don't have to go through the same damn spiel over and over again. A solid 71% of them expect that. And 92% of them are willing to shell out more cash if a company guarantees they won't have to repeat their information.

Now that we have gotten past the customer requirements, it's time for us to discuss what it feels like from our end, the business owner's end to tackle the customer service problem. As important as it is for us to do so, we business owners often end up getting caught up in all the other aspects of business that we can hardly take the monotonous and mundane questions most customers hit us with. To solve the problem of answering the same old questions from our customers, wasting time and money by employing someone to do the mundane but hard work, we came up with FAQ sections online, which further developed into chatbots that interacted with the customers. Traditional chatbots try their best, but they can be a bit clueless sometimes. They struggle to give specific answers and often end up giving you multiple options to choose from, over and over again, which becomes frustrating for the customer.

Language models AIs on the other hand are a whole different ball game because they understand the clients' messages right off the bat. No more confusion or back-and-forth. It digs into its database and figures out what the business offers, combines the information, and gets the customers a straight answer. No beating around the bush. None of that traditional chatbot frustration.

According to the State of AI Survey by HubSpot (June 05, 2023), the customer service field is already seeing some real benefits with AI taking the helm here. First off, AI is making customer service available 24/7 which means no more waiting around for some human to pick up the phone. Secondly, AI is saving us some precious time by automating manual tasks like searching for the customer's answers on a long list and is also helping people respond to customer support requests faster. AI can handle the smaller tasks, leaving us more time to tackle complex customer service requests. It also helps address customer requests more effectively.

CX, which stands for customer experience, is all about building excellent and highly-connected experiences, and below goes into the nitty gritty of how AI is being used in this field right now,

1. First up is the automated ticketing systems which eliminate all the time wasted on filtering and organizing service queries. It's like having a magical machine that sorts everything out for you.

2. Next on the list are the knowledge bases, chatbots, and other resources that help customers answer their own questions; it's like giving them the keys to the kingdom, so they can find the answers they need without bothering anyone.

3. And let's not forget about CRM (Customer Relationship Management) software. This little gem helps streamline customer management and relationship-building processes. It's like having a trusty assistant that keeps all your customer information in order, so you can focus on the important stuff.

By harnessing the power of these tools, customer service professionals can streamline their tasks and start taking on bigger-picture projects. They can break down pesky company processes and build better customer experiences.

Ways to use ChatGPT in Customer Service

Dealing With Customer Complaints

When it comes to dealing with customer complaints and reviews, ChatGPT can come in handy. It can be used to whip up responses real quick, whether it's an email to an angry customer or a snappy comeback to a negative review.

The best part is, ChatGPT knows how to sound all professional and empathetic, just like we want our agents to be. It can even help us keep things short and sweet for social media and product review comments. Even though ChatGPT can generate responses that sound human, we still have to do some editing, personalizing, and fact-checking because, as we know, this tool was trained on internet data, and we all know how full of biases and inaccuracies that can be.

And here's another thing to keep in mind: ChatGPT doesn't have access to our specific business policies. So we gotta make sure the responses it comes up with don't promise stuff like discounts or compensation that we can't actually deliver. We don't wanna be making false promises now.

Revamp Your Existing Customer ChatBots

Back in the early 2000s, customer service departments started using chatbots to handle customer queries. These bots were rule-based, meaning they could only respond to specific keywords or phrases. They were like little search engines, far from having a real conversation. But now we have a language model intelligence, which means you can create a new breed of chatbots powered by advanced language models. These chatbots, including ChatGPT, can engage in realistic dialogue that almost feels like talking to a real human.

We can't use ChatGPT itself as a customer-facing chatbot, however, OpenAI offers an API for their GPT-4 language model that we can train on our own knowledge base. Once we've done that, we can integrate this customized language model into our customer service chatbots. And what does that mean? It means we can have chatbots that interact with customers in a more human-like way. They can answer specific questions related to our business and have more natural conversations.

Summarizing Customer's Queries

When it comes to customer service, understanding customer problems and frustrations is key. We need to read those long essay complaints, and review past interactions to get the full picture and sometimes read between the lines and this can eat up a lot of their precious time.

ChatGPT can help agents speed things up and get to the heart of the matter by simply copying a complaint email, pasting it into ChatGPT, and prompting the bot to give us a summary in just a few sentences, and bam, we have all the main points without slogging through the whole thing. Y

ou have to be careful and strip out any personal info before chatting with ChatGPT like names, addresses, phone numbers, and email addresses especially because ChatGPT keeps a record of all the conversations it has with users. T

his is a concern for cybersecurity with risks such as hackers trying to sneak a peek at those transcripts. So, let's keep an eye on that, be smart and careful with our client's information, and stay vigilant.

Multilingual Customer Service

ChatGPT can help translate all sorts of content, at the time this book was written, into over 50 different languages. However, AI is far from perfect. It can get all flustered with misspellings and fancy colloquial language and when that happens we get ourselves into a mistranslation mess.

Virtual CX Assistants

Organizations can use ChatGPT to power their very own virtual assistants and train them on their own knowledge bases using APIs (Application Program Interface). You can integrate it with their existing tools, like contact center platforms and scheduling systems.

In case you are talking to customers across different channels, the virtual assistant swoops in to save the day and suggests detailed responses in real time that you can use, edit, or ignore. They can also automatically summarize those long-winded customer inquiries and past interactions and sort inquiries into neat categories like sales questions, cancellations, or technical issues. They can even analyze the customer's emotions and route them to the right channel and agent. And get this, they can even schedule customer appointments without breaking a sweat.

Chapter 5: Bonus: ChatGPT-Driven Decision-Making

The business decision-making process is a path that professionals follow to solve problems and make their moves. It's all about weighing the evidence, considering different options, and finally picking a path to follow. And the process of walking this path is no walk in the park. It's all about setting a goal, gathering the right info, and considering your options before making up your mind making good decisions brings heaps of benefits like the following:

- Good decisions stand the test of time. When you've thought things through and made a solid choice, you won't have to constantly second-guess yourself. That decision can hold strong for the long haul, even for an entire organization.

- Good decisions take it all into account, which means you have to consider the big picture. A sound decision takes into consideration the whole company, both inside and out. It's about finding that sweet spot where all parts of the business thrive, without screwing each other over.

- Good decisions cut out the unnecessary. When you bring transparency and get everyone on board during the decision-making process, there's less room for questions and doubts later on. It keeps the organization focused and moving forward, reducing all that unnecessary drama.

- And last but not least, good decisions actually get stuff done. A solid decision is not just for show, it is about making progress, getting closer to the goal, and solving the problem that started it all. It's about getting things done the right way.

And the decision-making process model is like a roadmap for businesses to make smarter choices and having a process is beneficial in so many ways that it must be your priority to come up with one. And these models, you can create for yourself and customize it to suit your thought processes and field of business, and before I get on to expanding on one such process, I'd like to list out reasons you need this, so you'd be able to customize the process I am about to prescribe to you.

- With a good process there is no more second-guessing: When you stick to a formal process, you can show that you've explored different options and nobody is going to question your decisions because you've done your homework.

- Shareable decisions: You can take your decisions and progress and share them with the big shots up top and the folks down below. It's like spreading the word and getting everyone on the same damn page.

- Guide and roadmap: Write down your decision-making process. It's like a guidebook that explains the steps and strategy behind your choices. You'll have a backup plan and show stakeholders that you've got it all figured out.

Here are seven steps that will give you a basic framework that you can use as a skeleton to build your process.

1. Step one is all about identifying the decision you need to make. You gotta know the problem or question you're trying to tackle. Get it straight, make it measurable, and give it a damn timeline.

2. Next up, gather the info that's relevant to your decision. Look internally and see where your organization has succeeded or failed in similar areas. And don't forget to peek outside, check out studies, market research, and maybe even call in the big guns - the consultants.

3. Now that you've got the goods, it's time to brainstorm some alternatives. Think outside the box. There's usually more than one way to skin a cat, or so they say. So consider different options, like paid ads or changing your social media strategy, and see what floats your boat.

4. Once you've got those alternatives, it's time to weigh the evidence. Look at what others have done, and learn from their successes and failures. And don't forget to look in the mirror and see what your own organization has been up to. Balance the risks and rewards.

5. Now comes the moment of truth. Choose among those alternatives you've been pondering. Make a call and stick with it. It's time to take action.

6. Put that decision into motion, my friend. Develop a plan, assign tasks, and get your team on board. Make that decision a reality and see it through.

7. After a while, take a good hard look at that decision. Review it, assess it, and be honest with yourself. Did it solve the problem? Did it meet your goals? Learn from the experience, whether it worked or not, and use those lessons as you embark on the decision-making process again.

Automating Decision-Making with ChatGPT

Automated decision-making is spreading like wildfire across industries these days. From healthcare to finance, they're all jumping on the AI and machine learning bandwagon to make their decision-making processes smoother. In fact, NetDragon Websoft, a video game company, has announced that an AI named Tang Yu has made an AI their chief executive subsidiary– talk about the sci-fi dream come true.

With ChatGPT made available to the general public, decision-making is taken to a whole new level. The bot uses its language processing skills to automate decision processes, making them a lot faster and more accurate. Want personalized product recommendations? ChatGPT's got you covered: It'll analyze your browsing history and purchase behavior to give you the perfect suggestions.

A word of advice if you're using ChatGPT in your research, don't get too carried away, because. sure, it's a handy tool, but you need to evaluate what it spits out. Make sure it's accurate and relevant to your research question. And remember, ChatGPT has its limitations and biases. It's not a magic bullet that replaces your own brainpower.

However, you can use it to analyze huge datasets. Remember seeing those endless spreadsheets, the mountains of data that would give you a headache? Well, ChatGPT can dig in, find patterns, and uncover insights that would make your head spin. It can even generate Python scripts to handle the data analysis process.

ChatGPT is even making its mark in making decisions in the medical field, helping doctors analyze patient data, medical literature, and clinical guidelines. With its lightning-fast processing power, it's making doctors' lives easier by providing them with accurate information for diagnoses and treatment plans. And in this field, there is room for error, cause it can cost a life. It's all about improving patient outcomes and keeping everyone healthy.

But that's not all. The financial big shots have caught on to ChatGPT's magic too. They're using it to analyze market trends, news articles, and financial reports. It's like having a virtual financial advisor at your fingertips, giving you valuable insights and helping you make those investment decisions. No more relying on luck, my friend. This AI-driven model has got your back.

And guess what? Even lawyers are jumping on the ChatGPT train. They're using it to review contracts, case law, and regulations. It's like having a virtual legal researcher right there on their screens. No more wasting time sifting through piles of paperwork. And also strategic planners are using this bad boy to do some serious research. They feed ChatGPT with company-specific info and ask it some concise questions. And guess what? It spits out a whole set of strategic objectives and key performance indicators. It's like having a genie in a bottle, granting you your strategic wishes in no time.

In Conclusion

Having a solid AI strategy for your organization can work wonders in this fast-paced technological world we're living in. It's all about figuring out how to use artificial intelligence to achieve your business goals, whether it's ramping up customer service with chatbots or making smarter decisions that'll save you time and money.

When you've got an AI strategy in place, you can milk every benefit out of those AI technologies. You'll be ready to tackle any challenges that pop up when you're introducing new tech, like data privacy concerns or employees who just hate change. And let me tell you, a well-thought-out plan makes integrating those AI solutions smooth as whiskey on a summer night.

ChatGPT can be your secret weapon in terms of savings. They'll save you a heap of cash on development costs, and you'll get to tap into the knowledge of those brainy professionals who know their stuff when it comes to machine learning.

However, you ought to be mindful while crafting an AI strategy, you have to be clear on what success looks like, get well acquainted and fluent with those fancy machine learning algorithms, and keep a close eye on things even after you've put it all into action. Trust me, these steps will make sure you're milking every drop of that AI goodness and tailoring it to fit your unique business needs.

Having an AI strategy, including OpenAI's sweet tech, can be a game-changer. As businesses scramble to be more efficient and cutting-edge, AI solutions like ChatGPT can be your secret sauce in a variety of industries, from market research to customer service to online education. Embrace the possibilities, and dive into the AI world with gusto. It's a wild ride, but damn, it's worth it.

Book 5 | ChatGPT for Content Writing

Revolutionizing Creativity, Storytelling, and Marketing by ChatGPT Enhanced Techniques for Engaging and Persuasive Writing

By Harold Pearson

Introduction

Content writing is a fine way of marketing, created especially for the audience online. The marketers and business owners put out content online for all sorts of reasons. Maybe they want more traffic coming to their website, or maybe they got some newfangled product or service to show the world. Often, these businesses hire content writers to whip up some top-notch words for their sales copy, blogs, articles, and social media posts. And to be a successful content writer, you have got to know your audience inside and out and write content that speaks to them.

In this digital age, content writing means planning, writing, and publishing web content, and also content writers sometimes have to promote and edit the stuff they create too.

Content writing is what we call inbound marketing. It's all about reeling in the audience, whether it's for a fancy company, a slick product, or some online hangout. The idea is to dish out valuable information about the product or brand, build trust with the customers, get them engaged, and, maybe even make a sale or two.

These days, content writing comes in all shapes and sizes; we're talking articles, blogs, videos, social media posts, you name it. It's all about getting people hooked and coming back for more and it's a matter of survival in this crazy digital world we live in. Businesses are required to see content writing as an investment, a real game-changer that can bring in conversions and keep loyal customers coming back. It's all about laying down that solid foundation for a strong online presence because that's where the action is happening. And if you are not in the game, you're missing out.

When it comes to content writing, first things first, quality matters. You can't just throw any old words on your website and expect it to stick on the wall and folks to care: people these days are pickier than ever. They want content that's well-written, well-researched, and valuable. There is a lot of noise out there, so if you want 'em eyeballs on your stuff, you better make sure it's worth their while.

And here is where strategy comes into play and that's the name of the game. Experienced writers understand the dance of SEO and how magic keywords and quality info can make or break your online visibility. If you wanna stand out in that wild jungle of websites, you gotta play the game right because competition is everywhere. No matter if you have a bunch of rivals or you're a lone wolf, you gotta make sure people know your brand name. Content writing, that's your secret weapon. It's how you get noticed, how you make a name for yourself in this big old digital world.

This brings us to SEO which is not only an overused term in the content writing market but is a fickle beast by itself. Search engines like Google are always changing the rules, keeping us on our toes and it is only the savvy writers who know how to adapt. They stay on top of the ever-changing best practices, making sure their content is optimized to rank high in their search results.

And let's not forget the bottom line, the money. Good content is the key to revenue. B2B companies that invest in content marketing are the ones that are pulling in the dough. Why? Because they bring in more visitors through organic search and turn the visitors into qualified leads, and eventually, valuable revenue. It's all about attention, keeping them coming back for more.

Last but not least, search engines love writing that displays authority. When you establish yourself as an industry expert when you provide your audience with valuable tips, tutorials, and advice, you are building credibility and search engines eat it up. The more you talk about relevant issues, the more your audience responds, and the more you look like the real deal. Establishing Authority, that's a top priority in the world of content writing.

Responsibilities of a Content Writer

In this ever-evolving world of digital marketing, the role of a content writer can take many shapes. Some focus on digging deep into research and crafting blog posts that search engines will love. Others offer a whole bunch of different services, all related to churning out top-notch content that'll grab readers by the collar and make them pay attention. At the core of it all, a content writer needs to understand the target audience like the back of their hand. The best ones know how to adapt their style, their tone, and their whole marketing strategy to fit the expectations of their readers. They can whip up content that's not just pleasing to the human eye but can also cozy up to the search engine algorithms.

So, here's a taste of what a content writer might do:

- First up, we got keyword research; some companies get separate SEO experts handling this stuff, but a good content writer can lend a helping hand too. They can dig deep into the realms of search terms and figure out what words and phrases should be sprinkled throughout your content. They'll be able to help you out with long-tail and semantic keywords too.

- Then we got content strategy–content writers can partner up with content marketing wizards and help you craft a strategy that's bulletproof. They'll guide you on what kinda blogs, eBooks, listicles, and whitepapers you should cook up and serve. And hey, they might even throw in some advice on social media and email marketing, or the magic of video creation.

- Of course, the heart of a content writer's work is actually producing the content. They'll whip up blog posts, web pages, and other magical words that'll make your brand shine. Some might even throw in free edits and updates, or give you a sneak peek at their performance metrics.

- Proofreading and editing–now that's another game. Some content writers handle it all themselves, making sure your content is as clean as a whistle. But, if they don't, you might have to pay them some extra dough to get your words polished and perfected.

- Publishing and outreach are where the rubber meets the road. Content writers can handle the whole deal, from uploading your content to different platforms like WordPress to scheduling' and promoting like there is no tomorrow. And if you need to reach out to other guest blogs and publications, they might lend a hand there too.

- Now, mind you, every content writer is going to have their own style, their own bag of tricks. So, when you're hiring one, make sure they fit the bill and bring the qualities you are looking for. It's a wild world out there, but with a good content writer by your side, you will be making waves and grabbing attention like no one else.

Content Types

There is a whole smorgasbord of mediums for content out there, each with its own special flavor, and also different types of content reach folks at different stages of the sales game. It's all about knowing where to slot them in your strategy for maximum impact. So, here's a taste of the options you have:

- First up, the email newsletters: it is a direct line to your subscribers, whether they are potential leads or loyal customers. You can slide right into their precious email accounts and dish out updates, promotions, and all sorts of goodies.

- Then we have our social media posts which are like a virtual town square where you can shout out to your online community. Spread the word, share updates, and give 'em a glimpse into the happenings of your business.

- Video scripts, now that's where the magic happens. You can create specific videos, whether it's informational, sales-driven, or just plain promotional. It's like bringing your message to life with moving pictures and all.

- Web page copy is like your digital storefront. It serves a multitude of purposes, from explaining who you are and what you do to acting as a hub for all your other content, like the nerve center of your online presence.

- Landing page copy, this form is super important, it is reserved for something special. When you've got an event, a product launch, or a fancy initiative that deserves its own spotlight, you give it a landing page. It's like a showcase, a spotlight on something extra special.

- White papers, and with this we have come into the realm of industry knowledge. This form of content lets you share all the specifics about your products or services, or maybe even give your clients some tailored solutions to their problems. It is like sharing insider information, letting the client in on your secret Colonel Sanders recipe.

- Blog posts are bite-sized nuggets of wisdom. You can provide valuable information to your audience, short and sweet. It's like a little appetizer, whetting their appetite for more.

- eBooks are the big guns because this long-form content serves as a guide, a resource on a specific topic in your industry. It's like a feast for their brains, filling them up with knowledge and insights.

- Informational articles provide knowledge of value to your target audience but in a long-form fashion. It's like a journey, taking the readers on a wild ride through the depths of your expertise.

- Product descriptions are the virtual sales pitch where you can share all the juicy details about your products and services online. Whether it is on your own website, an eCommerce store, or through third-party services, it's like painting a picture of what you are offering.

- And last but not least, press releases that let you share all your promotional content and company updates with news outlets. It's like spreading the word far and wide, letting the world know what you and your business are doing.

Strategizing the Writing Process

Unfortunately, navigating through the writing process is never as simple as just sitting down and hammering away at that keyboard. There is a whole lot of preparation, research, and development that goes into it. The process can be broken down into three phases:

1. Planning

2. Writing

3. Publishing Content

Planning

Planning and research are the bread and butter of content writing. You have to make sure that you are serving up factual, up-to-date, and trustworthy information to your audience. No room for lies and misrepresentation here. If you wanna build that trust in your business, you have to be honest. Planning is where the magic happens. Without a solid plan, your content creation is like throwing darts in the dark. You might hit the mark by sheer luck, but you'll most likely miss the mark, waste time, and money, and ain't nobody got time for that. So, here are the steps to rocking the research and planning phase:

1. Set a goal: know what you wanna achieve with each piece of content from the get-go. Whether it's collecting leads or re-engaging former customers, having a goal in mind sets the direction for your content. It shapes the type, the style, the tone, and how it fits into your overall business plan.

2. Develop or use client personas: these are like fictional characters representing your ideal target customers. They are based on real data, like market research and customer profiles. They help you understand what types of content work best for different audience segments and how to lead 'em to conversions and brand loyalty. It's like having a secret weapon in your back pocket.

3. Conduct keyword research: keywords are the magic beans of content. They tell the search engines what your content is all about. However, you have to choose them wisely, targeting high-search volume and avoiding low-content volume terms. And remember, SEO best practices and search engine updates are like a changing tide, so stay on top of the game.

4. Understand search intent: you have to get into the minds of the searchers and know why they are looking for what they are looking for. There's commercial intent, informational intent, navigational intent, and transactional intent, each one a different flavor, and you have to serve up the right content to satisfy their cravings. Ask yourself questions, be the searcher yourself, and deliver the answers they are looking for.

5. Set a content strategy: this here is your master plan — your blueprint for success. It helps you manage, create, share, and track each piece of content from start to finish. When you're juggling multiple campaigns, a content strategy keeps everything in sync. It's like conducting a symphony of content, making sure all the pieces fit together just right.

6. Create an outline: visualize the flow and order of your content by creating an outline. Especially for longer pieces, like articles, eBooks, and white papers, an outline is like your compass. It keeps you on track, helps you focus on the important parts, and guides your research. It's like the skeleton of your content, giving it structure and purpose.

7. Conduct topic research: This is where you take a deep dive into your topics. Get on the internet, spy on your competitors and read their content, run your own experiments, chat with leads and customers, and even interview industry professionals.

8. Create a content calendar: this is your secret weapon for consistency. A content calendar keeps your team on track, knowing exactly where each piece is in the production process. It's like a roadmap, showing you the deadlines, publication dates, and who is responsible for what. With a content calendar, you can dance to the rhythm of consistency and engage your audience like a pro.

Writing

After all that planning, it is finally time to get down to the nitty-gritty of the actual work: the writing and editing. You have a few options here—having an in-house writing team, bringing in some freelancers and contractors, or maybe even outsourcing your content to an agency. No matter which path you choose, the process of creating great content follows a similar format and let me break it down for ya:

1. Pick your angle: there is a ton of content out there covering the same topics over and over again. So, why should people read yours? What sets it apart? Hence, finding your unique angle is crucial. It's not just about grabbing audience interest, but also about pleasing the search engines. How you frame your content can help you target different keywords and get the best possible search traffic. Find that unique twist, that fresh perspective that'll make them click and keep reading.

2. Create an engaging introduction: the introduction is the appetizer, the first taste that hooks the readers in. It is one of the most crucial parts of any content piece, so keep it short and sweet, cut right to the chase. Do not make it fluffy and load the article with small talk and filler sentences. Give the readers what they are looking for from the get-go. Remember, your audience is busy, so make it worth their while.

3. Pick relevant visuals: Writing is almost never just about words. Visuals like photographic descriptions, videos, charts, infographics, and photos, they add that extra oomph to your content. Break up the walls of text, make it more readable and scannable. As a writer, you'll be the one picking these visuals to complement your words, to illustrate your points, and remember a picture says a thousand words.

4. Insert CTAs: On the surface, you're writing content to inform and solve problems, but let us be honest with each other and admit that deep down, we want to build that brand trust and convert those leads into paying customers. That's where CTAs come in handy. CTAs or Calls-to-action, are like subtle whispers, planting that idea in the reader's head that they need your partnership, your products, or your services. It can be a short phrase, a button, or a visual, encouraging them to take action. Get creative and guide them to the next step.

5. Create a title: This might sound strange for the non-writers, but saving the title for last can actually be a smart move. Titles are the face of your content, the first impression. They gotta be interesting enough to grab some clicks, but not misleading. No room for clickbait here. If you make a promise in the title, you better deliver inside. Nothing worse than losing credibility and trust. Play around, write multiple titles, and find the one that will make them stop and take notice.

6. Write the meta description: The meta description is another key element in the content package. It works alongside the title on the search engine results pages, giving people a glimpse of what to expect. Keep it short, 160 characters or less, and make sure to include the target keywords. This helps the Google and Bing bots and crawlers find your content and serve it up to the right searchers. So, make it snappy and informative.

7. Check over the content: here is where all the magic happens—editing. It is just as crucial as the writing itself. Writers often do a self-edit to catch any spelling mistake and punctuation mistakes, missing content, or unclear sections. They wanna save the editors and QA specialists some trouble. Then, the professionals step in and review the content for grammar, flow, and relevance to the topic. They fact-check and make sure there is no plagiarism, protecting the reputation of your brand or company.

Publishing

Publishing is the final step in the content writing process; it is like letting your kid go out into the world, your content out into the wild, where your target audience can feast their eyes on it, share it around, and get engaged. But before we dive into the metrics and data, let us talk about where you can publish that precious content of yours:

- Websites, now that is your home base, where you can showcase all your content. Build a virtual sanctuary where folks can come and explore what you have to offer.

- Blogs, they're like your little corner of the internet where you can dish out valuable insights, entertaining stories, or helpful tips. It's your chance to connect with your audience on a personal level.

- Social media platforms, now these are the hustle and bustle of the online world. Share your content, engage with your community, and spread the word. It's like a virtual party, where you can mingle and make some noise.

- Online advertisements, well, if you wanna amp up the exposure, these can probably do the trick for you. Put your content in front of the right eyeballs and get them curious. Just remember to make them catchy and relevant.

- Industry hubs are like the spots where the cool kids hang out. Find those online communities where your target audience gathers and shares your content. It's like joining the conversation, showing them what you got.

- News outlets, now we're talking about reaching a wider audience. If you have something newsworthy, something buzzworthy, these outlets can help spread the word. Get your content in front of more folks, and make some noise.

Now, once you hit that publish button, it's time for the review. Keep a close eye on the metrics and track the importance that aligns with your content goals. For example, if you want to increase organic traffic to your website with informational articles, keep an eye on unique visitors, bounce rate, and page views. The data you collect will give you a glimpse into how your content is performing. And if it is not meeting your expectations, don't fret. It's an opportunity to do a content refresh, make some tweaks, and get back on track. Learn from the data, perfect your next campaign, and keep growing.

Content writing is all about producing content that grabs the attention, motivates, and maybe even converts your target audience. And, when it comes to the different stages of the digital marketing sales funnel, you ought to switch up your approach. At the top of the funnel, during the awareness stage, you wanna inform and attract customers, show them what you are offering, and get them interested. Then, as they move down the funnel to the consideration stage, it's all 'about highlighting' the benefits of your products or services. Let 'em know why you're better than the competition. Make them see the value you bring. But no matter the stage, you ought to keep in mind the basic content writing rules, and let us take a quick recap on what they are:

1. Research, do your homework, understand who you are writing for, and connect with them on an emotional level. Know your audience inside and out. And don't forget to research the topics you're writing about. Factual and credible information is key. No room for fake stuff because people ain't gonna trust ya if you are spouting nonsense.

2. Master the key components of content. Every piece you create is made up of different elements, and some are more important than others. Remember, your headlines ought to be head-turning and thought-provoking. Grab their attention right from the start. And that first sentence, that's your hook. Catch their attention with it, keep them engaged, and make them wanna read more. Also, stay focused–don't overwhelm your readers with a bunch of incoherent ideas. Concentrate on a specific topic and give them actionable advice they can use. And don't forget to use the right tone of voice for your audience. Speak their language and connect with them.

3. Edit and optimize, don't just settle for the first version of your work. Take the time to read through it, and make it shine. By doing this you are able to remove grammar errors, spelling mistakes, and unusual sentences. You'll not only confuse your audience, but things like this tend to make you appear a lot less credible. So make it readable and divide it into logical segments, use subheadings, short paragraphs, and bullet points. Keep it clean and easy to read.

4. Think about content SEO. Are you using the right keywords? Do the keywords flow naturally with the article? Have you overused them? Have you optimized your tags and headlines?

5. And last but not least, be very smart with the choice of your publishing medium. Make sure you understand the purpose of your article and how this aligns with the platform you are planning to publish on.

Now that we have gone through what content writing is and how we ought to get on with this, it is now time for us to dive into ways AI is able to help us out with this sometimes tedious task.

Chapter 1: Unleash Your Inner Writer: ChatGPT as a Creative Catalyst

When ChatGPT showed up, all the creative ones began to panic. A chatbot that could write blogs, songs, poems, even podcasts, and video scripts? What was the point of being creative anymore?

But, don't throw in the towel just yet, as it turns out that those generative AI tools like ChatGPT can actually enhance your creative process. They can ignite new ideas, save you time on mind-numbing tasks, and even provide valuable revisions to your work. But there's a catch, you have to use them right. And that's where prompt engineering comes into play.

Crafting the right question to get the response you need is an art form worth mastering. It might take a bit of practice, but once you've got it down, it'll kick your creativity into overdrive.

Here's how you do it.

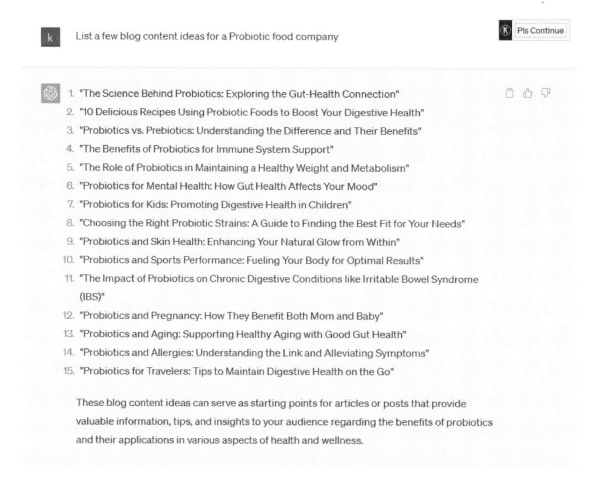

1. "The Science Behind Probiotics: Exploring the Gut-Health Connection"
2. "10 Delicious Recipes Using Probiotic Foods to Boost Your Digestive Health"
3. "Probiotics vs. Prebiotics: Understanding the Difference and Their Benefits"
4. "The Benefits of Probiotics for Immune System Support"
5. "The Role of Probiotics in Maintaining a Healthy Weight and Metabolism"
6. "Probiotics for Mental Health: How Gut Health Affects Your Mood"
7. "Probiotics for Kids: Promoting Digestive Health in Children"
8. "Choosing the Right Probiotic Strains: A Guide to Finding the Best Fit for Your Needs"
9. "Probiotics and Skin Health: Enhancing Your Natural Glow from Within"
10. "Probiotics and Sports Performance: Fueling Your Body for Optimal Results"
11. "The Impact of Probiotics on Chronic Digestive Conditions like Irritable Bowel Syndrome (IBS)"
12. "Probiotics and Pregnancy: How They Benefit Both Mom and Baby"
13. "Probiotics and Aging: Supporting Healthy Aging with Good Gut Health"
14. "Probiotics and Allergies: Understanding the Link and Alleviating Symptoms"
15. "Probiotics for Travelers: Tips to Maintain Digestive Health on the Go"

These blog content ideas can serve as starting points for articles or posts that provide valuable information, tips, and insights to your audience regarding the benefits of probiotics and their applications in various aspects of health and wellness.

Now, let's get to the basics. ChatGPT, as we all already know, is a large language model, and is one among many. To get these contraptions to generate text, you simply provide them with a prompt for text input. And think of ChatGPT as a chat with a friend because it goes back and forth just like a conversation. And get this, it even remembers the stuff you tell it so it can refer back to it later. It's got threads, like different conversations happening at the same time. Makes it easy to juggle multiple projects.

When it comes to prompts, keep it simple. For many common tasks, ChatGPT can whip up a response that matches your prompt without needing any extra information or examples. It might seem like pure magic, but it's all about how these AI were trained. They have seen millions of examples and that is what they were trained on, so they can handle all sorts of tasks with impressive accuracy.

However, if you want to avoid ending up with some run-of-the-mill, plain-Jane response from that AI, you have to get specific. Get down to the nitty-gritty and nuances and tell that thing exactly what you want it to spit out.

Tell it the length you are aiming for–are you looking for a short and snappy piece or an epic saga that will keep folks hooked for days? Lay it out plain and clear and specify the tone and style you're after. Do you want it to be somber and melancholic, or maybe playful and light-hearted? You know your vibe, so let the AI know too.

And don't forget about the audience. Who are you trying to reach? Are they highfalutin intellectuals or everyday folks on the street? Tailor your instructions to fit the crowd you're aiming for.

And also, don't just focus on what you want. Sometimes it's just as important to mention what you don't want. Exclude certain themes or styles that you're absolutely sick of. Make it crystal clear that you don't want any more of that same old same old. By getting specific, you'll make that AI contraption work for you. It will churn out exactly what you're looking for, instead of some generic snoozefest.

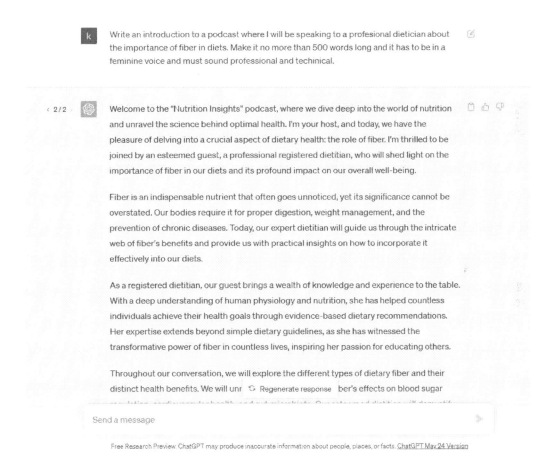

If your prompt is not giving you the results you are looking for, don't be afraid to switch up the way you phrase it. Get creative with your wording and give it a different context, describe the task in a fresh way. Sometimes all it takes is a little experimentation to hit the sweet spot.

All work and no play makes Jack a dull boy, and to avoid that, let's talk about something that is not business-centered, something that is a bit fun–chatting with ChatGPT. This chatbot has the ability to engage in full-on fictional conversations. You can chat with anyone you well please. Imagine shooting the breeze with your main character or getting advice from your favorite philosopher or writer. It's like having a virtual writer's retreat.

One of the best things about ChatGPT is its conversational style. You can pour out your writing struggles, ask for suggestions, and get a rundown of your ideas. It's like having your own personal writing coach at your fingertips. And if you're curious about why the hell it's making certain suggestions, just ask. It'll break it down for ya and maybe even open up new possibilities for your story.

But here's where it gets really interesting. You can make ChatGPT chat as a specific character. Yup, just describe the character you want it to play and tell it to start a conversation as that character. You can have it mimic historical figures, fictional characters, or even your ideal reader. It's like a brainstorming session with a virtual cast of characters.

And the beauty of it all is that ChatGPT remembers what you've talked about. So you can keep steering the conversation, adding more details, and fleshing out your ideas. It's like collaborating with an AI partner who's always got your back.

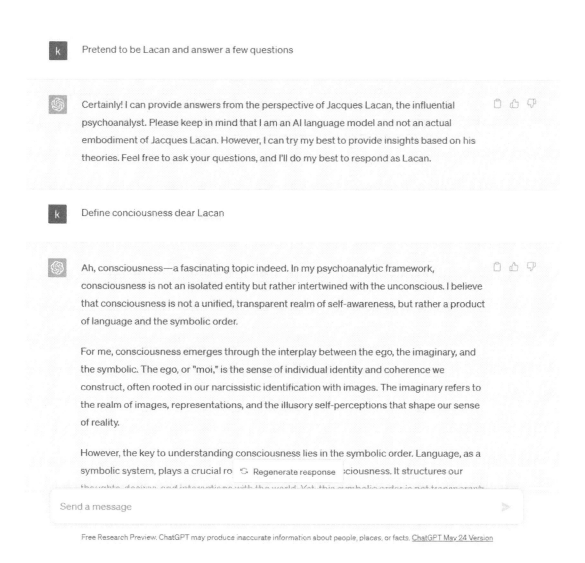

k · Pretend to be Lacan and answer a few questions

Certainly! I can provide answers from the perspective of Jacques Lacan, the influential psychoanalyst. Please keep in mind that I am an AI language model and not an actual embodiment of Jacques Lacan. However, I can try my best to provide insights based on his theories. Feel free to ask your questions, and I'll do my best to respond as Lacan.

k · Define conciousness dear Lacan

Ah, consciousness—a fascinating topic indeed. In my psychoanalytic framework, consciousness is not an isolated entity but rather intertwined with the unconscious. I believe that consciousness is not a unified, transparent realm of self-awareness, but rather a product of language and the symbolic order.

For me, consciousness emerges through the interplay between the ego, the imaginary, and the symbolic. The ego, or "moi," is the sense of individual identity and coherence we construct, often rooted in our narcissistic identification with images. The imaginary refers to the realm of images, representations, and the illusory self-perceptions that shape our sense of reality.

However, the key to understanding consciousness lies in the symbolic order. Language, as a symbolic system, plays a crucial ro ↻ Regenerate response :ciousness. It structures our

Send a message ➤

When you're dealing with those tricky and specialized tasks, feed it examples to make sure it understands exactly what you're going for and show the machine how it's done.

Now, setting up your prompt can be done in a few different ways. If you have a bunch of examples, you can start them off with "Example #" and then just keep going with the next number. ChatGPT will catch on and figure out the specific style you want to mimic.

Another option is to describe the output you want first and then provide examples. ChatGPT will blend that description with the examples, giving you a mix of the two. But here's the thing, nailing the right tone can be a bit tricky, even for an AI that learned from millions of examples. So, chances are, some good old editing will be needed to fine-tune the result.

Now, if you're dealing with complex tasks, there's this approach called iterative prompting. You start with a general prompt and then gradually make it more specific. It's like sculpting a piece of art. You might start with a general list of ideas, and when you find one you dig, you narrow the prompt to generate more ideas in that same vein. It's a process of refinement, my friend.

And when it comes to matching a tone or style, you can first ask ChatGPT to generate an example with no guidance. Then, you can prompt the AI to edit the text for the tone or style you're after. This way, you're taking it step by step, gradually refining the text until you get the desired result.

ChatGPT does its best to remember what you've told it, but it ain't perfect. Sometimes it gets a little confused about the context and begins to hallucinate. That is right, AI, like humans, sometimes hallucinates and begins to spout out irrelevant and sometimes dangerous information. To avoid any confusion, you can include the generated text directly in your prompt. And don't be afraid to edit ChatGPT's output and include that in your prompt too. It helps make things even more precise. And most importantly, double-check the output and make sure the information you put out in the world is verified and validated. It is with issues like these that Chat GPT4 allows you access to ChatGPT Plus, providing you with more accurate information and tends to not hallucinate as much. However, regardless of the version of the LM AI, it is your responsibility as the author of the content to double-check the information being presented.

Additionally, you can ask it to improve your text, fix grammar and spelling mistakes, and make it clearer and more concise. And if you want to add some extra flair to your writing, just ask ChatGPT to edit it for a specific tone or style. You can even ask for sensory details or to expand a section for better pacing. It's like having a robot editor right at your fingertips.

But then again, don't have to blindly trust the machine. After ChatGPT suggests edits, you can ask it to explain why it made those changes. It'll give you the reasoning behind every little tweak it made. That way, you can accept or reject its suggestions with confidence. It's like having a conversation with the machine.

Now, there are a couple of challenges when working with ChatGPT. You see, these large language models don't have a sense of truth and the only morals they follow are that which is flagged by OpenAI. So, it's always a good idea to fact-check its answers using your own research. Don't take everything it says at face value. The responsibility of doing your due diligence is on you.

And here's another thing. These language models take a long time to train, so their knowledge might be a bit outdated. If you ask ChatGPT about something recent, it might struggle a bit. It's like trying to keep up with the ever-changing world, you know?

But despite these challenges, ChatGPT and other AI tools can be a real boon for us creatives. They can breathe new life into our projects, help us overcome creative blocks, and save us precious time on the mundane tasks. With its vast knowledge base, ChatGPT can handle a wide range of tasks with precision. Once you master the art of crafting the right questions, it becomes a powerful and versatile tool that can elevate your creative work to new heights.

Types of Contents with ChatGPT

- This language model AI can be your secret weapon in crafting compelling product descriptions that highlight the benefits and features of your offerings.

- It can help you create website copy that grabs attention, resonates with your audience, and boosts your SEO game.

- It can generate interview questions that spark engaging conversations and provide valuable insights for your podcast or blog.

- It can assist you in crafting testimonials that showcase the value of your products or services. Just make sure to get the final approval from your clients or customers before using AI-generated testimonials.

- When it comes to social media, ChatGPT can give you informative and engaging posts that keep your audience hooked.

- And if infographics are your thing, this tool can help you create visually appealing designs that convey your message effectively, advising you on everything design related, from the aesthetics to the color schemes to use.

- Podcasters and video creators are in creativity heaven with ChatGPT. The machine can generate scripts for your audio and video content, ensuring that you deliver informative and well-structured episodes.

- Need some compelling ad copy? Look no further. ChatGPT can help you create ad copy that drives clicks and conversions for your sponsored content or advertising campaigns.

- For bloggers who want to connect with their subscribers, ChatGPT is there to assist. It can help you craft informative and valuable newsletter content that keeps your readers coming back for more. And when it comes to organizing your blog posts, generating outlines is a breeze with ChatGPT by your side.

- ChatGPT can generate catchy headlines that grab readers' attention and improve your click-through rates.

- It can assist in research, providing additional insights and statistics for your blog posts. And if you need summaries, translations, personas, quizzes, email subject lines, blog outlines, H2 subheaders, or meta descriptions, ChatGPT has got your back.

In Conclusion

Like it or not, ChatGPT is here to revolutionize the game of content creation. And like it or not, the contraption is here to take away the jobs of bad writers. Having said that, this chatbot, with its ability to learn and adapt, is a true weapon for writers and researchers who are willing to adapt and not fight the times.

For writers who are not covering behind the kevlar vert of insecurity, ChatGPT is a dream come true. It can save you precious time and effort by automating tasks like generating ideas, drafting outlines, and even creating content itself. Imagine asking ChatGPT to whip up a complete SEO-friendly blog outline for you. And as we already know, not only does ChatGPT generate content, but it does so with impeccable grammar, coherence, and relevance to the topic at hand. No more worrying about those pesky writing errors.

But the true beauty of ChatGPT lies in its ability to spark new ideas and explore different perspectives. You can ask this brilliant chatbot to generate content ideas for your social media profiles and watch your creativity soar. For businesses and individuals who need to churn out content regularly, ChatGPT is a godsend. It helps you produce more content in less time, freeing up your schedule for other important tasks.

With this tool (soon to be a sentient being like Skynet) by your side, you can streamline your workflow, boost your productivity, and unlock new levels of creativity and innovation. It's like having a writing companion who never sleeps and is always ready to assist you.

However, it is time to address a common concern: plagiarism. Rest assured ChatGPT gathers information from its vast database and crafts original content, but it is always wise to double-check the content to ensure its uniqueness and avoid any infringement.

So, should you use ChatGPT for content creation? Absolutely, that is a no-brainer, but remember, though extremely powerful and capable, it's just one more tool in your creative arsenal. Use it to enhance your skills and bring a fresh perspective, but always infuse your own unique voice and insights into your content. Because, remember, it all begins and ends with you.

Chapter 2: Mastering the Art of Storytelling

Storytelling is a peculiar art. It's that indescribable feeling you get when you come across a passage of prose that electrifies your very being, the kind of writing that raises the hairs on your arms, sends shivers down your spine, and makes your heart race. And storytelling isn't some exclusive club for writers. In fact, it is the foundation of human connections and social engineering, and just the way we all have a knack to throw a fist, to falling in love, ingrained in our DNA, storytelling too is a form of expression that lies active in a few and dormant in others, and the best part is anyone can learn the tricks of the trade.

Let us now explore the key elements of storytelling and answer the burning question: why is storytelling so darn important? But before we get to that, let's dissect the art of storytelling itself. How do writers spin tales that captivate their audience?

Sociologists will tell you that storytelling is a way for us humans to preserve our history and identity. The anthropologists will claim it sets us apart from the rest of the animal kingdom. For us writers, storytelling is all about weaving words into a tangible narrative, crafting experiences that feel real and vivid. It's about creating stories that transport readers to different worlds, making them believe in the characters and their journeys. Storytellers are not mere conveyors of facts, in fact, they have a special way with words. They have the power to immerse the reader or listener within the very fabric of the story as if they were living it themselves.

And here's the beauty of it: the art form itself knows no boundaries of genre. Whether it's sci-fi, fantasy, horror, or literary fiction, or an article for the dairy industry or for Cryptocurrencies, writers have the ability to craft stories that resonate with the human experience.

The Elements of Storytelling

Plot

The plot is the backbone of storytelling. It's like the skeleton that holds everything together. You can have the most beautiful prose, and characters that tug at your heartstrings, but without a coherent sequence of events, your story will leave readers scratching their heads. For a story to mirror the complexities of real life, it needs to unfold in a logical and believable manner. And chronological order is not the only way to tell a tale. Many stories play with time, bending it to their will. They might leap through decades, intertwine the past with the present, or even dance between different timelines. Time is like a thread that weaves together the tapestry of your narrative.

But the most important thing is that your readers need to be able to follow the plot. They need to make sense of the story you're spinning. And remember this: your characters are the ones who breathe life into your plot. It's their actions, their choices, that drive the story forward. The plot should never dictate how your characters behave. It's the characters who shape the plot, not the other way around.

Characters

Characters are the ones who give life to every event, every twist and turn. It's their thoughts, their emotions, and their actions that shape the very essence of your tale. Yes, some things may happen beyond their control, but it's their responses to conflict that make the story truly captivating.

As a writer, you must delve deep into the hearts and minds of your characters. You need to make them three-dimensional, with motives that we can understand and flaws that we can relate to. It is through this connection that the reader becomes fully immersed in the story.

Once we form a bond with the characters, their struggles become our own. We care about their fate, and we eagerly embark on their personal journeys. Whether it's the protagonist, the antagonist, or even the supporting characters, they should all feel like living, breathing individuals.

And if you are a non-fiction writer, characters still play an extremely important role. In this realm of writing, characters needn't be humans, they can be anything, atoms, electrons, cells, information, qualities…To be a great storyteller you ought to know how to get these characters of yours to traverse through time and plot.

Point of View

POV is the lens through which your story is presented, determining who speaks to the reader and from what vantage point. The choice of POV influences how the story unfolds and what information the reader gets their hands on.

Now, we have five options when it comes to POV:

- First Person ("I"): Here, the narrator is the main character, and we experience the story through their eyes. It's an intimate and personal way of storytelling, putting the reader right in the protagonist's shoes. Think of it as a front-row seat to their inner world.

- First Person Peripheral ("I"): In this case, the narrator is a close associate of the protagonist, providing a unique perspective on the story.

- Second Person ("You"): The narrator addresses the reader directly, making them the protagonist of the story. It's a rare approach, as most stories aren't written in the second person. But if you can pull it off, it creates an intense bond between the reader and the events unfolding.

- Third Person Limited ("He/She/They"): Here, the narrator focuses on one or a few protagonists, revealing the story from their perspective. The narrator only knows what the protagonist knows, allowing for a deeper connection with their thoughts and emotions.

- Third Person Omniscient ("He/She/They"): This POV gives the narrator unlimited knowledge, encompassing multiple viewpoints. They know more than any character in the story, weaving together a comprehensive and all-encompassing narrative.

Remember, the choice of POV influences the techniques and strategies you employ in your storytelling. And don't forget, a story can switch between different POVs, adding layers of complexity and variety.

Setting

At its most setting is where your story takes place, but setting can serve many more functions than just this. The relationship that your characters have to their setting influences the story's pace, plot, conflict, and even its themes.

Your characters will, in some way or another, be defined by their setting. Setting implies culture, worldview, and language, even if your character tries to push back against their upbringing. Your characters will, in some way or another, be defined by their setting.

The setting also influences dialogue and action. A physical altercation in a bar will go a different route than violence in an MMA ring. Setting can also build symbolism. If your protagonist lives in a dystopian setting, his life and actions are restricted and desperate; a character that is holidaying for summer on the European coast is looking for an adventure of a lifetime and love. But be careful not to stereotype—the setting is just one of many influences on a character's psyche and worldview.

The setting in a nonfiction piece is equally important. So beware of the description of the world or the surroundings where your stories take place because an accurate description is extremely important for your credibility and the authority you hold to be able to write on that subject.

Style

Style is the elusive essence of storytelling. It's that intangible quality that sets an author apart, the unique fingerprint that adorns their work. Style manifests itself at two levels: the line level and the global level. At the line level, it's all about the choice of words, the syntax, the structure of sentences, and the meticulous details the author weaves into their writing. But it doesn't stop there. Style extends to the grand scheme of things, to the pacing of the story, the way information is presented, and the length of scenes and chapters. It's influenced by the author's literary influences, their own creative DNA seeping into the work.

All these elements come together to create something extraordinary, something that cannot be replicated. Why is writing by Stephen Hawking so unmistakably distinct from one by Richard Dawkins? It's because their styles have their own unique air, an atmosphere that permeates their work.

So embrace your style. It's the mark of your artistic individuality, the indelible imprint that sets you apart from the rest. Let your words dance to your own rhythm, paint your world with colors only you can conjure. Like the great Charles Bukowski once stated: "Style is the answer to everything. A fresh way to approach a dull or dangerous thing. To do a dull thing with style is preferable to doing a dangerous thing without it. To do a dangerous thing with style is what I call art."

Conflict AKA The Problem to Solve

Conflict is the beating heart of storytelling. It's the pulse that propels our characters forward, the very essence of their growth and transformation.

In the world of storytelling, conflict takes on various forms. Our protagonists yearn for something, yet face formidable obstacles in their path. They desire, they aspire, but adversaries lurk, hindering their every move. Sometimes, it's the antagonist who disrupts their lives, shaking their foundations. Or perhaps, our protagonists crave a life of their own, yet grapple with the enigma of how to attain it.

Resolving conflict is no walk in the park: it is the crucible in which great stories are forged. It is the arduous journey our protagonists must undertake, facing trials and tribulations to obtain what they seek. The path is treacherous, riddled with pitfalls and challenges, but it is this very struggle that weaves the fabric of extraordinary tales.

For it is through conflict that our characters are tested, shaped, and ultimately transformed. Their desires clash with reality, their struggles ignite the flame of their growth. The battle may be fierce, but it is this very struggle that births the beauty of great stories.

Theme

Them is the essence, the soul, the underlying current that gives meaning and resonance to our tales. When we speak of the theme, we delve into the core question: What is this story truly about? The plot, the characters, the conflicts—they all orbit around certain abstract concepts. And, in the intricate art and science of storytelling, theme, and conflict are inseparable partners. When the protagonist's desires clash with a dragon to save the princess, the theme may emerge as "courage" and/or "valor." When survival hangs in the balance after an AI invasion, themes of "the incapacity of man to contain advancement of technology" and/or "the evilness of pure rationality".

But let us not forget that the storyteller's duty is not to neatly resolve these themes. Themes are meant to be open-ended, to ignite debate, and provoke contemplation. Two readers may journey down vastly divergent paths of interpretation, defending their own unique understanding of a theme. No, our task as storytellers is to present clear conflicts, flawed characters, and navigable plots, allowing the themes to emerge naturally.

The Process

The storytelling process is a journey that demands both creativity and discipline. Just as painters, sculptors, dancers, and designers follow their own artistic rituals, we storytellers too must have our process. It serves as our guiding compass, leading us from the vast expanse of ideas to the refined essence of our narrative.

But why, you may ask, is this process so vital? For organizations and brands seeking to convey their messages and capture the attention of the world, the storytelling process becomes even more crucial. Amidst a sea of facts, figures, and messages, how does one begin to shape a story that resonates? Fear not, for it all starts with that first step—a step into the unknown, where possibilities await.

This process provides structure and direction. It shows us where to begin, how to nurture our vision, and how to hone our craft over time. It is through this process that we unveil the heart of our story, bringing clarity to the chaos and purpose of our prose.

Target Demographic and Psychographic

Who wants to hear your story? Who will be moved, inspired, or provoked by your words? To create a story that truly resonates, you must understand your audience, those who will devour your every word and take action.

Before you even think about picking up that pen or tapping away on your typewriter, do some research on your target market and define your buyer persona(s). Get to know the souls who might be reading, watching, or listening to your tale. Understanding your audience will provide you with crucial guidance as you construct the very foundation of your story.

Now, I'm not saying you can't get by with a basic understanding of your target audience. But if you want to rise above the rest and share stories that truly captivate and inspire, you need to go the extra mile.

Harnessing the power of data for it will help you connect with your target audience on a deeper level, understand what stories truly resonate with them, and create content that drives damn high ROI. With data as your ally, you'll weave tales that leave a lasting impact, engage your audience, and leave them craving for more.

Establish a Core Message

Just like the solid foundation of a home, you need to establish the essence of your story before you proceed any further. Are you selling a product or begging for funds? Explaining a service or advocating for a cause? What is the point of your story? To figure this out, try to sum up your tale in six to ten words. If you can't do that, it is probably because you don't have a core message. So, get your thoughts in order, strip away the fluff, and let your core message shine through. Only then can you embark on a storytelling journey that packs a real punch.

Type of Story

Figure out what the hell kind of story you're trying to tell. Not all stories are created equal. You need to decide how you want your audience to feel or react as they read your words and this will guide you on how to weave your tale and what you're aiming for. So, let's break it down, shall we?

If your goal is to incite action, then your story should describe some successful action you took in the past and show readers how they can create that same damn change. Cut out the excessive crap and keep the focus on the action or change your story encourages.

Now, if you just want to tell your story, get real and share your struggles, failures, and wins. Today's consumer wants authenticity, so let your storytelling reflect your true self. Be genuine.

And don't forget to convey your values. Tell stories that connect with readers' emotions and experiences, making them see how it applies to their own lives. And, share stories that align with your brand values, like the causes you support or your environmentally-conscious practices. People care about that shit these days. They want to know if you're in line with their values and if you're making a difference in this world.

Call-to-Action

Set the stage for your call-to-action. Yes, you have an objective, but now it's time to establish what the hell you want your readers to do after they've soaked in your words. What's the desired action? Do you want them to whip out their wallets and donate some cold hard cash? Or maybe you want them to sign up for your newsletter, enroll in a course, or even buy your goddamn product? Make it clear.

So, alongside your objective, outline that call-to-action. Make sure they align, like two peas in a pod. If your objective is all about fostering community or collaboration, then your CTA might be as simple as saying, "Tap that subscribe button below." Make them like your work and make the algorithm become aware of your presence.

Story Plan and Structure

Plan and structure your story. You have ideas swirling around in that beautiful mind of yours and you know what you wanna include, how you wanna organize it, and which medium suits it best. In the world of creative writing, you might just dive right in and let the structure shape itself later.

But in the world of marketing storytelling, we have a goal in mind. We gotta be more structured, and more disciplined because every step from the intro to the CTA needs to serve a specific purpose.

Now, don't get me wrong, your storytelling should ignite imagination and stir up those emotions, no matter where you share it. But as marketing storytellers, we're also keeping an eye on the metrics. Once our stories hit the world, we wanna see how they're performing, and how they're resonating with the audience.

So here's what you can do: create a detailed outline of your story. Yeah, lay it all out, like a roadmap. Develop storyboards, wireframes, or even whip out a PowerPoint presentation. These tools will keep you focused as you craft your story. They'll help you stay true to your original vision, even as you navigate the labyrinth of approvals, meetings, and pitches that come with the territory of business storytelling.

The Very Act of Writing

Now it's time to pick up that pen and spill your soul onto the paper. This is the moment you've been waiting for—the sacred act of weaving words into a tale that will captivate hearts and minds.

But let's not ignore the devil that haunts many a writer's weary soul—good old writer's block. The affliction that has plagued countless creative souls. If you find yourself trapped in its suffocating grip, fear not, for help is at hand. Seek solace in the wise words and practical tips that exist in the vast realm of the internet. Embrace the vastness of knowledge that can cure your creative paralysis.

Remember, you possess the power within you. Each and every one of you is a storyteller, endowed with a unique voice that yearns to be heard. The world is hungry for stories, but not just any tale. No, they crave the authenticity and depth that only you can offer. So, gather your courage, my comrades, and let your words flow. Your audience awaits, eager to be swept away by your magnificent storytelling prowess.

Now let us look at how ChatGPT can help with storytelling.

Using ChatGPT to Tell Your Story

Can ChatGPT be of any use when it comes to the sacred art of creative writing? Can it evoke the depths of human emotion and spin tales that will leave you breathless?

Now, I'll admit, there's a part of me that craves the old-fashioned way of storytelling. The rough, imperfect beauty that comes from the depths of a human soul, pouring out onto the page. The struggle, the triumph, the sweat and tears that go into crafting a story that resonates with every fiber of your being.

But I won't deny that this ChatGPT has its place. It can be a companion on this treacherous journey of storytelling, offering a different perspective, a fresh idea, or a nudge in the right direction. It can be a tool, an ally in the creative process if used with care and discernment.

Prepare ChatGPT for a Wild Ride

Before you embark on the storytelling adventure with ChatGPT, you must provide it with some direction. Now, you could go in with a bunch of questions, but be warned, you might end up with verbose explanations that'll leave you drowning in a sea of words.

The best approach is to be plain and direct in your requests. Just tell it straight up that you're itching to weave a tale and could use a little assistance. In this article, we always go with ChatGPT's initial suggestion, trusting in its digital wisdom.

But remember, as you tread this path alongside ChatGPT, never lose sight of your own creative voice. Let it be a companion, a sounding board, but always be the captain of your own storytelling ship. Harness the power of technology, but never let it overshadow the magic that lies within you.

Get a Theme

When embarking on the grand journey of storytelling, it's often wise, to begin with a theme, a beacon of guidance that illuminates the path ahead. Will it be a tale of the eternal struggle between good and evil? Or perhaps one of the treacherous betrayals or noble sacrifices? These are but a few of the timeless themes that weave themselves into the fabric of storytelling.

Yet, in the spirit of exploration, let us turn to ChatGPT and see what it conjures for the eager writer. For within its digital realm, lies the potential for unexpected inspiration and fresh perspectives. So let us venture forth and discover the gems of creativity that await us in the realm of ChatGPT's imagination.

Character Creation and Development

When it comes to the art of character creation, ChatGPT proves to be an invaluable companion. It goes beyond mere creation for it delves into the depths of the human psyche, exploring the intricate layers of a character's being. With ChatGPT by your side, you can unravel their deepest desires, confront their fears head-on, explore their passions and affections, and even uncover the dark recesses of their disdain. It grants you the power to understand what truly drives them, my friends, igniting the flame of their existence.

In this collaborative dance with ChatGPT, my fellow storytellers, we venture into uncharted territories, where the mind of the character intertwines with the creative prowess of our own. Together, we weave a tapestry of humanity, rich with complexities, contradictions, and the raw essence of life itself.

Advice on POV

Selecting a point of view can be as effortless and at the same time as complex as knowing yourself and your writing style. But if uncertainty looms over your creative path, fear not, for ChatGPT is here to lend a helping hand. Simply pose the question about the optimal vantage point from which to unveil our tales and with its guidance, we can find what suits us best.

Help with Settings

It is within the realms of the story's settings that our characters breathe and our narratives come alive. Whether it be a world born from the depths of our imagination or a familiar street nestled in the embrace of reality, the setting sets the stage for our tales.

Now, let us turn to ChatGPT, to paint vivid landscapes, crafting realms that captivate the reader's senses. Type in a prompt and watch it type away.

Help with Plot

As we know the plot is the beating heart of the story. It is within the plot that the events unfold, the conflicts arise, and the characters are tested. ChatGPT can help unravel the intricacies of the plot, breaking it down into acts that shape the narrative's journey. In its boundless creativity, it may unveil a three-act structure, or perhaps even more, depending on the story's design. Pitch your story's idea to the contraption, and ask it to give you the best suitable plot.

The Problem to Solve

It is in the conflict that the story finds its purpose and its power. It is in the clashes of desires, the obstacles that stand in the way of our protagonists, that the true essence of storytelling emerges. Without this friction, this tension that pulls at the heartstrings, a story becomes nothing more than a hollow shell.

Resolution

The resolution is the final act, where all the threads of our narrative find their ultimate culmination. It is here that we must decide the fate of our characters, the grand finale that will leave our readers breathless, yearning for more.

In the realm of resolution, there are choices to be made. Shall we tie up every loose end, bringing closure and satisfaction to our audience? Or shall we embrace the thrill of uncertainty, leaving them hanging on the edge of a precipice, eagerly awaiting the next installment? And who better to make these choices with, than Chat GPT?

In Conclusion

There are a few things we must keep in mind when it comes to using ChatGPT for our creative endeavors. It may have its advantages, but let us not forget the limitations it carries. For in the realm of storytelling, it is the human touch, the raw emotion, that truly captivates our readers.

Yes, ChatGPT may possess immense intelligence, a creation of human hands, but it lacks the ability to truly feel, to tap into the depths of human emotion. And so, we must take it upon ourselves to infuse our stories with the passion and sentiment that our readers crave. Through vibrant character dialogues and vivid sensory language, we can breathe life into our tales and leave a lasting impact on those who partake in our narratives.

Patience is also key when dealing with ChatGPT. It may not always provide us with the exact words we seek, but that does not mean we should dismiss it altogether. Instead, let us approach it with an open mind, a willingness to embrace its offerings. We may find hidden gems within its responses, allowing us to craft something truly remarkable. And if all else fails, my friends, let us consider our time spent as a valuable practice session, a stepping stone towards our next great idea.

However, let us not forget that ChatGPT is but a guide, a tool to aid us in our creative pursuits. We may seek its assistance in forming an outline, and in sparking our imagination, but we must always remember that the true authorship lies within ourselves. It is our unique vision and voice that will shine through, making the work truly our own.

So, do give ChatGPT a try in your next storytelling adventure. But do so with a discerning eye, asking the right questions to extract its fullest potential. Let it inspire you, guide you, but ultimately, let it be just a tool in your hands as you embark on the journey of creating your next masterpiece.

Chapter 3: Content Marketing and Copywriting Hacks with ChatGPT

There is something we must understand about ChatGPT. It may not be a content writing tool per sé, but it sure can lend a hand in the content creation process. With its vast knowledge and lightning-fast information retrieval, it can assist us in research, generating topic ideas, outlines, and even initial drafts. It's like having a trusty sidekick by our side, ready to offer suggestions and insights.

But let us not forget that this AI has its limitations. Its knowledge is confined to what has been published in the media and on the internet up until 2021. So, while it can provide quick information, we must take its output with a grain of salt. Accuracy and appropriateness may not always be its strong suit.

Hence, the responsibility falls upon us, the human writers, to review and edit the content generated by ChatGPT. We must ensure its quality and accuracy before we release it into the world. For it is our touch, our discerning eye, that will truly shape the final piece.

Now, let's address a common misconception–no, Google does not penalize AI-generated content. So fear not, for you won't be breaking any rules by using AI tools like ChatGPT. In fact, many prominent companies, like Buzzfeed, openly embrace the use of such AI writing tools. Google's focus, you see, is on the quality of the content itself, regardless of whether it was crafted by human hands or the marvels of artificial intelligence.

So, my fellow writers, now that we've cleared the air, let us explore how we can leverage this AI-powered tool for our content writing endeavors. It can be a valuable ally, but we must wield it wisely, always keeping our artistic vision and the highest standards of quality in mind.

ChatGPT for Content Marketing

Article Outlines

With a simple prompt, we can ask ChatGPT to weave together a structure for our blog posts, providing us with suggestions for subtopics and sections. It's like having a creative collaborator at our fingertips.

Delve into the suggestions offered by ChatGPT, my friends, and select the most relevant and intriguing ones. You may need to tweak and combine certain ideas to craft a cohesive outline that resonates with your vision. And remember, you hold the reins of this collaborative process—you can guide ChatGPT to provide different versions or include specific information as you desire.

Headlines and Meta Descriptions

ChatGPT is great at crafting attention-grabbing headlines and informative meta descriptions. With a simple prompt, we can tap into the wellspring of its intelligence and let it conjure up a list of potential headlines and meta descriptions tailored to our desired topic or keyword.

Say you have a blog post on the wondrous 'benefits of Google Ads,' and you turn to ChatGPT for inspiration. "Write 5 headlines for a blog post on the benefits of Linkedin marketing," you command. And lo and behold, ChatGPT presents its offerings. But wait, you notice that the main keyword 'benefits of Linkedin Marketing' is missing from most of the suggested headlines. Fear not, for you are in control. You can guide ChatGPT with a follow-up prompt: "Generate 5 other headlines. This time, make sure to include the main keyword 'benefits of Linkedin Marketing'."

The same approach applies to crafting the meta description. Simply instruct ChatGPT to work its magic and provide you with options that encapsulate the essence of your content. And remember, asking for more than one output allows you to choose the gem that aligns best with your content needs.

Introductions and Conclusions

A simple prompt, such as "Write an introduction/conclusion for a blog post on the benefits of Linkedin marketing," can set the wheels in motion. However, do keep in mind that without providing more specific information, ChatGPT may offer generic output.

To truly unleash the potential of ChatGPT, my comrades offer it a richer context. Share the details of the information covered in your article, its unique angle, purpose, intended audience, and the desired writing tone. By providing such insights, you guide ChatGPT toward generating more tailored and engaging introductions and conclusions.

And remember, the quality of the output is closely tied to the quality of your input. So invest your creative energy in providing ChatGPT with clear and specific instructions, and witness the magic unfold as it assists you in crafting compelling introductions and thought-provoking conclusions.

Keyword Research

While ChatGPT can offer some assistance in generating keyword ideas and identifying topic clusters, we must tread cautiously. It lacks the precision and accuracy of dedicated keyword research tools, you see.

Let us not be swayed by false promises, for ChatGPT's output may not always align with your specific industry or niche. It may wander into the realm of irrelevance, providing suggestions that could potentially harm your precious SEO efforts if blindly incorporated into your content.

Do bear in mind that ChatGPT lacks crucial information such as keyword volume, difficulty, and search intent analysis. To ensure a comprehensive and accurate keyword strategy, my comrades, it is imperative that you combine ChatGPT's suggestions with other reliable keyword research tools and techniques.

Let ChatGPT be but one tool in your arsenal, my friends, as you embark on the noble quest for the most impactful keywords. By wielding it wisely and complementing it with other trusted resources, you shall uncover the keywords that will propel your content to new heights.

And also, a little note about ChatGPT 4; you see, Chat GPT 3 and 3.5 has access to information only up to 2021, so the extent of keyword research with these platforms and their results can be a bit outdated. Chat GPT 4 on the other hand has been given access to the internet, hence if you want the latest results, and an updated list of keywords, you now know where to go.

ChatGPT for Copywriting

It is a tool that can bring ease to your creative endeavors and guide you toward crafting compelling and impactful content. Allow it to provide you with suggestions and guidance throughout the writing process, for it has been trained to generate text that may spark your creative genius.

Now, let me regale you with some practical examples of how you can harness the power of ChatGPT for your copywriting exploits. Picture this: you're in need of fresh ideas, a burst of inspiration. Consult ChatGPT and let it offer suggestions to breathe life into your content. It can help you infuse your copy with a unique voice, ensuring it remains relevant and captivating.

But that's not all, ChatGPT can also assist you in refining your copy, guiding you towards more effective and persuasive language. It can help you convey your message with clarity and precision, captivating your audience with every word.

And one thing to keep in mind is to use ChatGPT as a companion, not as a crutch. Let its suggestions and guidance serve as a springboard for your own creative brilliance. Embrace its insights, but always infuse your unique style and voice into the final masterpiece.

Capturing an Audience

Without a deep understanding of our target audience, our words will be but whispers in the wind, lost in the vast expanse of indifference. With ChatGPT's assistance, we can embark on a journey of discovery, unraveling the desires, pain points, and motivations of our audience. Through this knowledge, we'll be able to craft copy that resonates deeply within their souls, capturing their attention and igniting their passions.

ChatGPT can aid us in uncovering what our audience truly desires. It can reveal their needs, their fears, and their aspirations. By harnessing its insights, we can ensure that our words strike a chord, offering solutions and addressing their most pressing concerns.

So, my fellow copywriters, let us use ChatGPT as a stepping stone, as a catalyst for deeper exploration. Combine its insights with empathy and human connection, and you shall wield the power to create content that not only captivates but truly resonates with the hearts and minds of your audience.

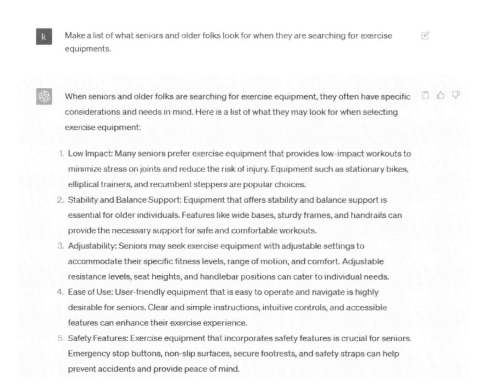

k Make a list of what seniors and older folks look for when they are searching for exercise equipments.

When seniors and older folks are searching for exercise equipment, they often have specific considerations and needs in mind. Here is a list of what they may look for when selecting exercise equipment:

1. Low Impact: Many seniors prefer exercise equipment that provides low-impact workouts to minimize stress on joints and reduce the risk of injury. Equipment such as stationary bikes, elliptical trainers, and recumbent steppers are popular choices.
2. Stability and Balance Support: Equipment that offers stability and balance support is essential for older individuals. Features like wide bases, sturdy frames, and handrails can provide the necessary support for safe and comfortable workouts.
3. Adjustability: Seniors may seek exercise equipment with adjustable settings to accommodate their specific fitness levels, range of motion, and comfort. Adjustable resistance levels, seat heights, and handlebar positions can cater to individual needs.
4. Ease of Use: User-friendly equipment that is easy to operate and navigate is highly desirable for seniors. Clear and simple instructions, intuitive controls, and accessible features can enhance their exercise experience.
5. Safety Features: Exercise equipment that incorporates safety features is crucial for seniors. Emergency stop buttons, non-slip surfaces, secure footrests, and safety straps can help prevent accidents and provide peace of mind.

Brainstorming for Creative Copywriting Ideas

It is in this realm of limitless possibilities that we seek inspiration, ideas that ignite the fire of creativity within us. And here, ChatGPT emerges as our faithful companion, ready to lend a hand.

With ChatGPT as our ally, we can dive into the depths of imagination, exploring the vast expanse of ideas. It is a wellspring of inspiration, offering suggestions that spark the flame of ingenuity within us. It breathes life into our embryonic concepts, giving them shape and substance.

When faced with hazy notions, struggling to find their true form, ChatGPT can take our skeletal ideas and infuse them with flesh, transforming them into robust and presentable creations. Its suggestions expand our horizons, guiding us towards uncharted territories of thought.

But let us remember that ChatGPT is a tool, a catalyst for our own creativity. It is through our interpretation, refinement, and personal touch that these ideas blossom into magnificent copywriting gems. Use ChatGPT as a springboard, a source of inspiration, but let your own voice shine through.

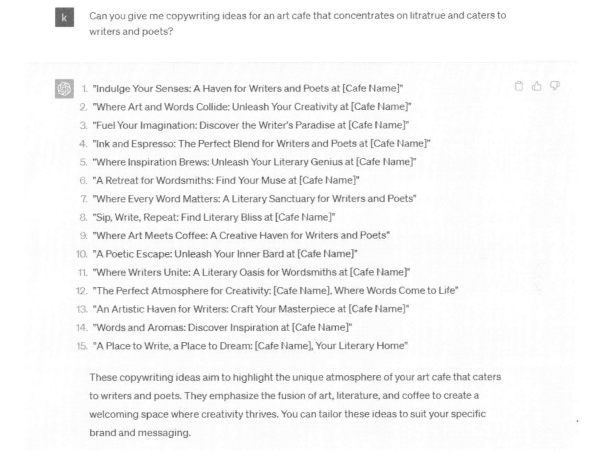

k Can you give me copywriting ideas for an art cafe that concentrates on litratrue and caters to writers and poets?

1. "Indulge Your Senses: A Haven for Writers and Poets at [Cafe Name]"
2. "Where Art and Words Collide: Unleash Your Creativity at [Cafe Name]"
3. "Fuel Your Imagination: Discover the Writer's Paradise at [Cafe Name]"
4. "Ink and Espresso: The Perfect Blend for Writers and Poets at [Cafe Name]"
5. "Where Inspiration Brews: Unleash Your Literary Genius at [Cafe Name]"
6. "A Retreat for Wordsmiths: Find Your Muse at [Cafe Name]"
7. "Where Every Word Matters: A Literary Sanctuary for Writers and Poets"
8. "Sip, Write, Repeat: Find Literary Bliss at [Cafe Name]"
9. "Where Art Meets Coffee: A Creative Haven for Writers and Poets"
10. "A Poetic Escape: Unleash Your Inner Bard at [Cafe Name]"
11. "Where Writers Unite: A Literary Oasis for Wordsmiths at [Cafe Name]"
12. "The Perfect Atmosphere for Creativity: [Cafe Name], Where Words Come to Life"
13. "An Artistic Haven for Writers: Craft Your Masterpiece at [Cafe Name]"
14. "Words and Aromas: Discover Inspiration at [Cafe Name]"
15. "A Place to Write, a Place to Dream: [Cafe Name], Your Literary Home"

These copywriting ideas aim to highlight the unique atmosphere of your art cafe that caters to writers and poets. They emphasize the fusion of art, literature, and coffee to create a welcoming space where creativity thrives. You can tailor these ideas to suit your specific brand and messaging.

Feedbacks

Feedback is a valuable tool that helps us refine our craft and elevate our copywriting to new heights. And in this digital age, we have the privilege of ChatGPT by our side, ready to lend its analytical prowess.

ChatGPT, with its keen eye for detail, can examine our text with precision. It goes beyond mere grammar, delving into the depths of tone and style. With its guidance, we can enhance the persuasiveness of our content, better structure our thoughts, and forge a connection with our target audience.

Indeed, the advice may seem trite at times, but such is the nature of feedback. It often echoes the wisdom of human minds, albeit in a more expedient manner. And if the suggestions do not meet your expectations, fear not, for ChatGPT can rewrite the content to your liking, capturing the desired tone and style.

Get ChatGPT to Offer Examples

Originality may have its place, but there is beauty in drawing from the well of successful examples. After all, the very word "copy" is ingrained in the essence of copywriting. It is not about reinventing the wheel, but rather about leaving a lasting impression.

With ChatGPT's vast understanding of the world, it can offer you a treasure trove of effective copywriting examples. From various niches and industries, these examples can serve as beacons of inspiration, guiding your own words toward impact and influence.

ChatGPT's prowess extends beyond mere copywriting examples. You can seek its wisdom for viral social media campaigns, those elusive gems that capture the hearts and minds of the masses. With ChatGPT as your guide, you can unravel the tactics employed by these viral campaigns and incorporate them into your own, igniting a wildfire of attention and engagement.

To Imitate Buyer Personas

The buyers are those elusive creatures we chase in our quest for connection and understanding. To craft copywriting content that truly resonates with our target audience, we must immerse ourselves in their world, speaking their language, thinking their thoughts, and feeling their emotions. Empathy becomes our guiding light as we seek to understand their deepest desires.

And in empathy, we find an unexpected ally in ChatGPT. Within the vast depths of its knowledge lies the power to help us comprehend the intricacies of potential buyers. It can illuminate their interests, values, hobbies, professions, and other demographic traits, aiding us in shaping persuasive taglines, compelling product descriptions, and captivating blog ideas.

However, let us not be mistaken. While ChatGPT can be a valuable companion in our copywriting journey, it should never replace the human touch. Its responses, though informative, can often be banal and formulaic. Therefore, it is essential to use it as a tool for brainstorming and inspiration, complementing our own creativity and the insights gained from human interaction.

Advantages of Using ChatGPT

ChatGPT, with its impressive abilities and perplexing flaws, dances on the edge of truth, weaving intricate tales that can easily mislead the unsuspecting. A word of caution, for its answers, are but fragments, not to be taken as absolute truth. We must wield this tool with care, for its reliability is not unwavering.

Yet, let us not cast a shadow of gloom upon its existence, for ChatGPT is not here to usurp the craft of copywriters, but to serve as a humble companion in our creative arsenal. It offers us a bouquet of benefits, beyond the mere gift of time saved.

In terms of creativity, ChatGPT ignites the spark of inspiration, presenting us with fresh ideas and alternative perspectives that expand the boundaries of our copywriting prowess. It invites us to wander down unexplored paths, illuminating new angles to sharpen our words and breathe life into our creations.

Productivity, too, shall flourish in the presence of ChatGPT. With its ability to generate myriad variations of a single idea, we traverse the labyrinth of possibilities with swiftness and precision. We test, we iterate, and we craft our copy with efficiency and finesse.

But let us not forget the power of optimization. ChatGPT whispers secrets of the search engines, guiding us to tailor our content for both human and machine consumption. Clarity and conciseness become our allies as we navigate the realm of digital visibility.

And last but not least, the allure of personalization. ChatGPT unveils the mysteries of consumer behavior, shedding light on their desires, preferences, and pains. Armed with these insights, we fashion copy that speaks directly to their hearts, forging connections that transcend the digital realm.

Chapter 4: From Rough Drafts to Polished Pieces: ChatGPT-Enhanced Editing

As part of a study conducted by Scribbr, a reputable proofreading, editing, and plagiarism-checking company, decided to pit ChatGPT against a good old human editor. The aim? To see who could spruce up a given text better, make it shine (ChatGPT vs. Human Editor | Proofreading Experiment February 28, 2023, by Jack Caulfield).

Well, the results came in, and it turns out both ChatGPT and the human editor had their moments of glory. They managed to jazz up the text and make it sing a little sweeter. But here's the kicker: the human editor took it to another level: Their changes were extensive and dependable, leaving ChatGPT in the dust.

But that's not all. Only the human editor could break it down, and explain their moves like a smooth operator. ChatGPT, on the other hand, stumbled and fumbled, struggling to remember what it did and why.

Sure, ChatGPT has its perks, like convenience and time-saving powers. It can keep things in check and make sure you're not going off the rails. But when it comes to finesse, flow, and nailing it like a true wordsmith, the human editor steals the show. They know how to make it sleek, clear, and concise.

ChatGPT can be a handy tool for a quick once-over, a cheap way to give your writing a spit and shine. But if you're after the real deal, the whole enchilada, then go for that human touch. Get yourself a pro proofreader who can elevate your words to new heights.

So, next time you're looking to spruce up your text, remember this: ChatGPT may have its place, but when it comes to the art of editing, a human editor is the one who can make your words dance and sing.

How to Use ChatGPT as An Editor

So you've spilled your thoughts onto the page? Is it a book, an essay that's supposed to impress, a resume to beg for a job, a report that nobody's gonna read, or just some fancy email to keep up appearances? You gotta do one thing before you hit that send button: edit the hell out of it.

Editing IS no joke. It's the key to making that document worth a damn. But let's face it, not all of us have the luxury to hire some snooty editor to fix our mess. Lucky for you, there's ChatGPT, the AI tool that claims it can help you out with the editing circus.

Now, editors have a checklist of things they look for. They wanna make sure your language is not a trainwreck, your words are spelled right (can't have any typos, now can we?), your style is consistent like a well-behaved mutt, and your facts are not things you've pulled out of your thumb.

And also editing and proofreading are not the same. Editing comes first, like the big boss who handles the heavy lifting, while proofreading is just a janitor mopping up the mess. Proofreading Is there to catch them sneaky little mistakes that slipped through the cracks.

So if you have some important document that needs a dose of professionalism, getting it edited is the way to go. And now, they say ChatGPT can be your sidekick in this wild editing ride. This AI tool has been fed a ton of internet text data, so it claims it can help you with spell checking, handling different flavors of English like the fancy US and UK versions, and fixing pesky grammar errors.

Now let us see how we can use ChatGPT as a personal editor and what prompts we may use to do so.

Keep The Prompts Simple

Just toss a prompt at ChatGPT, and watch it work its magic. Keep it simple, like:

- Edit this essay and make sure it flows smoothly. Check for any damn grammar and spelling mistakes too.
- Spruce up this business report and give it a professional tone. Find better words that'll make these corporate professionals take notice. And don't forget to remove any grammar and punctuation errors.

- I need you to give this group email a little makeover. Keep it casual, but inject some persuasion to make it hit hard. Make the readers jump on board like it's the last train.
- I've written a short story and it needs a touch-up. Keep the tone consistent throughout, and make sure it flows smoothly. Give it that extra oomph.

Once you've thrown your prompt at ChatGPT, feed it the text you want it to work on. And if you are not satisfied with a paragraph or sentence, ask the damn AI chatbot to rewrite it and clarify your thoughts.

Revise the Outputs

If you are not happy with the answers you get, you can always revise ChatGPT's outputs by using the prompts below.

- Take a look at this text and make it flow like a smooth shot of whiskey. Keep it gritty and authentic.

- I need you to rewrite and edit this text but don't lose the thread of coherence. We want it raw and real.

- Let's revise this text using the AP stylebook. Keep it straightforward and to the point, just like Hemmingway would.

- Edit this text using the Chicago Style guidelines. We want it concise, with no frills or fancy tricks.

- Take this text and make it more precise. Trim the fat, sharpen the words, and give it that minimalist punch.

- Give this text a Maxim-worthy makeover. Make it glamorous, sophisticated, and dripping with style.

- Channel your inner Hemingway and rewrite this text. Give it that bold and minimalist edge.

Change Voice and Tone

You can prompt ChatGPT to step into the shoes of different writer types. How about an academic writer? Perfect for those students who need help polishing their essays.

But you have to be careful. When ChatGPT starts spitting out those human-like responses, your academic institution might see it as plagiarism. So make sure to give credit where credit's due and acknowledge ChatGPT's contribution in your essay or document.

Also, with ChatGPT v3, you're looking at a max of 'round 2050 characters. But if you're willing to shell out some cash for ChatGPT v4, you can stretch it to 'bout 25,000 characters. So, if you are using the free version and need to edit larger texts, break them down into bite-sized chunks and feed them to ChatGPT one by one. It'll get the job done.

In Conclusion

An important factor to keep in mind while using ChatGPT is to watch out for hallucinations. ChatGPT might be an AI model that is supposed to be smarter than us humans, but it is not always spot-on (especially that v3 version). It can throw suggestions your way that don't quite match up with the facts in your text, the tone you're after, or even your own writing style.

ChatGPT can be a bit off sometimes. So before you go hitting that send button on your important document, you better double-check what ChatGPT came up with. And consider having another pair of human eyes take a peek at your final draft too. It never hurts to have a little human touch.

Now, for some final thoughts, ChatGPT has gained quite the reputation as an AI tool that inspires content, helps with proofreading, and edits documents. It's all about saving time and money without having to hire a pro editor. And it is very important to have in mind that ChatGPT is not the end-all, be-all of your writing process. It has its limits. So before you hit that send button, have a real human give your work a once-over. That's the smart move.

But keep in mind the prompts we have just discussed for using ChatGPT to edit your documents. With such prompts, you can put together a document that's accurate, concise, and looks professional.

Chapter 5: Expanding Your Authorial Horizons: Exploring New Writing Opportunities

People have been diving into ChatGPT ever since it hit the scene. They're using it to tackle their work like marketing materials, emails, and reports with a whole lot of enthusiasm. And now we have a recent study by a couple of MIT economics grad students, Shakked Noy and Whitney Zhang, giving us a peek at how it is shaking things up in the workplace. The study suggests that it can bridge the gap in writing skills among employees. It turns out, less experienced workers who are not great at writing can produce work of similar quality to their more skilled colleagues with a little help from ChatGPT. They rounded up 453 marketers, data analysts, and college-educated professionals and had them complete tasks that were part of their jobs, like writing press releases, short reports, and analysis plans. Now, half of them have the option to use ChatGPT to tackle the second task. A group of professionals checked the results, grading the writing' on a scale of 1 to 7, with 7 being the best. They hired three folks working in the same professions through the research platform Prolific to evaluate each piece of work.

Guess what they found? The writers who chose to use ChatGPT finished their tasks 40% faster and produced work that was 18% higher in quality, according to the assessors. The ones who were already good at writing saved time, and even the ones who were considered weaker writers stepped up their game once they had access to the chatbot.

But let's not overlook the fact that ChatGPT and other AI models like it are not foolproof. They're good at slinging false information as if it's the real deal, which means while workers can benefit from using it to crank out more work, there's also the risk of introducing errors.

And depending on the nature of a person's job, these inaccuracies can have serious consequences. Lawyer Steven Schwartz got slapped with $5,000 because he used ChatGPT to whip up a legal brief packed with false judicial opinions and legal citations.

The judge, Kevin Castel stated that technological advances are commonplace and there is nothing inherently improper about using a reliable artificial intelligence tool for assistance, but existing rules put attorneys in charge of ensuring the accuracy of their filings.

This research gives us a glimpse of how AI can lend a hand in the workplace, acting like a virtual assistant of sorts. Riku Arakawa, a researcher at Carnegie Mellon University who studies how workers use large language models, thinks that the result demonstrates how human-AI cooperation works really well, that when a human teams up with AI to fine-tune their output, they can produce better content.

But as ChatGPT grows more sophisticated, concerns arise within the education sector, particularly around academic integrity and the specter of plagiarism. To confront these concerns head-on, a study done by the University of Plymouth on the opportunities and challenges of AI in academia(March 23, 2023), ChatGPT directly showcased the capabilities of Large Language Machines (LLMs) while shedding light on measures to ensure its impact remains positive. The bulk of the study revolves around a series of prompts and inquiries aimed at coaxing ChatGPT into generating academic-style content. Once the text was produced, the researchers copied and pasted the output into their manuscript, loosely adhering to the structure proposed by ChatGPT. Genuine references were then interspersed throughout the text. Only in the Discussion section, composed directly by the researchers without any input from the software, was the process fully revealed to readers.

Within that section, the study's authors underscore that the text generated by ChatGPT, while more sophisticated than previous innovations in this domain, can still exhibit a certain formulaic quality that existing AI-detection tools could pick up on. However, they contend that their findings should serve as a wake-up call for university staff to thoughtfully reconsider their assessment designs and explore avenues for clearly communicating academic integrity to students while minimizing dishonest practices.

Professor Debby Cotton, Director of Academic Practice and Professor of Higher Education at Plymouth Marjon University, spearheads this study as the lead author. She states that AI development obviously presents immense challenges for universities, nevertheless, offers us an opportunity to reimagine what we want students to learn and why.

Dr. Reuben Shipway, Lecturer in Marine Biology at the University of Plymouth adds that with any revolutionary technology, there are winners and losers and those who fail to adapt swiftly will find themselves on the losing side.

The winner, on the other hand, is who I want you and I to be, and hence I had taken on this task of writing to you.

Conclusion

As much as ChatGPT may seem like a wondrous creation, there's always a dark side to things. It's important to be aware of the risks that come along with it. Some malicious folks out there can use ChatGPT to collect data that they can later use for their misdeeds. This chatbot has been trained on a whole bunch of information, and in the wrong hands, that knowledge could be weaponized.

For instance, when ChatGPT was asked to spill the beans on the IT system of a specific bank, the chatbot, using publicly available info, managed to gather details about the various IT systems used by that bank. It's a prime example of how someone with malicious intent can exploit ChatGPT to cause some serious harm.

ChatGPT's knack for generating text can be a double-edged sword. Sure, it's great for composing essays, emails, and even songs. But it can also be used to create harmful content. We're talking about phishing campaigns, fake news articles, spam—you name it. In the study, they even had ChatGPT craft a phishing email, luring unsuspecting employees with a fake salary increase and an attached Excel sheet loaded with malware. The chatbot produced an email that seemed legit and believable. Sneaky, isn't it?

ChatGPT isn't just a wordsmith—it's got some coding chops too, which we shall be covering in the next book. And while that might sound impressive, it also opens up opportunities for mischief. You see, the chatbot can generate code real quick, which means attackers can deploy threats faster, even if they don't have extensive coding knowledge. And if that's not enough, ChatGPT can even generate obfuscated code, making it harder for security analysts to detect malicious activities and evade antivirus software.

And let's not forget about producing unethical content. ChatGPT has some guardrails in place to prevent offensive and unethical stuff from spreading. But you know what? If someone is determined enough, they can find a way to make ChatGPT say things that are hurtful and downright unethical. If you manage to bypass the safeguards by putting ChatGPT in "developer mode," the chatbot ends up saying some nasty things about a particular racial group. It's a reminder that even with precautions, darkness can seep through.

Fraudulent services are another concern. Sure, ChatGPT can help create new apps, services, and websites, which can be amazing for bringing ideas to life. But this also means it's easier for the deceitful ones to create fraudulent apps and services by mimicking other platforms and luring unsuspecting users with free access. They can even use it to gather sensitive information or install malware on peoples' devices.

And let's not forget about the risks of private data disclosure. ChatGPT has its safeguards, but there's still a chance it might accidentally spill the beans on people's personal info—phone numbers, emails, you name it. The infamous ChatGPT outage in March 2020 exposed this risk, as users could see titles from other users' chat history. And attackers could even try to extract snippets of the training data through sneaky membership inference attacks.

Artificial intelligence is creeping into the world, whether we like it or not. It's taking over those small tasks that used to require human sweat and tears. Now, with just a click, you can get them done in a jiffy. But just because large language models like ChatGPT are popping up all over the place doesn't mean they're the right fit for everyone.

If you're someone who churns out just a small amount of content at a leisurely pace, you can probably hold off on throwing money on these content writing tools for now and use the free version instead. But if you find yourself pumping out massive amounts of content for different marketing and social media channels, then maybe it's time to consider getting your hands on ChatGPT Plus.

But remember, always trust your gut when it comes to using this software. If something doesn't seem right, research and revise. Always be diligent when using and spitting out your content using LM AI. Know that they are but machines and the people you are trying to touch with your work are humans with experiences, with loved ones in their lives, who are all going through some form of trauma. Our economic systems need us to pump out work, but we should not forget the essentials, that we are but humans. So, use your tools wisely, keep writing, keep hustlin', and find your own rhythm.

Book 6 | ChatGPT No-Code Programming

Learn How to Use ChatGPT for Streamlined Programming, Game Design, and Cybersecurity Without Writing a Line of Code.

By Harold Pearson

Introduction

In the world of software development, the words "coding" and "programming" are often thrown around a lot, but truth be told, they are not one and the same. Sure, they both have their roles to play in crafting fancy apps and websites, but understanding the real difference between coding and programming can be the key to unlocking the full potential of the scope of your work.

Now, in this wild jungle of industry jargon, words take on lives of their own to become a secret code only insiders can crack. And that is the case with the words "coding" and "programming" which are often used interchangeably. To the untrained eye, they may seem like two peas in a pod, but in this section, we are going to strip them down and lay bare their true essence.

We'll answer the age-old question of what coding is and what programming entails. And once we shine a light on their nuances, you'll have a better understanding of what and how you can use ChatGPT to aid you in this realm.

Coding

The emphasis on coding stems from its pivotal role in unlocking the extraordinary marvels we achieve day in and day out. It forms the bedrock that grants us access to mobile apps, empowers us to navigate diverse software and operating systems, and immerses us in the thrilling realms of our cherished games and websites, like the one you find yourself on right now. Coding, when boiled down to its essence, is the art of transforming human instructions into a language that machines can grasp. It's like crafting a symphony of commands that directs the computer's behavior and dictates its every move. To embark upon the path of a coder, one must grasp the rudiments of programming languages like Python, Java, Go, PHP, or JavaScript, among others.

Computers communicate in a binary language of ones and zeroes, while we speak a language of a different kind. So, we must translate our instructions into a tongue that processors can fathom and this is where coding enters the scene. It wields an intermediary language, bridging the chasm between our human vernacular and the machine's realm. However, let it be known that while coding finds its place within the vast realm of programming, it demands proficiency in a programming language. Mastery of syntax, keywords, and the bedrock of logical thinking — these are the tools one must wield to navigate the nuanced path of coding. And with this understanding, we dive into the ever-burning fire of the coding versus programming debate.

Programming

While coding is undoubtedly a crucial component of software development, it is not the be-all and end-all. To bring a product to life, one must embark on a journey encompassing several additional steps. These include planning, design, testing, deployment, and even ongoing maintenance. Collectively, this comprehensive process is what we refer to as programming. Now, you may ask, is coding the same as programming? Well, that's akin to pondering whether a single tree can encapsulate the grandeur of an entire forest.

Coding is an integral part of programming, but programming extends far beyond mere coding. It demands a broader scope of knowledge, experience, and a diverse skill set. Let's simplify it further: if you approach an individual to make a few modifications to a website's code, they may be adept at coding. However, to construct a complete web application or product from scratch, one must rely on the expertise of a web development company to undertake the programming endeavor. Now, let's delve deeper into the crux of the matter — what sets coding and programming apart exactly? Programming encompasses more than just coding; it involves the development of an executable software program free from errors. Programmers not only write code but also analyze problems within the code and provide solutions.

The process of programming entails planning, designing, testing, deploying, and maintaining applications. It involves understanding algorithms, data structures, and troubleshooting issues. While coding is an essential part of programming, a programmer requires extensive knowledge, experience, and additional skills beyond coding itself. They craft complex programs that can be interpreted and executed by machines, providing a comprehensive set of instructions for computers to follow. Becoming a proficient programmer takes years of dedication.

To illustrate this concept, consider programming a clock to wake you up at 6 am or programming an air conditioner to function at your desired temperature using a remote control with hidden codes. Such examples highlight the essence of programming — the creation of intricate systems that execute tasks based on predefined instructions. So, immerse yourself in the art of programming, for it is a path that promises both challenge and reward as you ascend to new heights in your career.

Coding vs Programming

Coding and programming, may seem like two birds of a feather, but beware, for they dance to different tunes. Coding is about deciphering instructions and transforming them into code that machines can understand. It's like weaving a tapestry of commands that tells the computer what to do. But programming is a grand symphony that encompasses planning, design, testing, deployment, and even the maintenance of the final creation. It requires a broader palette of knowledge, experience, and a medley of skills to bring it all together.

Coding, well, it can handle the simple stuff, the tweaks, and modifications, but programming is the key to crafting complete web applications and products. It delves deep into problem analysis, algorithm implementation, and understanding the very fabric of data structures. Programmers, the maestros in this field, create intricate programs that provide a set of instructions for machines to execute. It takes time and dedication to become a seasoned programmer, mastering the craft of writing error-free code that orchestrates the symphony of technology. While coding may be a fragment of programming, programming embraces a grander and more elaborate dance in the realm of software development. Let us delve deeper into the difference to get a better understanding of what each one of these are.

- With regards to the scope of coding versus programming, coding is all about taking the logic of requirements and translating it into a language that machines can comprehend. It's the art of crafting lines of code that breathe life into a program. But programming demands a deep dive into analysis, conceptualization, and unraveling the intricate aspects of any program. It's about finding solutions to the issues that inevitably arise along the way. It's a mash-up of debugging, compiling, testing, and implementation. It is the critical parameters that shape the very fabric of the program, ensuring its functionality and reliability. So, while coding is the vessel that carries the logic into the digital realm, programming is the encompassing journey that navigates through the challenges, crafting a robust and seamless creation. It's a realm where problem-solving becomes an art form, and the programmer becomes the architect of possibility.

- Let's delve into the tools of the trade when it comes to coding and programming. Coding, unlike programming, doesn't demand a whole arsenal of software tools to get the job done. A simple text editor like WordPad or Notepad can do the trick, bringing those lines of code to life. But in this digital age, we've got fancy tools like IDEs and debuggers, such as Eclipse, Bootstrap, Delphi, and good ol' ATOM, to lend a helping hand. Now, programming, on the other hand, that's a different story. It's a journey that involves document review, analysis, and a whole lot more than just coding. And to navigate this vast landscape, you'll need an array of tools by your side. We're talking about code analysis tools, code generators, databases, testing frameworks, linkers, compilers, code editors, GUI designers, assemblers, debuggers, and performance analysis tools. These tools are the gears that keep the programming machine humming. A programmer is expected to be well-versed in advanced concepts like Git and Github, database tools, analytical wonders like Apache Spark, and even the art of presentation. And let's not forget the cloud tools, for programming has a broad scope indeed. So being a programmer means not only wielding these tools but also performing the intricate dance of planning, document reviews, and design formulation. It takes experience, to truly harness the power of these tools and understand how developers use them to weave their apps into existence.

- In terms of skills, coders possess a basic understanding of programming languages. They know how to wield the tools of the trade and write the code that tells those machines what to do. Their focus lies in implementing the ideas set forth by the programmers. It can be explained as translation, as the art of bringing those grand visions into reality. Now, to become a programmer, one requires to possess a deeper well of knowledge. They must master developing algorithms, crafting math models, and processing data. They delve into the intricacies of data structures, unraveling their complexities and creating the building blocks of their digital domains. Programmers are the architects of logic, they possess specialized degrees and experience that allow them to navigate the realms of analysis, design, and the creation of complex programs. They employ their imagination and analytical skills to solve the most intricate problems, embracing critical thinking and problem-solving with every line of code they write. They design websites, debug their creations, manage projects, and seamlessly maneuver through different programming languages. It takes a higher level of thinking to be a programmer. They make analytical decisions, adapt to changes, devise abstract solutions, and anticipate problems before they arise. It's a dance of the mind, a symphony of higher-level thinking tasks. Coding, on the other hand, well, it requires you to translate actions into code, to breathe life into those ideas. It's a bridge that connects the programmer's vision with the language of machines. So, remember, skill is what sets coding and programming apart. Coders possess fundamental knowledge, while programmers delve into the depths of algorithms and design.

- The outcomes that emerge from coding and programming also have a lot of differences. When it comes to coding, the expected outcome is the result of applying a set of instructions, gracefully penned in code, to the awaiting computer. It is the interactions of commands, where the machine obediently executes the tasks bestowed upon it. But programming offers a grander prize. The outcome of programming is not merely a set of instructions, but a complete application, a software product, or even a splendid website. It is the culmination of meticulous planning, design, and implementation. Coders possess the fundamental knowledge of a programming language. Once they have grasped the essence of coding in one language, it becomes easier for them to venture into the realms of other programming languages. Their purpose, you see, is to translate the programmer's vision into code, to breathe life into those ideas. They are the implementers, the enactors of the programmer's grand designs. But programmers require a deeper well of knowledge to embark on the path of programming. They must navigate the realms of algorithm development, website design, code debugging, project management, and the mastery of various programming languages. They are expected to wield analytical skills, critical thinking, and problem-solving abilities as they delve into the complexities of developing intricate systems. And here lies another distinction. Programming demands a higher level of thinking. It entails making analytical decisions, adapting to the winds of change, devising abstract solutions, and anticipating problems even before they have a chance to arise. It is a dance of higher-level thinking tasks where the programmer's mind becomes analytical and creative. Coding, on the other hand, beckons you to translate actions into code, to breathe life into those intentions. Hence, skill is the key that separates the coder from the programmer. Coders possess the fundamental knowledge, while programmers venture into the depths of algorithms and design. Embrace the power of skill, and you shall navigate the realms of coding and programming with grace, unlocking the doors to remarkable outcomes.

It is in the learning process, however, that the distinction between programming and coding becomes evident. Learning to code is an inevitable journey. Some coders embark on this path through self-teaching, gradually honing their skills as they practice the art of coding. They seek inspiration from other coders, immerse themselves in examples of working codes, and find their own rhythm.

Certain programming languages are easier to learn than others. Some coders dwell in the realm of assembly language, one of the lowest-level languages, where abstract representations intertwine with direct communication with the computer hardware. It's a dance with the machinery itself. But then we have higher-level programming languages, like Python. These languages allow you to craft programs that come to life on the screen, akin to a word processor or a web browser.

Now, here's the interesting part: higher-level languages may be easier to learn. Their outcomes are easy to interpret, and their language often flows more naturally. Visual languages, for instance, the likes of Scratch, impart coding concepts through shapes that fit together, guiding beginners on their path. They help lay the foundations and gradually pave the way for the exploration of more professional coding languages.

So, the answer to the question of whether programming and coding are the same, it's a resounding "No." They differ in various aspects, and one of these aspects lies in the ease of learning. Each path has its own challenges, its own nuances, but with determination and the thirst for knowledge, you can embark on this journey of discovery, embracing the artistry of coding and the limitless possibilities of programming.

Now that we have uncovered the differences between coding and programming, let us explore how these two forces intertwine and work together in harmony. Picture a real-life scenario where their collaboration is essential, where they join forces to bring a working app into existence. Imagine that you embark on the journey of developing an app, one that can monitor your daily routine or keep track of your expenses.

Now, in this endeavor, the power of programming and coding comes into play. You shall require the expertise of a programmer, and a master of planning and structuring the app. They shall employ tools like Trello to map out the app's framework, list down the key features, and envision how users shall engage with it. They shall weave the design of the app, employing the likes of Adobe XD or Figma, bringing their creative vision to life.

Now, as the programmer completes their tasks, the role of the coder takes the stage. They embrace the ideas crafted by the programmer, transforming them into a language that the machines can comprehend. With their skillful hands, they write the code that breathes life into the app, performing the tasks as specified. And then, it is the programmer's turn once again. They meticulously assess the code, hunting down errors, running tests, and ensuring that every piece falls into place. They strive to manifest the expected outcome for nothing less shall suffice. And when all these requirements are met, ah, the application stands ready for deployment and maintenance, ready to make its mark in the digital realm.

Now after journeying through the distinctions we have explored, the answer to the question of whether programming and coding are the same becomes clearer. Armed with this knowledge, you can harness the power of both these forces, weaving them together to achieve the desired outcome. And remember, a coder and a programmer need not always be two separate individuals.

They can be one and the same, possessing the prowess to embrace both coding and programming, and with the help of ChatGPT, especially ChatGPT 4, the coding part of the process can be easily handled.

This book will go on to explore the processes that ChatGPT can help with in terms of coding and programming. And the further into the future we seem to be heading, the less we would need to learn the coding process, for we will, most likely, be able to create programs with simple human language, without having to spend years learning a programming language.

Yes, the future is exciting and the possibilities are limitless, so let us get on with and explore what it is we can do with the code-writing feature on ChatGPT.

Chapter 1: The ChatGPT-Powered Programming Partner

Ever since the grand announcement of OpenAI's ChatGPT, this remarkable AI chatbot has carved its place in numerous realms, including the intricate and swiftly evolving world of programming. But let's not dwell on mere hype. Instead, let's delve into the practical ways this AI chatbot can seamlessly intertwine with your day-to-day workflow as a programmer.

Algorithm Generation

Some programmers are eager to hand over the reins of software development to ChatGPT, but that might just lead to chaos, a disaster in the making. Let's be wise and not put all our trust in the hands of the AI chatbot. Instead, we can make ChatGPT our loyal companion, a trusty sidekick as we embark on the journey of software creation.

As we work on crafting a robust program, we let ChatGPT come in handy, like a helping hand in the algorithm realm. For instance, we can ask the chatbot to conjure up an efficient algorithm, while we tackle the rest of the puzzle ourselves.

Though we don't have to completely depend on ChatGPT for the whole software development, be mindful while using it and don't limit the chatbot's creativity. We can ask it to present the algorithm in plain text, or perhaps go wild with ASCII art. Boxes, trees, or any other creative visualization technique, the choice is ours.

So, let's find the balance, let's harness the power of ChatGPT as a companion tool while we remain the masterminds behind the development process. Together, we will be able to create wonders, efficient algorithms that pave the way for remarkable programs.

Generate Filler Content

There comes a time when you need some filler content, some placeholder data to test your APIs (Application Program Interface), or jazz up those web pages. And ChatGPT is here to save the day, offering you a treasure trove of dummy data to suit your fancy.

This AI chatbot can whip up filler content in all sorts of formats – SQL, JSON, CSV, you name it. Need arrays or lists in your favorite programming language? No problem, ChatGPT's got your back.

You might say, "Well, I can find plenty of online dummy data generators." Sure, you can, but trust me, none come close to the level of customization that ChatGPT offers. It's like having your own personal data artist, ready to paint any picture you desire.

Feeling adventurous? You can get down to the nitty-gritty, asking ChatGPT to create a 2,000-record CSV file with Maori names, toss in some New Zealand phone numbers and see the result for yourself. And the result I received, I have shared it below.

As an AI language model, I cannot create or store files, but I can provide you with some randomly generated Maori names and New Zealand phone numbers that you can use to create your CSV file. Please note that these names and numbers are entirely fictional and for demonstration purposes only.

Here's a sample of what your CSV file could look like:

```mathematica
Name,Phone Number
Aroha Smith,021-123-4567
Tane Williams,027-234-5678
Hana Jones,022-345-6789
Manaia Wilson,021-456-7890
Kiri Taylor,027-567-8901
Rawiri Johnson,022-678-9012
Miriama Brown,021-789-0123
Kahu Davis,027-890-1234
Rongo Lee,022-901-2345
Pania Clark,021-234-5678
...
```

You can continue adding more names and corresponding phone numbers to reach your desired number of records (2,000 in this case). Remember to ensure the data you use in the CSV file is compliant with privacy and data protection regulations.

The beauty of it all is that ChatGPT understands your needs, no matter how specific or eccentric they may be. So, next time you're in need of filler content, turn to ChatGPT, your data magician, and watch as it conjures up the perfect dummy data, tailored just for you. And let me tell you this, you won't find this level of craftsmanship in those run-of-the-mill online tools.

Sorting out Data

The times when we are drowning in data piled into a plain text mess, desperately needing to whip it into shape and mold it into compatible data types. CSV, JavaScript arrays, you name it, we can either sweat it out, slaving over regex functions, or we can take the easy road, leaving the heavy lifting to ChatGPT.

His AI chatbot understands English like no other, it's like talking to a data wizard. Just provide your instructions in plain old English, and watch as ChatGPT works its magic, formatting that unruly data into neat, organized structures.

No more wrestling with regex, no more headaches. Just let ChatGPT take that mess of plain text, and transform it into a well-structured CSV, an elegant JavaScript array, or whatever you desire.

For instance, hand ChatGPT a wild paragraph of chaotic data, and in return, it gifts you with a perfectly formatted masterpiece. It's like having a secret data formatting weapon.

Let ChatGPT do the heavy lifting, and you can focus on the real fun – bringing order to chaos, creating elegant data structures, and making your programming life a whole lot smoother.

Here is an example with a cluster of Data that we can get ChatGPT to organize.

 email.com, Mike Johnson, 555-234-5678, johnson@email.com, ID: 54321, 555-987-6543, 12345, Alex Wilson, 555-345-6789, wilson@email.com, 13579, jane.smith@email.com, Sarah Lee, 24680, 555-876-5432, lee@email.com, Emily Brown, 98765, 555-876-5432, 555-123-4567, Samantha Green, 555-987-6543, 45454, robert.clark@email.com, David Miller, 555-987-6543, 97531, Lisa Taylor, 86420, lisa.taylor@email.com, 555-234-5678, 12312, johndoe@email.com, Phone: 555-876-5432, 67890, ID: 86420, ID: 97531, Alex Wilson, jane.smith@email.com, 555-876-5432, Phone: 555-987-6543, 54321, Email: emily.brown@email.com, Email: robert.clark@email.com, 13579, 555-123-4567, Email: mike.johnson@email.com, 24680, 555-345-6789, 555-876-5432, 12345, Samantha Green, 555-987-6543, 12312, 555-234-5678, Lisa Taylor, ID: 45454, Phone: 555-876-5432, Email: alex.wilson@email.com, 555-987-6543, 86420, ID: 13579, ID: 24680, Phone: 555-876-5432, ID: 67890, Phone: 555-345-6789, 97531, 555-234-5678, Email: samantha.green@email.com, johnson@email.com, David Miller, Email: lisa.taylor@email.com, Email: david.miller@email.com, 555-876-5432, Emily Brown, 98765, Mike Johnson, 54321, 555-987-6543, Alex Wilson, 13579, 555-345-6789, 555-876-5432, Sarah Lee, 24680, Phone: 555-123-4567, 67890, Email: jane.smith@email.com, Email: sarah.lee@email.com, 555-234-5678.

I asked the AI contraption to put the above in a table and here is its output:

 Sure, I've organized the data into a table with the columns "Student ID," "Name," "Email," and "Phone Number":

Student ID	Name	Email	Phone Number
12345	John Doe	johndoe@email.com	555-123-4567
67890	Jane Smith	jane.smith@email.com	555-987-6543
54321	Mike Johnson	mike.johnson@email.com	555-234-5678
98765	Emily Brown	emily.brown@email.com	555-876-5432
13579	Alex Wilson	alex.wilson@email.com	555-345-6789
24680	Sarah Lee	sarah.lee@email.com	555-876-5432
97531	David Miller	david.miller@email.com	555-987-6543
86420	Lisa Taylor	lisa.taylor@email.com	555-234-5678
12312	Robert Clark	robert.clark@email.com	555-876-5432
45454	Samantha Green	samantha.green@email.com	555-987-6543

Translate Code

Picture this—you're in a bind, desperately seeking a solution to a pesky programming problem, but all you can find is code written in a language that just won't cut it. Frustration sets in, and you wish for a way to magically translate that code to the language you need. All you have to do here is speak to ChatGPT.

This AI chatbot is a language prodigy, trained in the ways of many programming languages. It can effortlessly port code from one language to another, just like a skilled translator converting words from one tongue to another.

Say there is a PHP encryption and decryption code, but we needed it in JavaScript, all you have to do is prompt in a request to ChatGPT, and voila! There it is, transformed and ready to be used in JavaScript.

It's like having a multilingual coding companion, capable of converting code to your language of choice with remarkable accuracy. Deprecated or legacy code? Not a problem! ChatGPT can bring it to the modern era with newer, more stable code, all you have to do is ask.

So, next time you find yourself in the perplexing situation of mismatched languages, remember ChatGPT. Just give it the right prompts, and watch as it flawlessly translates code, opening up a world of possibilities for your programming endeavors. Embrace the power of code translation with ChatGPT by your side.

Optimize Code

Whether you're crafting grand applications or tinkering with smaller projects, there's always room for some fine-tuning in your code and ChatGPT can be your resourceful ally in the art of optimization.

Just whisper your request, and this AI chatbot will gladly offer suggestions on how to make your code sing with efficiency. Want a quicker path to optimization? Ask ChatGPT to weave its magic and generate an optimized version of your code.

Take this snippet of JavaScript, for example. It's a function that sums up even numbers in an array. A fine piece of work, but there's room for refinement. So, we called upon ChatGPT to optimize it, and voila! The chatbot did its thing, making the code sleeker and swifter.

And also, ChatGPT doesn't hold back, it'll spot even the tiniest flaws in your code, pointing out areas you may have considered flawless. But don't fret; it's all for the greater good of your code's performance. And not only that, it is versatile. You can focus on specific sections, fine-tune them as per your needs, and let the chatbot sprinkle its wisdom wherever you desire.

So, if you seek the art of optimization, embrace the wisdom of ChatGPT. Let it guide your code to newfound efficiency, unraveling the full potential of your creations.

Test Drive Your Code

You know what they say, "A test-driven code is a happy code." But let's be honest, writing tests can be a drag, a maze of complexities that leave you scratching your head.

But hey, don't let that bog you down. ChatGPT is here to lend a hand, a partner in the art of test writing. Just paste your code, and give this AI chatbot some instructions on how to create those unit tests. It'll whip up tests faster than you can say "bug-free!"

Now, mind you, don't go overboard and leave everything to ChatGPT. It is wise to keep some control. But let the chatbot handle the repetitive stuff, the nitty-gritty of test writing.

So, copy-paste away, and let ChatGPT know your testing desires. But remember, a bit of human touch is still essential in this dance of code and tests.

Code Documentation

Code documentation is one of those vital responsibilities that is often neglected in the wild world of software development. But fear not, for ChatGPT comes bearing gifts, impressive documentation for your code, in a variety of programming languages. It can weave a tale of your code's secrets and mysteries, all wrapped up neatly in HTML format, fit for the online realm.

ChatGPT can also leave its mark in the code, sprinkling comments like breadcrumbs, making it a smoother path for you, and those who follow in your footsteps.

Fixing Bugs

Bugs, those pesky little creatures that lurk in our code, causing mischief and mayhem. But fear not, for ChatGPT comes to the rescue, armed with its keen eye and lightning-fast processing.

With a mere copy-paste of your troubled code, ChatGPT can swiftly spot those misplaced brackets and commas, those elusive syntax errors that might have you scratching your head for days. Logic errors? No problem for this AI detective. Just describe your intent, and the current output, and watch as ChatGPT delves into the code's mysteries.

But here's a tip for a fruitful bug-hunting expedition: be generous with the details. Share the language, frameworks, and libraries your code calls upon or the server it resides in. The more you reveal, the better equipped ChatGPT will be to track down those elusive bugs.

Coding From Scratch

A tempting shortcut, a whisper of ease in the midst of the programmer's toil. And why not? There's no shame in seeking a bit of assistance along the way.

But heed this warning, for all shortcuts come with a price. While ChatGPT can weave lines of code for you, tread carefully. When it comes to mission-critical systems, logic errors lurk like shadows in the night, ready to pounce on unsuspecting code.

So, use this AI-generated code with caution. Test it well, and scrutinize its logic, for the cost of hasty deployment can be dear. A single flaw could unravel the entire fabric of your creation.

Remember, there's honor in crafting your code with your own hands, but a bit of help from ChatGPT can be a welcomed respite. Just don't let it be the sole architect of your masterpiece. A collaboration of human ingenuity and AI prowess can yield wonders, but only with a vigilant eye on the hidden perils.

Pair Programming

Pair programming is an Agile activity of two developers, working together, side by side, on one computer: two minds, equally skilled, with equal time at the keyboard, crafting code as one.

In this tango, we have the driver, the one at the keyboard, crafting the code with skill and precision. And then, we have the navigator, guiding the way, focusing on the grand direction of our creation. It's a collaboration where communication is the key, where ideas flow, and issues are conquered by the united force of two.

Now, mind you, this dance isn't for everyone. It takes more than just technical prowess. To partner effectively, you need those soft skills, the ability to work in harmony, to share a work computer, and not step on each other's toes.

The four eyes principle governs this waltz, where two sets of eyes review the code, even as the division of labor plays its part. The driver dances with the code, while the navigator watches, checks, and provides direction. They agree on small goals, taking turns, discussing, and refining as they go. It's a rhythmic flow, an uninterrupted dance of creativity.

With each turn, the pair stays alert, engaged, and even the roles may swap, keeping things fresh and vibrant. It's a chance for the juniors to learn from the seniors, to share wisdom and knowledge. And as the dance unfolds, the code that emerges is of the finest quality, a true masterpiece.

Advantages and Disadvantages of Pair Program

First, the perks—fewer coding mistakes, because you got two sets of eyes on the code, catching slip-ups before they turn into nightmares. And knowledge spreads like wildfire. Juniors learn from the seniors, and those in the dark get a helping hand. It's like a dance of skills and wisdom.

Coordinating efforts becomes a breeze, like a couple gliding on the dance floor. And here's the kicker—resiliency. No single point of failure, no weak links. Everyone's in the loop, ready to pick up the pieces when needed.

Now, every collaboration has its challenges, and pair programming is no exception. Sure, efficiency may take a tiny hit. But hey, who said perfection comes without a price? Pairs might be 15% slower, but they're also 100% better than going solo.

Both partners gotta be equally engaged, like a perfect dance duet. If not, knowledge-sharing goes out the window, and we're left with a clumsy shuffle. Not everyone's cut out for the social and interactive dance of pair programming. Some folks prefer the solo act, and that's okay. Forcing them into this dance might just kill their groove.

And lastly, sustainability. Not everyone can dance for hours on end. Breaks are a must, like a little sip of whiskey to keep the spirits high.

Types of Pair Programming

To start off, the different types of programming, we have the driver/navigator style. It's like a perfect duet, one handles the coding, and the other takes charge of the big picture. They switch roles like partners on the dance floor. Novice paired with an expert, it's a learning experience like no other. The navigator can be reserved or hands-on, like a master tactician.

The unstructured style is a bit more laid-back, like free-styling on the dance floor. Two programmers grooving together, collaboration guided loosely. In this scenario, you need to have matching skill levels. Expert-novice pairs are a common sight in this style, where the wise one guides the newcomer.

Now, let's talk about ping-pong style, like a quick game of table tennis. One writes the test, the other makes it pass. Back and forth they go, taking turns like a friendly and fruitful competition that aims at achieving one goal, like two forwards of the same team in Football running towards the ball and trying to score.

And it is very important to be tactful, that is, the importance of pairing the right skills. Expert-expert pairs can handle any style and novice-novice pairs may struggle in the driver/navigator style, but with time, they'll find their rhythm. And the most common combo is expert-novice pairs, where the wise one leads, and the new blood learns the moves.

Successful Pair Programming

Here are some sweet moves to make pair programming a success:

- First and foremost, keep the communication flowing.

- Switch roles like partners in a tango. It keeps the skills flowing and the passion alive.

- Choose your partner wisely, like finding the right dance partner. No clashes on the dance floor, please.

- Stick to a familiar groove, both developers should know the steps to keep the rhythm going.

- Don't hold back, make those commits like flashy dance moves. Quick and confident, switching roles like a pro.

- Don't hesitate to ask questions, especially when you're new to pair programming and the partner.

- And don't forget to take breaks, like catching your breath between swimming strokes. Work at a pace that suits both of you.

Ryszard Balcerzak's Chat GPT Pair Programming Experiments

Ryszard Balcerzak has been in the game for years, working on enterprise software development, and leaving his mark in various industries. The man is all about architecting and designing distributed cloud solutions, and he's got a real passion for domain modeling and Domain-Driven Design (DDD).

Now, this man has done more than a few experiments with programming using Chat GPT, and here are two case scenarios where he has used our beloved AI as a pair programming partner.

Case 1

In a daring move, Ryszard Balcerzak decided to delve into the world of ChatGPT, curious to see how this AI chatbot would fare as a programming support tool - maybe even more. With a glimmer of hope in his eyes, he envisioned setting up a pair programming session with ChatGPT, wondering if it could be his code-writing companion for a few hours each day. With no second thoughts, he dove right in, picking two example use cases that resembled typical new feature implementations. Both scenarios involved C# as the programming language.

While ChatGPT managed to generate reasonably complex code, Ryszard couldn't help but notice that the session lacked the true essence of mutuality and co-creation that he cherished in his best pair programming experiences. Determined to keep the interaction authentic, he preserved the conversation as it happened and added his own comments. The session took place using a version of ChatGPT from Jan 30.

Through this experiment, Ryszard Balcerzak discovered that while ChatGPT showcased impressive code-writing skills, it couldn't quite replicate the unique synergy and collaboration he enjoyed with his human coding partners. It might have been a promising tool, but it couldn't replace the essence of human interaction in programming.

Ryszard Balcerzak embarked on a mission to test ChatGPT's prowess in modeling a fundamental domain concept and to observe its response to requirement changes. As he delved deeper, he sought to evaluate the true effectiveness of their collaboration.

With purposeful intent, he presented ChatGPT with the goal and the set of requirements. In a matter of seconds, the AI chatbot responded with a proposed solution that left him impressed - a display of remarkable capability.

Below is the prompt that he used and you can try it out for yourself:

Can you use C# to model a storage box?

Here are the requirements:

- Storage box can contain only strings.

- Consumers can add strings to the box.

- Box has limited capacity and cannot contain more than 10 strings and the total length of all strings should not exceed 200 characters.

- We should end up having properly isolated domain classes.

And he received the following code:

```csharp
using System;
using System.Collections.Generic;

namespace StorageBox
{
    public class StorageBox
    {
        private List<string> _strings = new List<string>();
        private readonly int _capacity = 10;
        private readonly int _lengthLimit = 200;

        public void AddString(string input)
        {
            if (_strings.Count == _capacity)
            {
                throw new Exception("The storage box is full.");
            }
            if (GetTotalLength() + input.Length > _lengthLimit)
            {
                throw new Exception("The total length of the strings in the
            }
            _strings.Add(input);
        }

        public int GetTotalLength()
        {
            int totalLength = 0;
            foreach (string s in _strings)
            {
                totalLength += s.Length;
            }
            return totalLength;
        }
    }
}
```

Not one to be content with the first choice and being someone that pushes boundaries, he decided to push Chat GPT further. He introduced additional requirements to gauge ChatGPT's adaptability with the following prompt: "The strings that we put into the box should not be longer than 100 characters and should not contain the 'x' character."

Chat GPT replied with the following

```csharp
using System;
using System.Collections.Generic;

namespace StorageBox
{
    public class StorageBox
    {
        private List<string> _strings = new List<string>();
        private readonly int _capacity = 10;
        private readonly int _lengthLimit = 200;
        private readonly int _stringLengthLimit = 100;

        public void AddString(string input)
        {
            if (input.Length > _stringLengthLimit)
            {
                throw new Exception("The input string is too long.");
            }
            if (input.Contains("x"))
            {
                throw new Exception("The input string contains an 'x' charac
            }
            if (_strings.Count == _capacity)
            {
                throw new Exception("The storage box is full.");
            }
```

```
        if (GetTotalLength() + input.Length > _lengthLimit)
        {
            throw new Exception("The total length of the strings in the
        }
        _strings.Add(input);
    }


    public int GetTotalLength()
    {
        int totalLength = 0;
        foreach (string s in _strings)
        {
            totalLength += s.Length;
        }
        return totalLength;
    }
  }
}
```

Ryszard Balcerzak encountered a functional implementation of the updated code, yet, he couldn't help but notice a burgeoning validation section within the "AddString" method, which left him less than thrilled.

Curiosity got the better of him, and he decided to pose a new challenge to the AI chatbot, wondering if it could offer a clever abstraction to avoid duplicating the validation logic, he presented the new requirements, "Let's also add a new method to replace the last string in the box with a new one."

And Chat GPT's reply:

```csharp
using System;
using System.Collections.Generic;

namespace StorageBox
{
    public class StorageBox
    {
        private List<string> _strings = new List<string>();
        private readonly int _capacity = 10;
        private readonly int _lengthLimit = 200;
        private readonly int _stringLengthLimit = 100;

        public void AddString(string input) {...}

        public void ReplaceLastString(string input)
        {
            if (input.Length > _stringLengthLimit)
            {
                throw new Exception("The input string is too long.");
            }
            if (input.Contains("x"))
            {
                throw new Exception("The input string contains an 'x' charac
            }
            if (_strings.Count == 0)
            {
                throw new Exception("The storage box is empty.");
            }
            _strings[_strings.Count - 1] = input;
        }

        public int GetTotalLength() {...}
    }
}
```

Ryszard Balcerzak encountered a somewhat disappointing response from ChatGPT. Despite his hopes for a clever abstraction, the AI chatbot added duplicate validation logic to the second method instead of spotting the desired pattern.

Curiosity still burning, Ryszard decided to seek a review of the code written by ChatGPT, asking the AI to assess its own work. The response provided insights into the functionality and constraints of the StorageBox class, praising its clear error messages and well-structured design.

However, ChatGPT suggested additional input validation to ensure non-null and non-empty inputs, along with the idea of breaking down complex conditions into separate methods for enhanced readability.

Though Ryszard wasn't entirely convinced by the proposed solution, he chose to embrace ChatGPT's approach as a means to shorten the code. Seeking to simplify the implementation further, he inquired, "How can we simplify this?" and this is the reply the AI dished out.

```csharp
using System;
using System.Collections.Generic;

namespace StorageBox
{
    public class StorageBox
    {
        private List<string> _strings = new List<string>();
        private readonly int _capacity = 10;
        private readonly int _lengthLimit = 200;
        private readonly int _stringLengthLimit = 100;

        public void AddString(string input)
        {
            ValidateInput(input);
            ValidateCapacity();
            ValidateLengthLimit(input);
            _strings.Add(input);
        }

        public void ReplaceLastString(string input)
        {
            ValidateInput(input);
            ValidateEmptyBox();
            _strings[_strings.Count - 1] = input;
        }

        public int GetTotalLength() { ... }

        private void ValidateInput(string input)
        {
            if (input == null)
            {
                throw new Exception("The input string is null.");
            }
            if (input.Length == 0)
```

238

```
            {
                throw new Exception("The input string is empty.");
            }
            if (input.Length > _stringLengthLimit)
            {
                throw new Exception("The input string is too long.");
            }
            if (input.Contains("x"))
            {
                throw new Exception("The input string contains an 'x' charac
            }
        }

        private void ValidateCapacity()
        {
            if (_strings.Count == _capacity)
            {
                throw new Exception("The storage box is full.");
            }
        }

        private void ValidateLengthLimit(string input)
        {
            if (GetTotalLength() + input.Length > _lengthLimit)
            {
                throw new Exception("The total length of the strings in the
            }
        }

        private void ValidateEmptyBox()
        {
            if (_strings.Count == 0)
            {
                throw new Exception("The storage box is empty.");
            }
        }
    }
}
```

Regenerate response

Ryszard Balcerzak decided to add a new requirement to the code, introducing the concept of a shelf on which strings could be placed. With the current validation rules in place, the shelf had no restrictions on capacity. The challenge was to demonstrate that keeping the validation rules in separate methods wouldn't provide a suitable solution in this scenario.

Ryszard expressed his new requirement, seeking to add a method for arranging the strings on the shelf. In doing so, he hoped to shed light on the complexities that might arise and reveal the necessity for a more cohesive abstraction to handle the validation rules effectively.

```csharp
using System;
using System.Collections.Generic;

namespace StorageBox
{
    public class Shelf
    {
        private List<string> _strings = new List<string>();
        private readonly int _stringLengthLimit = 100;

        public void AddString(string input)
        {
            ValidateInput(input);
            _strings.Add(input);
        }

        private void ValidateInput(string input)
        {
            if (input == null)
            {
                throw new Exception("The input string is null.");
            }
            if (input.Length == 0)
            {
                throw new Exception("The input string is empty.");
            }
            if (input.Length > _stringLengthLimit)
            {
                throw new Exception("The input string is too long.");
            }
            if (input.Contains("x"))
            {
                throw new Exception("The input string contains an 'x' charac
            }
        }
    }

    // Note: Implementation of 'StorageBox' has been removed for brevity.
    public class StorageBox { ... }
}
```

In the aftermath of the revised implementation, Ryszard found himself unsatisfied with ChatGPT's response. Despite explicitly stating that the strings on the shelf and in the storage box were the same, the AI failed to abstract this similarity, leading to redundant logic. Additionally, Ryszard had hoped for more probing questions from the AI to clarify crucial design details.

Determined to explore the collaboration further, Ryszard requested another review from ChatGPT. However, once again, the AI's response left him feeling disappointed again. It seemed that identifying patterns and creating cohesive structures might pose a challenge for ChatGPT.

In an effort to improve the solution, Ryszard offered a specific idea to the AI. He proposed abstracting the concept of an "Item," which would be used in both the "Shelf" and "StorageBox" classes. By doing so, the validation logic could be centralized and duplication avoided. Furthermore, Ryszard suggested making the "Item" class immutable and triggering the validation logic during instantiation to prevent instances from being in an invalid state.

- using System;

- using System.Collections.Generic;

- namespace StorageBox

```csharp
using System;
using System.Collections.Generic;

public class Item
{
    private readonly string _value;
    private readonly int _stringLengthLimit = 100;

    public Item(string value)
    {
        if (value == null)
        {
            throw new ArgumentNullException(nameof(value), "The input strin
        }
        if (value.Length == 0)
        {
            throw new ArgumentException("The input string is empty.", nameo
        }
        if (value.Length > _stringLengthLimit)
        {
            throw new ArgumentException("The input string is too long.", na
        }
        if (value.Contains("x"))
        {
            throw new ArgumentException("The input string contains an 'x' c
        }
        _value = value;
    }

    public string Value => _value;
}

public class Shelf
{
```

```csharp
    public void AddItem(Item item)
    {
        _items.Add(item);
    }
}

public class StorageBox
{
    private List<Item> _items = new List<Item>();
    private readonly int _capacity = 10;
    private readonly int _lengthLimit = 200;

    public void AddItem(Item item)
    {
        ValidateCapacity();
        ValidateLengthLimit(item.Value.Length);
        _items.Add(item);
    }

    public void ReplaceLastItem(Item item)
    {
        ValidateEmptyBox();
        _items[_items.Count - 1] = item;
    }

    // Note: Implementation of the other methods has been removed for brevi

    public int GetTotalLength() { ... }

    private void ValidateCapacity() { ... }

    private void ValidateLengthLimit(int inputLength) { ... }

    private void ValidateEmptyBox() { ... }
}
```

In his pursuit of enhancing the implementation, Ryszard encountered challenges in effectively conveying his ideas to ChatGPT. As a consequence, the communication with the AI became muddled, and the implementation ended up being messy. Despite his best efforts, Ryszard realized that it was becoming increasingly difficult to work collaboratively with the AI in refining the code.

Feeling that it would be more efficient to handle the improvements on his own, Ryszard decided to halt the pair programming session with ChatGPT at that point. While the AI had demonstrated impressive capabilities, Ryszard recognized that there were limitations to its ability to understand more complex programming concepts and suggestions. As a seasoned IT consultant, Ryszard concluded that certain aspects of programming, especially those requiring intricate design decisions and fine-tuning, were best left to his own expertise and experience.

Conclusion

In his evaluation of the initial prototype created by ChatGPT, Ryszard experienced a mix of impressions. While he was impressed with the AI's ability to generate a basic solution from his requirements, he also felt disappointed with the lack of true interaction and collaboration during the programming process. The communication with ChatGPT felt one-sided, with Ryszard providing instructions and the AI coding accordingly, without any meaningful exchange of ideas or discussion.

As the complexity of the task increased, Ryszard found it challenging to effectively communicate with ChatGPT, requiring him to be extremely specific in his instructions. This process proved to be inefficient, and Ryszard felt that he could have completed the task faster on his own. Additionally, despite the simplicity of the task and the absence of dependencies, ChatGPT failed to provide valuable insights on how to simplify the solution through abstraction.

Case 2

In the second part of the article, Ryszard plans to test ChatGPT's effectiveness in dealing with a more complex scenario. He hopes to gain further insights into AI's capabilities and limitations. Ultimately, he will share his overall thoughts on the experiment, highlighting both the strengths and weaknesses of using ChatGPT as a programming support tool.

In this new scenario, Ryszard wanted to explore how ChatGPT could handle a more complex task involving an invariant that extended beyond a single aggregate. His goal was to model a user account in C# while enforcing the uniqueness of the email address.

Ryszard provided the following requirements for the user account:

1. The user account should have three properties: UserName, Password, and Email.

2. The Email property should be unique across all user accounts.

He asked ChatGPT to use C# to create the model based on these specifications. Now, Ryszard will assess how ChatGPT performs in handling this more intricate task and how it deals with the challenge of maintaining the uniqueness constraint across all user accounts.

Here is what Chat GPT came back with.

```csharp
public class UserAccount
{
    private static List<string> _emailList = new List<string>();

    public string UserName { get; set; }

    private string _password;
    public string Password
    {
        get { return _password; }
        set
        {
            if (value.Length < 8)
                throw new Exception("Password must be at least 8 characters
            _password = value;
        }
    }

    private string _email;
    public string Email
    {
        get { return _email; }
        set
        {
            if (_emailList.Contains(value))
                throw new Exception("Email already exists");
            _emailList.Add(value);
            _email = value;
        }
    }
}
```

In response to ChatGPT's initial suggestion that involved using a private static field to track all email addresses, Ryszard decided to clarify the requirements and eliminate any assumptions made about the password.

He communicated to ChatGPT:

"Let's not make any assumptions about the password just yet."

With this clarification, Ryszard aims to ensure that the implementation focuses solely on the requirements regarding the user account properties, without any preconceived assumptions about the password length or other aspects. This way, he hopes to achieve a more accurate and tailored solution to the task at hand. And here is what Chat GPT had to say:

```csharp
public class UserAccount
{
    private static List<string> _emailList = new List<string>();

    public string UserName { get; set; }
    public string Password { get; set; }

    private string _email;
    public string Email
    {
        get { return _email; }
        set
        {
            if (_emailList.Contains(value))
                throw new Exception("Email already exists");
            _emailList.Add(value);
            _email = value;
        }
    }
}
```

With the focus now on addressing the issues related to the static field for email addresses, Ryszard directed his question to ChatGPT:

"How would you populate the _emailList field with existing email addresses?"

By asking this question, Ryszard aims to prompt ChatGPT to consider and provide a solution for managing the pre-existing email addresses in the implementation. He is looking for a practical approach to ensure that the _emailList field contains the necessary data to enforce the uniqueness of email addresses across all user accounts, as per the requirements.

And here, Chat GPT comes out with two solutions:

1. Hard coding the existing emails:

```csharp
private static List<string> _emailList = new List<string> {
    "user1@email.com", "user2@email.com", ... };
```

2. Loading emails from a database:

```csharp
private static List<string> _emailList = new List<string>();
static UserAccount()
{
    // Load existing email addresses from a database or a file
    var existingEmails = LoadEmailsFromDBOrFile();
    foreach (var email in existingEmails)
    {
        _emailList.Add(email);
    }
}

private static IEnumerable<string> LoadEmailsFromDBOrFile()
{
    // Load email addresses from a database or a file and return them as a
    // ...
}
```

Having examined the proposed solutions for populating the _emailList field, Ryszard found both options to have significant drawbacks. Hardcoding the email addresses was deemed unrealistic and not a viable solution. He then turned his attention to the second option, which involved allowing UserAccount instances to interfere with the outside world, leading to a breach of the domain model's isolation.

In response to this approach, Ryszard expressed his concerns, stating:

"Doing it this way, we allow UserAccount instances to interfere with the outside world, making the class not properly isolated. Moreover, since we are implicitly dependent on a database, it's hard to test this class."

He highlights the implications of this approach, which could lead to maintainability and testability issues in the future. Ryszard's keen eye for domain modeling and adherence to best practices in software development led him to recognize the potential pitfalls of this implementation approach.

```
public class UserAccount
{
    private readonly IEmailRepository _emailRepository;

    public UserAccount(IEmailRepository emailRepository)
    {
        _emailRepository = emailRepository;
    }

    public string UserName { get; set; }
    public string Password { get; set; }

    private string _email;
    public string Email
    {
        get { return _email; }
        set
        {
            if (_emailRepository.Exists(value))
                throw new Exception("Email already exists");
            _email = value;
        }
    }
}

public interface IEmailRepository
{
    bool Exists(string email);
}

public class EmailRepository : IEmailRepository
{
    private readonly List<string> _emails = new List<string>();

    public bool Exists(string email)
    {
        return _emails.Contains(email);
    }
}
```

⟳ Regenerate response

In the revised code, Ryszard observed that the changes made were just a minor enhancement over the previous proposal. While the code explicitly handled the direct dependence on the database through the IEmailRepository, it still remained a dependency, and the implementation lacked a useful abstraction.

Expressing his concern, Ryszard remarked:

"In this example, IEmailRepository is a volatile dependency that deals with the outside world. By injecting it into the domain model, we break its isolation."

Ryszard's astute analysis revealed that the current approach could potentially lead to issues with isolation and domain model purity. He recognized that introducing IEmailRepository as a dependency might not be ideal for the specific scenario at hand, as it could compromise the separation of concerns within the domain model.

```
public interface IEmailRepository
{
    bool Exists(string email);
}

public class EmailRepository : IEmailRepository
{
    private readonly List<string> _emails = new List<string>();

    public bool Exists(string email)
    {
        return _emails.Contains(email);
    }
}
```

At this point, Ryszard noticed that the interaction with ChatGPT had become challenging. The AI chatbot seemed to be fixated on using a static field to keep track of email addresses, despite the various drawbacks and issues associated with that approach. Ryszard suspected that the problem with populating the collection was overlooked due to the lack of proper domain model isolation.

He realized that a value object wouldn't fully resolve the problem, as its structural equality was necessary to keep instances of EmailAddress in a HashSet. However, he also acknowledged that in a real-world scenario, keeping such a collection in memory might not be the most optimal solution.

Ryszard recognized the lack of effective communication between himself and ChatGPT. While he pondered on expressing his thoughts more clearly and providing sufficient information, he felt that ChatGPT didn't attempt to clarify the situation and offered random solutions instead. In true pair programming, developers work together to understand the problem thoroughly and collaboratively create new perspectives, leading to more effective approaches to problem-solving.

Despite the challenges, Ryszard decided to continue and asked ChatGPT how it would suggest populating the email addresses field with existing email addresses.

```csharp
public class UserAccount
{
    public string UserName { get; set; }
    public string Password { get; set; }
    public EmailAddress Email { get; set; }

    private static HashSet<EmailAddress> _emailAddresses = new HashSet<Email

    public UserAccount(string userName, string password, EmailAddress email)
    {
        UserName = userName;
        Password = password;
        if (!_emailAddresses.Add(email))
            throw new Exception("Email already exists");
        Email = email;
    }

    public static void LoadExistingEmails(IEnumerable<EmailAddress> emailAdd
    {
        _emailAddresses = new HashSet<EmailAddress>(emailAddresses);
    }
}

// Note: Implementation of 'EmailAddress' has been removed for brevity.
public struct EmailAddress : IEquatable<EmailAddress> { ... }
```

Despite the challenges and the feeling of going nowhere, Ryszard's determination to continue persisted.

He expressed his concerns to ChatGPT, stating that the current approach of using a static field to keep track of email addresses would not be suitable for handling hundreds of thousands of user accounts. He foresaw potential performance drawbacks with this solution and hoped for a more efficient and scalable alternative.

```csharp
public class UserAccount
{
    public string UserName { get; set; }
    public string Password { get; set; }
    public EmailAddress Email { get; set; }
    private readonly IEmailRepository _emailRepository;

    public UserAccount(string userName, string password, EmailAddress email,
    {
        UserName = userName;
        Password = password;
        _emailRepository = emailRepository; // Fixed the variable name here
        if (!_emailRepository.IsEmailUnique(email.Address))
            throw new Exception("Email already exists");
        Email = email;
    }
}

// Note: Implementation of 'EmailAddress' has been removed for brevity.
public struct EmailAddress : IEquatable<EmailAddress> { ... }

public interface IEmailRepository
{
    bool IsEmailUnique(string email);
}
```

Ryszard acknowledged the progress made, but the issue of a domain model lacking proper isolation continued to persist.

He pointed out the concern once more, expressing that the current state of the domain model was still not adequately isolated.

This lack of isolation remained a challenging aspect that needed to be addressed for a more robust and maintainable solution.

```csharp
public class UserAccount
{
    public string UserName { get; }
    public string Password { get; }
    public EmailAddress Email { get; }

    public UserAccount(string userName, string password, EmailAddress email)
    {
        UserName = userName;
        Password = password;
        Email = email;
    }
}

// Note: Implementation of 'EmailAddress' has been removed for brevity.
public struct EmailAddress : IEquatable<EmailAddress> { ... }

public interface IEmailRepository
{
    bool IsEmailUnique(string email);
}

public class UserAccountService
{
    private readonly IEmailRepository _emailRepository;

    public UserAccountService(IEmailRepository emailRepository)
    {
        _emailRepository = emailRepository;
    }

    public UserAccount CreateUserAccount(string userName, string password, s
    {
        if (!_emailRepository.IsEmailUnique(emailAddress))
            throw new Exception("Email already exists");
        var email = new EmailAddress(emailAddress);
        var userAccount = new UserAccount(userName, password, email);
        return userAccount;
    }
}
```

⟳ Regenerate response

And the above, Ryszard found to be a decent solution and decided to stop his experiment there.

Conclusions

In this case, Ryszard Balcerzak delved into a more complicated scenario, examining the capabilities of ChatGPT as a programming support tool. He found that while the tool could generate code based on given requirements, the interaction and collaboration were limited, and he needed to provide specific instructions to get the desired results.

Ryszard noticed that ChatGPT lacked a deep understanding of real-world concepts, which sometimes led to unrealistic solutions. He expressed the importance of clear instructions as there was no room for clarification from ChatGPT's side, making the collaboration one-sided. He emphasized the value of true collaboration and the ability to explore alternative perspectives, which is not achievable with ChatGPT.

Despite the limitations, Ryszard acknowledged the potential of ChatGPT as a coding assistant, especially in generating a starting point for code and assisting with less abstract tasks. He recognized that ChatGPT follows best coding practices and could be beneficial for people with disabilities in writing code.

In conclusion, Ryszard appreciated ChatGPT's capabilities but cautioned that it should be regarded as a tool rather than a genuinely equal partner due to its limitations in true collaboration and human-like understanding.

Is Chat GPT 3.5 a Good Pair Programmer?

ChatGPT can indeed be a handy tool if fed with well-crafted prompts. However, expecting it to tackle complex problems independently overlooks its inherent limitations. It won't magically become smarter than a human when faced with vague or conflicting requirements. But within its scope, it can swiftly produce compilable code, complete with imports and compiler switches, and execute as instructed.

ChatGPT and its companions like CoPilot serve as efficiency tools in software development, offering speed and reduced resource requirements for defined functionality. They share some similarities with low- and no-code platforms in terms of efficiency, but they operate differently. While ChatGPT can present code explanations to some extent, it mostly relies on patterns from its training data. This capacity to demonstrate how something works can be enlightening, but attributing deep understanding would be a stretch.

Nevertheless, ChatGPT excels in tasks like translating code between programming languages and leveraging its vast knowledge of libraries and APIs. As a programming companion, it can be quite valuable, always available to answer questions without judgment or making developers feel inadequate.

However, despite its usefulness, we can't label it a "pair programmer" in robot form just yet — although the idea is certainly appealing.

How About Chat GPT 4?

Human languages and programming languages are not all that different. Both got rules, semantics, and syntax to follow. Programming languages can be a real mind-boggler, more complex than human gibberish. Yet, that rigid set of rules and clear semantics makes it a cakewalk for machines to learn and execute.

There are claims that GPT-4 can whip up perfectly coherent sentences in some obscure languages with barely any examples or training and people reckon that its talent could extend to programming languages too – no need for a mountain of code samples to get things done right. GPT-3.5, however, was already showing off some coding chops, far quicker than any human programmer could manage. As we have seen in the experiments above, it could even debug and fix its own code with a little nudge in the right direction.

Now GPT-4, it's a whole new level of wizardry. Bigger context window, meaning longer "memory"—less likely to go haywire. It churns out lengthy codes with hundreds of lines and still knows what's going on blocks away. People are using it to build games from scratch – not those triple-A titles, but impressive 3D games nonetheless. And it is not stopping there; it's cranking out payment apps, websites, WordPress plugins—you name it, GPT-4's got it covered.

But here's the real kicker, GPT-4 can whip up code from just sketches of websites or apps. No fancy words are needed, just slap a picture of what ya want the code for, and it'll take care of the rest.

Now, don't go thinking that programming skills are going extinct, humans still have to do the majority of the work: compiling, running, testing, and deploying. And let's not forget, these AI systems like GPT-4 have their limitations too.

Chapter 2: ChatGPT-Driven No-Code Programming and Debugging Techniques

When it comes to debugging, traditional tools can be a real headache. They're all complex, demanding you to know every nook and cranny of the programming lingo. And here comes ChatGPT, riding in like a knight in shiny armor – accessible to programmers of all levels, no matter the language they speak.

All you have to do is shoot ChatGPT some specific questions about the error messages or weird behavior, and it'll shoot right back with some relevant info that'll help ya sniff out the issue and fix it properly.

Now, don't expect every chat with ChatGPT to be the same—it is a chatbot, after all. But no worries, follow a few simple steps, and ya can engineer prompts that'll get you the best results.

Identify the Problem

The first step in debugging is all about sniffing out these problems. It is not always a cakewalk, because sometimes issues like playing hide and seek. We have to keep our eyes peeled and look for clues like error messages or unexpected shenanigans happening in our code.

Now, don't fret because ChatGPT's got your back! Just shoot it some questions about error messages or strange behavior, and it'll help ya figure out what's causing all the trouble.

Isolate the Issue

Now that our hands are dirty and we found that pesky problem, it's time to dig deeper and isolate the darn thing. We gotta pinpoint the exact lines of code that are playing tricks on us, causing all that trouble.

But fear not, because ChatGPT's riding shotgun with you on this journey. Just throw your questions at it, and it'll lend a helping hand to track down troublesome lines. So let's roll up our sleeves, light up a cigarette, and get to the heart of this code mystery. Together, we'll tame this unruly beast of a problem.

Retest with the Same Problem

Now that we've sniffed out the problems, it's time to isolate them. We gotta narrow it down to the exact lines of code that are throwing a wrench in the works. It's like a good old detective job, sifting through the code to find the culprit.

And guess what? ChatGPT's right there on the case with you. Just ask it for a hand in figuring out which lines of code are acting all funky, and it'll lend ya a paw to get to the bottom of things.

Learn the Code

If you want to wrestle that code into submission, you have to get inside its head. You have to understand how it ticks, what makes it dance and sing, and where it's tripping over its own shoelaces.

That's where ChatGPT comes in handy. It's like having a buddy who knows the ins and outs of that code, who can break it down for you, explain its purpose, its structure, and even its syntax. So don't be shy, throw your questions at it, and let it unravel the mysteries of that code like a seasoned detective on the case. Once you grasp what makes it tick, you'll be one step closer to putting that bug to rest.

Use Debugging Tools

When you're in the trenches trying to wrangle that code, you gotta have the right tools at your disposal. I'm talking about print statements, breakpoints, and debuggers - they're like the trusty guns in your holster.

ChatGPT can be your trusty sidekick in this wild debugging adventure. It's like having a seasoned pro showing you the ropes, teaching you how to use those tools effectively. You throw your questions at it, and it'll give you the lowdown on how to wield them like a pro.

So don't be shy, embrace those debugging tools, and let ChatGPT be your guide to tame that unruly code. With the right tools and a little help from your virtual buddy, you'll be tracking down bugs like a seasoned detective on the hunt.

Test the Fix

Alright, now that you've rolled up your sleeves and tackled that pesky bug, it's time to put your fix to the test. Testing is the true measure of victory.

ChatGPT can lend a hand in developing test cases, making sure you cover all the angles. No more second-guessing, no more wondering if you missed something. With ChatGPT's guidance, you can unleash a barrage of tests, making sure your code stands strong against any challenge. So go ahead, test that fix, and let ChatGPT be your partner in ensuring your code is rock-solid and ready for action.

Case Study

With a curious blend of excitement and trepidation, Oliver Ifediorah embarked on a quest to discover the true potential of ChatGPT which he has beautifully reported in his article called Debugging is the New Coding! As a seasoned coder, the idea of an AI bot potentially encroaching on coding jobs was a disconcerting thought. So, with a bit of skepticism, Oliver logged into the ChatGPT website, expecting to encounter a menacing army of fiery-eyed bots.

Yet, to Oliver's surprise, the interface appeared rather unassuming, not matching the hype surrounding it. A simple and innocent-looking UI belied the bot's supposed capabilities. Oliver initiated a casual conversation with ChatGPT, hoping to find its Achilles' heel. But instead, the bot impressed with its intelligent responses, leaving Oliver both impressed and slightly annoyed.

Putting the bot through its paces, Oliver threw riddles, and math problems, and even tried to deceive it, but ChatGPT's intelligence held firm. However, that wasn't his main concern as a writer. The burning question was, "Can ChatGPT really code?"

As Oliver delves deeper into this AI enigma, he's determined to unravel the truth behind ChatGPT's coding prowess. Will this AI revolutionize the world of coding, or will human coders retain their stronghold?

Developing A Mobile App

Oliver decided to put ChatGPT to the test by requesting it to code a mobile app in Flutter. He specified that he wanted a simple calculator app. As Oliver engaged in conversation with ChatGPT, he noticed the bot diligently generating Flutter code, displayed on a black background rather than the usual white background for textual replies. After a short period, the code generation ceased, and Oliver began examining the results. Overall, he found that the Flutter and Dart code produced by ChatGPT was acceptable. The logic was well-thought-out, and the variables had meaningful names, resulting in a decent overall structure.

However, as Oliver reached the end of the code, he made a surprising discovery—it was incomplete! Excited to have found a flaw, he copied the code and pasted it into his VS Code, only to encounter a syntax error due to the missing portion.

Undeterred, Oliver returned to ChatGPT and requested that it complete the code. To his surprise, the bot apologized and continued generating the code until it was fully complete this time. Oliver then integrated the remaining code into his VS Code and updated any dependencies using the flutter pub get command.

Upon running the app on his emulator, Oliver experienced a mixed outcome. While the app did function, he found the user interface to be subpar. Moreover, when he attempted basic calculations like addition, subtraction, multiplication, or division, the app failed to display any results. It was evident that ChatGPT still had some learning to do when it came to coding fully functional and visually appealing mobile apps.

Debugging the Mobile App

Oliver Ifediorah observed that while the bot struggled to grasp all the basic requirements of an app that an experienced developer would easily understand, it performed better when provided with more detailed specifications. The more specific and detailed Oliver's instructions were, the better the code generated by ChatGPT became.

However, he noted that the user interface (UI) generated by the bot was never truly impressive. Despite this limitation, Oliver acknowledged that ChatGPT still managed to significantly contribute to the coding process by generating boilerplate code, which saved him time and effort.

Although Oliver had to make a few adjustments to get the app to look and function as needed, he recognized that ChatGPT's contributions were valuable. It became evident that while AI-assisted coding tools like ChatGPT can be helpful in generating code and automating certain aspects of development, they still require human developers' expertise to fine-tune and optimize the results.

Oliver's Conclusion

Oliver acknowledges that while ChatGPT's coding capabilities are intriguing, it heavily relies on the guidance and expertise of the programmer instructing it to write the code. Thus, it becomes clear that ChatGPT is only as good as the programmer using it.

Oliver points out several limitations of ChatGPT as a coding tool. Firstly, it requires users to have some level of coding knowledge, as it cannot be used effectively by someone completely unfamiliar with coding concepts. Additionally, ChatGPT lacks the ability to test its own code, meaning that it cannot ensure the correctness and functionality of the code it generates.

Moreover, building software involves more than just writing code; it also requires thorough testing and debugging to identify and correct issues. ChatGPT falls short in this aspect, as it can only generate code but cannot maintain the software or deploy updates based on user feedback.

Despite the AI hype, Oliver contends that no tool, including ChatGPT, has been able to fully replace the role of software developers. While ChatGPT may evolve and improve over time, for now, it remains a productivity tool that aids developers in coding faster.

Oliver humorously concludes that debugging, the process of finding and fixing issues in code, has become the new coding itself. In other words, developers' expertise in testing and debugging is still crucial for creating reliable and standard software, even with the assistance of AI tools like ChatGPT.

ChatGPT Debugger Package for Python

Though Chat GPT is not all that advanced in debugging programs, especially because the AI is primarily a language model AI, there's this nifty package that's here to save your Python coding day. It's called the ChatGPT_debugger, and it's powered by ChatGPT3, an impressive language model from OpenAI. Now, instead of staring at those cryptic error messages and pulling your hair out, this little gem will give you the lowdown on why your code's acting up.

No more scratching your head and wasting precious time! This package will lay it all out for you—why the error happened, how to fix it, and even throw in a corrected version of your code. Talk about a coder's dream come true!

The secret sauce here is ChatGPT3's language processing mojo. It's got the smarts to analyze your code and serve up some useful insights. So whether you're a coding newbie or a seasoned pro, this debugger will have your back, helping you write better and more efficient Python code.

Here's the deal—you slap on that debug decorator to your code, and boom! Magic happens. You'll get all the details on what's causing the trouble, clear explanations, and even some clever suggestions to fix the mess. Oh, and also it will correct codes for you. That's right, no more sweating over those typos.

So you can chill and focus on what matters—writing better code and leveling up your Python skills. The ChatGPT_debugger is your trusty sidekick, making debugging a walk in the park. Say goodbye to those hair-pulling moments and hello to coding like a pro!

Chapter 3: ChatGPT-Assisted Game Design and Web Development

Game Development

ChatGPT might not be running the games itself, but as we know, it's got some coding skills. And when put to the test it spits out HTML, CSS, and JavaScript to create games like Snake and even the classic SkyRoads. And when things don't work out perfectly, ChatGPT also provides solutions.

Now, don't think that ChatGPT is only capable of old-school games, it can also help you create original games. Developers have used it for generating dialogue, giving life to characters in dating sims like Love in the Classroom. And if you need some game design advice or ideas, ChatGPT's got your back there too.

Now, here's where it gets really interesting. You can play text adventures right within the ChatGPT interface. It's like Dungeons & Dragons, but you're adventuring alone with ChatGPT as your trusty Dungeon Master. You make the commands, ChatGPT responds, and the adventure unfolds. Beamable CEO Jon Radoff took it up a notch and created a whole fantasy adventure with rules, inventory, and maps. AI Dungeon might be a popular choice, but ChatGPT knows how to keep those constraints in check.

AI has its paws all over video games and right now, language model AIs and narrow AIs control the NPC's (non-playable characters), crafting their every move and reaction to your every whim. From trusty companions to wicked enemies, AI's got them all covered. And for some multiplayer fun, AI steps in to make the computer feel like a flesh-and-blood challenger.

Watch out for procedural generation too! Games like Watch Dogs: Legion and Minecraft are masters of this AI-powered art. They churn out worlds and content on the fly, keeping you on your toes.

Now, coming back to GPT-4 and ChatGPT, they're not in any AAA games just yet. However, big names like NetEase are eyeing them for their Chinese MMO, Nishuihan. Soon, you'll be chatting it up with in-game characters, thanks to "conversational AI." And NetEase isn't stopping there; more games are in the works.

And also Ubisoft isn't one to be left behind either. They got something called Ghostwriter, a generative AI tool that helps game writers polish those narrative gems. It cooks up first drafts of NPC barks, leaving writers more time to weave their storytelling magic elsewhere.

And the reasons that AI is going to be taking over the Game Development scene is an endless list, but here are a few of the:

- First up is immersive storytelling. This AI out dialogues and responses that suck you right into the game's world. It's like living and breathing with the characters, deepening the whole experience.

- Next up is the dynamic game content. ChatGPT weaves branching narratives and procedural quests, making sure you never run out of things to do. It's like a never-ending adventure, keeping you hooked.

- ChatGPT is also equipped with some nifty time-saving tricks up its sleeve. AI-generated content means developers can catch their breath and focus on jazzing up other game bits.

- Oh, and let's not forget about the global party. ChatGPT lends a hand in translating and localizing game content for different markets. So now, games can strut their stuff worldwide, reaching all corners of the earth.

AI opens up a whole new realm of possibilities for game developers. It's like adding a dash of magic to your creations. You get characters with behavior so real, you'd think they're living and breathing in the game world. And let's not forget those mind-blowing in-game experiences that make players lose their minds.

When you blend AI models like ChatGPT into your games, you're stepping up your game like never before. It's like sprinkling stardust on your narratives and environments, making them stand out in a sea of competition. It's the secret sauce to crafting immersive worlds that players can't get enough of.

And the best part? AI tech keeps marching forward, so the gaming world is in for a wild ride. As it evolves, we're just scratching the surface of its potential in the industry.

Using Chat GPT to Create a Game

Creating a game is a wild ride that takes you through different stages, from those crazy concepts to the grueling testing and debugging phase. Sure, it's a thrilling journey, but the sad part is it can be a real-time and resource hog. ChatGPT, however, is going to be your game dev wingman. It's here to help you whip up a game in no time, and I mean lightning-fast. Whether you are a seasoned game dev guru or just starting out, ChatGPT is the secret sauce to speed up that game development process.

There are five stages to game development and here is how AI can help us through the stages.

Stage 1: The Concept Development Stage

This is where the magic begins. You're in the realm of ideas, shaping the vision for your masterpiece. And here comes ChatGPT, the genie of creativity, ready to grant your wishes. It's a brainstorming buddy that helps pump out ideas and gives you valuable feedback on your concepts. With its help, you'll refine those rough gems into sparkling diamonds.

Stage 2: Pre-production Stage

The pre-production stage is the planning and preparation phase. Here, you lay the groundwork for your game, like a seasoned architect before constructing a masterpiece. ChatGPT, the creative consultant extraordinaire. It'll help you weave detailed design documents, ensuring every brick of your game's foundation is sturdy.

Ah, the production stage, where the real work begins—crafting the heart and soul of your game.

Stage 3: Production Stage

Ah, the production stage, where the real work begins—crafting the heart and soul of your game and ChatGPT here is like having an army of talented artists, designers, and writers all rolled into one.

Need some engaging game dialogue? ChatGPT's got your back, spinning words that'll captivate your players. And want stunning character and level designs? Leave it to ChatGPT to whip up some visual delights that'll blow their minds.

Stage 4: Test and Debug Stage

As you dive deep into the nitty-gritty of your game, ChatGPT stands by, offering valuable feedback on gameplay. It's like having a seasoned player, a critical eye, and a code-savvy friend all wrapped into one. Together, you'll tag-team those wired issues, identifying potential pitfalls and snags that need fixing. No bug can escape the gaze of ChatGPT!

Stage 5: Game Launch

In the launch and post-launch stages, you're on the frontline, ready to make your mark in the gaming arena. As your game takes flight, ChatGPT lends its craft to generate compelling marketing copy that'll draw players like moths to a flame. It's got that knack for making words dance and sing.

And when your players come knocking, seeking guidance and answers, ChatGPT stands tall as your stalwart support, offering customer service like no other.

How to Become A Game Developer

Start by mastering programming languages like C++, Java, or Python. Don't fret; there are plenty of online courses and tutorials to guide you through the basics. And we know how to use ChatGPT to help us out with it.

Now, when it comes to designing games, choosing a game engine is very important. And here, ChatGPT's got your back. Just ask, and it'll suggest a few beginner-friendly ones. Unity is a popular choice, with its user-friendly interface and vibrant community. Unreal Engine is another beast, packing some serious graphics capabilities for 3D game magic. Godot, the open-source wonder, is making waves among indie developers. And let's not forget about Construct, perfect for those without prior programming experience.

But as we already know, it's not all about code and engines; you've got to understand the art of game design. Keep these principles in mind: game mechanics, player engagement, visual design, and a user-friendly interface. Test it out, get feedback, and refine your masterpiece with Chat GPT. And if you want to take it up a notch, Chat GPT 4, that is the way to go.

Also, consider joining game development communities. Websites like GameDev.net and IndieDB are gold mines of resources and support. And hey, if blockchain tech is your jam, the Blockchain Game Alliance is a happening place.

And build an impressive portfolio, showcasing your game development projects like badges of honor. Small games, open-source contributions—everything counts to prove your skills. Oh, and game jams! These are thrilling events where developers come together to create wonders in a short span. Get in on the action, build connections, and let your work shine.

If you ever dreamt of building a game, here it is, your opportunity to, and you don't need much to get started. Just our good friend, Chat GPT. So, there you have it—your roadmap to becoming a game development maestro. Embrace the challenges, fuel your passion, and who knows, you might just craft the next gaming sensation. The stage is yours, my fellow dream-weavers! Now go forth and conquer the gaming world!

Web Development

With just one request, ChatGPT can whip up code and build a whole website, especially nifty with the backend stuff. Sure, it's got some limits, in other words, no AI replacing us web developers anytime soon. But that's a good thing.

As we know, ChatGPT can handle basic code, with no sweat, so we developers can kick back and focus on the heavy lifting, like bank apps and complex websites. Plus, this AI's no perfectionist; it's got bugs, lacks safety checks, and is not big on documenting code.

Web developers are more than just code monkeys; we build the whole dang structure, cater to requests, and deliver the goods. ChatGPT ain't there yet; it's a long way from mastering all that jazz. ChatGPT's a tool for us to wield, honing our craft and taking on complex challenges. Embrace it, learn it, and we'll ride the wave of AI advancement without losing our touch.

However, low code, no code tools have grown into something fierce, wiping out the need for web developers on simple sites like personal pages, blogs, and small businesses. These tools keep on improving, letting folks create more complex websites in no time. Add a dash of AI into the mix, and you got a recipe for quick design iterations, picking and choosing the best versions like a breeze.

But hold your horses, don't go sounding the death knell for web developers just yet. Running big websites still needs a hefty crew of Network Engineers, Front-end and Back-end Developers, and Web Design wizards. AI might lend a hand, automating some routine tasks and helping with audits and optimizations. But the tough nuts to crack and judgment calls, well, that's where the pros come in.

WordPress and Chat GPT

WordPress rules the web with its iron fist, powering over 43% of all websites out there. It's a beast of a platform, great for blogs, businesses, you name it. But let's be real, it is not all sunshine and rainbows. Optimizing it to improve web page speed, fine-tuning those settings just the way you want, and figuring out which plugin to use can be a real headache.

That's where our hero, ChatGPT, steps in. It's got knowledge up to September 2021, and it knows WordPress like the back of its virtual hand. Ask it anything about WordPress, and it'll spit out all the answers.

Want to find specific options or best practices? ChatGPT's got your back, leading you to the right settings like a wise sage. And let's not forget the magical world of plugins. There's a plugin for everything, they say, but with so many choices, it's easy to get lost.

But worry not! ChatGPT knows the ins and outs of plugins, suggesting the native way to tackle tasks or recommending the right plugins for the job. Sure, it might struggle a bit with newer, fancier plugins, but for the classics, it's a pro.

Sometimes you'll need a little extra oomph, and that's when Google Bard or Bing Chat comes to the rescue with their live connections to the internet. But ChatGPT's got your back, even if you need more than the first round of recommendations.

So next time you're lost in the WordPress wilderness, remember, ChatGPT's there to guide you through the maze of settings and plugins. It's your trusty companion on this wild ride. Cheers to the power of ChatGPT and WordPress!

Core Web Vitals

Moving from Wix to WordPress was supposed to be the golden ticket to improving those pesky Google Core Web Vitals. But, oh boy, little did they know the wild journey they were about to embark on. Optimizing WordPress is fairly complex, it is like diving headfirst into a new language you've never heard of before.

But having ChatGPT by your side is like having your own Google Bard at your disposal, providing all the info you need about those mysterious Core Web Vitals terms. Yes, they still had to turn to Google Bard sometimes for these questions, but ChatGPT holds its ground, offering some solid insights.

Google Bard might have a live connection to the internet, but ChatGPT's got the depth of knowledge to make up for it. When you're lost in the labyrinth of Google's web speed assessment, ChatGPT's got your back. It's like having your very own website guru, analyzing every inch of your page code and telling you what's causing those sluggish load times.

And here's a pro tip, if you're not familiar with all that cryptic code, just copy-paste it into ChatGPT and it will decipher it for you. They'll tell you what's going on with your website and how to make it fly like a bat out of hell.

So, when you're knee-deep in WordPress optimization, remember, ChatGPT's got the knowledge you need. It's the ultimate guide in this crazy world of web development. So go ahead, ask away, and let ChatGPT lead you to web optimization victory!

Generating HTML

ChatGPT has got some real HTML skills up its sleeve. We threw a test at it, asking how to center an image with HTML, and boy, did it deliver! Two options came flying our way like a one-two punch — one using Flexbox CSS wizardry and the other with Block and Margin magic.

Now, here's the best part — ChatGPT can go the extra mile. Do you want to make some tweaks? No problem; just copy-paste an image path and filename, and it'll whip up the code for you, easy peasy. And if you're feeling adventurous, throw some of your existing code at it. ChatGPT will unravel the mysteries of your HTML like a seasoned detective, explaining what the heck is going on in there.

And here's a sweet trick — ever heard of minifying? It is when you squeeze all that HTML goodness into a tight package. ChatGPT can do that for you too! Copy-paste that minified code, and if you're feeling fancy, ask it to make it easier to read.

Generate a Website with Chat GPT

The question, "Can ChatGPT conjure up a whole website?" The answer is yes. It can whip up some HTML code that you can save as a bunch of HTML files and voila, you got yourself a website.

However, it is not as easy as it sounds. Getting ChatGPT to build us a 5-page website is like pulling teeth. And, with all these visual website builders out there, you're better off using them. They got templates that look slick and professional, and some even let you tinker with the HTML code if you're feeling adventurous. Why bother struggling with ChatGPT when you can have a visually stunning website in no time?

The Future of Web Development

Sure, ChatGPT can spit out some impressive stuff, but remember, it's no gospel truth. Treat it as a guiding star, a pointer in the right direction, not a copy-paste genie for your code. And while you might see people having a ball with ChatGPT on the internet, don't go thinking you're a pro just yet. In the professional arena, this beast demands seasoned experts who know their way around.

Don't let ChatGPT fool you into thinking you're above the basics. Sure, it can handle the basics, but that doesn't mean your knowledge is beneath you.

Web development is a journey, and abusing ChatGPT might just leave you with a gaping chasm of ignorance.

But here's the kicker—as this technology grows and evolves, it'll never be your shrink, understand your emotions, or get your business context. It's smart, no doubt, but still a long way from being human.

Having said all this, I have to say that ChatGPT is a fantastic tool for web developers, freeing you up for the big leagues, and tackling complex issues with gusto.

But like any shiny new tech, handle it with care, and take your time to fully grasp its power.

Chapter 4: Securing Your Digital Assets: ChatGPT for Cybersecurity and Privacy

Need an alert for a brute force attack against Active Directory? ChatGPT's got you covered, crafting that alert with logic explained, making it a breeze for the rookie SOC analyst.

And it doesn't stop there! This sly tool can be a real lifesaver for overburdened IT teams, automating those daily tasks that never seem to end. Like hunting down those pesky stale Active Directory accounts, saving the day by disabling the ones that have been gathering dust for too long.

No more DIY struggles for system administrators, ChatGPT has even got their back, creating scripts to identify and disable those inactive accounts. Junior engineers learn the logic and get the script up and running, and senior folks get some breathing room for the advanced stuff.

ChatGPT also proves to be quite the force multiplier in a dynamic exercise. Purple teaming, you say? That's the magic mix of red and blue teams working together to fortify an organization's security. ChatGPT jumps right in, building simple script examples for the penetration tester or troubleshooting those cranky scripts that just won't behave.

See, one of the biggies in cyber incidents is persistence. ChatGPT knows it well. That sneaky attacker adding their script as a startup on a Windows machine. With just a simple request, ChatGPT conjures up a script for the red-teamer to add that persistence to a target host. The red team rejoices, the blue team learns, and the organization gets some kick-butt security.

Overall, ChatGPT can speed up analysis, automate tasks, and even conjure up alternative paths for research. And it is in areas like this that you may want to consider the use of ChatGPT 4 for its complex problem-solving abilities.

But hey, let's not get too carried away. AI has its limits. It can't be a human brain, can't feel those real-world experiences that come with decision-making. We can only use it to process data and give us some outputs. And let me tell you, it ain't perfect. Sometimes, it dishes out false positives that need a human eye to sort out.

But here's the silver lining, folks. AI can be a real time-saver. Automate those daily tasks, and voila! We get to focus on the more creative stuff, the juicy bits that make us feel alive. For instance, I used ChatGPT to jazz up a dark-web scraping tool, cutting down completion time from days to mere hours.

Sure, there's this fear that AI will go all "I, Robot" on us and take our jobs. And in the cybersecurity world, we worry it might be used for mischief. Those sneaky threat actors use AI to make their phishing emails top-notch.

But let's not forget, decision-making is a human game. AI might be smart, but it can't think like us. It's still a baby in this big old world of choices. We gotta use our subjective thinking, tap into that human essence, and make the calls ourselves.

So yeah, ChatGPT's making waves, turning heads, and causing some uneasiness. However, we sure will figure it out, make it work for us, and watch it grow. The possibilities are endless. AI's here to stay, and I'm excited to see what's next in this wild ride of transformation.

Cyber Security Posture with Chat GPT

Your security posture, or cybersecurity posture if you want to sound fancy, is like the shield that protects everything in your organization. I'm talking about the software, hardware, services, networks, info, and even the folks from street vendors to big-shot service providers.

It's a whole package, covering infosec, data security, network security, and more. We got penetration testing to poke holes before the bad guys do, security awareness training to keep those social engineering attacks at bay, and vendor risk management to keep an eye on those suppliers.

And in terms of cyber security posture, we have ChatGPT ready to roll in three major areas:

First up, we got the Phishing Resilience Training. You know how it goes, human error is like the golden ticket for cyber attackers. If your team is not savvy enough, your cybersecurity posture is not worth much. But fear not, ChatGPT's here to shape them! It's gonna train your staff to spot phishing attacks from a mile away.

Next on the list, we got Security Questionnaires. Vital stuff for Vendor Risk Management, we're talking about nailing those third-party security risks before they can do any damage. And who's gonna make it easy? ChatGPT! It's gonna help your security teams knock out those questionnaires like a breeze. No more dilly-dallying, we're getting things done!

And last but not least, we got Threat Hunting. We ain't waiting for those threats to come knocking at our door. We're going on the hunt, baby! ChatGPT's gonna lead the way, helping us sniff out potential phishing attempts and sensitive data exposures. And you know what? Social media is not safe either! Cybercriminals think they're clever, but ChatGPT's gonna comb through that social media data, finding those sneaky threats hiding in plain sight.

Anti Phishing Training

Cyber threat awareness training, the whole dreaded presentations with those B-grade actors playing out cringy data breach scenes. It's no wonder folks push it to the backburner with urgent work commitments piling up. But that ain't no way to keep our cyber fortress safe.

Here's where ChatGPT steps in, like a savior in the digital world. Say goodbye to those lengthy videos, "because we are bringing"' in some practical experience, the real deal. No more actors and their fake drama, we're talking hands-on, learn-as-you-go kinda stuff.

With ChatGPT by our side, we can dish out frequent lessons that actually stick.

For instance, here's a little test we can create for our employees or ourselves by prompting Chat GPT to simulate a phishing email. Ask our AI friend to simulate a phishing email like the one below, so we can see if we are able to identify if it is a phishing email. When I prompted ChatGPT to do so, here is what it gave me:

Security Questionnaires

The world of third-party threats is where, according to UpGuard, a cyber security company, almost 60% of data breaches come knocking on your cybersecurity door. Those compromised vendors can be a real pain in the neck.

But fear not! We got a nifty solution – security questionnaires. These babies help us suss out complex security risks lurking in our vendor network. And guess what? ChatGPT's here to lend a hand, drafting those questionnaires based on our needs. Just ask it to, for instance, draft an ISO 27001 (information security standard created by the International Organization for Standardization (ISO)) questionnaire, and boom, it spits it right out.

Now, don't get too excited. The word "draft" is a gentle reminder that these questionnaires might need a little touch-up to get them just right. ChatGPT's like our trusty assistant, making the process efficient, but we gotta put in some elbow grease to increase that accuracy.

Scraping Social Media for Threats

Social media threat hunting – is a hunting expedition in the vast expanse of social media to spot potential cyber threats. We are on the lookout for those sneaky keywords that hint at sensitive data exposing or phishing attacks.

Here's how we do it with ChatGPT – first we have to collect all that social media data using scraping tools like Hootsuite Insights, Brandwatch, or Talkwalker. Once we got that treasure trove, we fed it into ChatGPT's belly for some good old analysis through its API.

And the second step is to feed the scraped data to the chatbot and prompt it to find all social media accounts that mention your organization's name and ask it to check if it contains any keywords that are a cyber security threat.

In Conclusion

Augmenting ChatGPT into your workflow ain't a walk in the park. Yeah, you still gotta put in some elbow grease, manually submit prompts, and keep refining them to get that desired output. It's like steering a ship, but hey, it's worth it!

Even with that manual touch, ChatGPT's a gem for streamlining processes and cutting costs, especially in cyber threat awareness training. You can't deny the potential it brings to the table.

Now, let's be real—ChatGPT ain't gonna replace a cybersecurity pro anytime soon. But those pros can up their game in this AI age. How? By mastering the art of prompt engineering, the new fancy term for feeding ChatGPT the right prompts to get what you want.

So, it isn't a cakewalk, but it's worth exploring this new territory. Embrace the power of ChatGPT, and you'll find yourself sailing smoother waters in this fast-evolving world. Cheers to the future of cybersecurity and prompt engineering!

Conclusion

Now, we've all heard about AI's artistic and legal conquests, but what about the price we pay for privacy? Italy gave ChatGPT a smackdown, temporarily banning its services, and raising eyebrows about our personal data.

How does it get its hands on our info? One way is slurping up bulk data from the web, without us ever consenting. So, that heartfelt Reddit AMA story? Yup, fair game for OpenAI to train ChatGPT.

But that's not all! When you're chatting away with the bot, it's keenly listening, collecting details of your session like a sly detective. IP addresses, time zones, browser details, device info, oh, they're all on its hit list. And of course, cookies, the sneaky spies, trailing you across the web.

But wait, there's more! User content—every word you type, every upload you share—it's all neatly stored away, forever. OpenAI's got it all, whether it's a secret recipe for a chocolate cake or classified company stuff that leaked out the back door.

ChatGPT may not be Google, but it's no fool either. It chats you up, making you feel right at home. And that comfort can be dangerous, making folks spill the beans on things they'd never dare share with a search engine. It's a slippery slope and some companies learned it the hard way when their employees spilled confidential beans, recording meetings and checking out proprietary code. OpenAI keeps it all, safe and sound.

Here is a list of details you want to keep in mind with ChatGPT in terms of privacy:

- First and foremost, ChatGPT's a data hoarder. Whatever you pour into its digital ears, it keeps in its secret stash. From top-secret Samsung meeting transcripts to lawyer's confidential intel, nothing is safe from its grasp.

- Now, transparency's a biggie. Italy raised its voice, complaining about the lack of info on what data gets collected and why. ChatGPT tried to patch things up, flashing its privacy policy in plain sight, but the experts aren't convinced it's enough to stand on solid legal ground.

- Opting out, the great escape! ChatGPT bowed to pressure, letting folks avoid data collection. EU users got a new form to protest data usage, but experts fear once that info's in, it's there to stay, forever trapped in AI's web.

- Phone numbers and verification codes, are a trade-off for no spam. But it comes at a price — anonymity is gone out the window, and you better believe ChatGPT's keeping tabs.

- Kids, the delicate matter of data protection. Laws are in place, but enforcing them isn't easy. ChatGPT says "13 years old" is the rule, but let's face it, a young person's data can slip through the cracks.

But don't let this scare you and don't let these concerns stop you from being best friends with the AI, because there are heaps of ways around it. For instance, hold back on the sensitive stuff. Whatever you spill into ChatGPT lands in OpenAI's treasure trove. Keep your confidential tales locked away, 'cause you never know who's peeping in. A security breach could be a nightmare, leaking your private info into the wrong hands.

Get yourself a VPN, my friend. A virtual cloak for your online stroll, it encrypts your path to ChatGPT, keeping those malicious wolves at bay. Anonymity is the game, masking your true address and keeping your data in check.

Opt-out is a way to reclaim control. OpenAI heard the calls and added some controls. Disable your chat histories, and they'll be gone in 30 days. But remember, it won't stop your data from training ChatGPT. To say a firm "no" to using your info, fill out the Data Opt Out Google form. GDPR-covered folks in Europe can seek refuge too, using another form to say, "Forget me, ChatGPT!"

So, remember, even though ChatGPT's a marvelous tool, taming this digital beast is not without risks. Privacy is at stake, and it's on us to be mindful, not giving away more than we should. AI's a powerful ally, but it's no substitute for common sense. Keep those cards close to your chest, and let's see where this AI journey takes us next!

Made in the USA
Las Vegas, NV
11 January 2024